A Taste of Barcelona

Big City Food Biographies Series

Series Editor
Ken Albala, University of the Pacific, kalbala@pacific.edu

Food helps define the cultural identity of cities in much the same way as the distinctive architecture and famous personalities. Great cities have one-of-a-kind food cultures, offering the essence of the multitudes who have immigrated there and shaped foodways through time. The **Big City Food Biographies** series focuses on those metropolises celebrated as culinary destinations, with their iconic dishes, ethnic neighborhoods, markets, restaurants, and chefs. Guidebooks to cities abound, but these are real biographies that will satisfy readers' desire to know the full food culture of a city. Each narrative volume, devoted to a different city, explains the history, the natural resources, and the people that make that city's food culture unique. Each biography also looks at the markets, historic restaurants, signature dishes, and great cookbooks that are part of the city's gastronomic make-up.

Books in the Series

New Orleans: A Food Biography, by Elizabeth M. Williams
San Francisco: A Food Biography, by Erica J. Peters
New York City: A Food Biography, by Andrew F. Smith
Portland: A Food Biography, by Heather Arndt Anderson
Chicago: A Food Biography, by Daniel R. Block and Howard B. Rosing
Kansas City: A Food Biography, by Andrea L. Broomfield
Rio De Janeiro: A Food Biography, by Marcia Zoladz
Madrid: A Culinary History, by Maria Paz Moreno
The Food and Drink of Sydney: A History, by Heather Hunwick
A History of the Food of Paris: From Roast Mammoth to Steak Frites,
by Jim Chevallier
The Food and Drink of Seattle: From Wild Salmon to Craft Beer,
by Judith Dern—with Deborah Ashin
Taipei: A Food Biography, by Steven Crook and Katy Hui-wen Hung
Miami: A Food Biography, by Kimberly Wilmot Voss
A Taste of Naples: Neapolitan Culture, Cuisine, and Cooking, by Marlena Spieler
The Eternal Table: A Cultural History of Food in Rome,
by Karima Moyer-Nocchi
A Taste of Barcelona: The History of Catalan Cooking and Eating,
by H. Rosi Song and Anna Riera
Vienna: A Food Biography, by Martina Kaller and Karl Vocelka

A Taste of Barcelona

The History of
Catalan Cooking and Eating

H. Rosi Song and Anna Riera

ROWMAN & LITTLEFIELD
Lanham • Boulder • New York • London

Published by Rowman & Littlefield
An imprint of The Rowman & Littlefield Publishing Group, Inc.
4501 Forbes Boulevard, Suite 200, Lanham, Maryland 20706
www.rowman.com

6 Tinworth Street, London SE11 5AL, United Kingdom

British Library Cataloguing in Publication Information Available

Library of Congress Cataloging-in-Publication Data
Names: Song, H. Rosi, 1970– author. | Riera, Anna, author.
Title: A taste of Barcelona : the history of Catalan cooking and eating / H. Rosi Song and Anna Riera.
Description: Lanham : Rowman & Littlefield, [2019] | Series: Big city food biographies series | Includes bibliographical references and index.
Identifiers: LCCN 2019007212 (print) | LCCN 2019007965 (ebook) | ISBN 9781538107843 (electronic) | ISBN 9781538107836 (cloth : alk. paper)
Subjects: LCSH: Cooking, Spanish—Catalonian style. | LCGFT: Cookbooks.
Classification: LCC TX723.5.S7 (ebook) | LCC TX723.5.S7 S66 2019 (print) | DDC 641.59467—dc23
LC record available at https://lccn.loc.gov/2019007212

♾️™ The paper used in this publication meets the minimum requirements of American National Standard for Information Sciences—Permanence of Paper for Printed Library Materials, ANSI/NISO Z39.48-1992.

To our mothers, He Young and Rosa Maria,
and to Noa, who was born with this book

Contents

Big City Food Biographies— Series Foreword

Cities are rather like living organisms. There are nerve centers, circulatory systems, structures that hold them together, and of course conduits through which food enters and waste leaves the city. Each city also has its own unique personality, based mostly on the people who live there but also on the physical layout, the habits of interaction, and the places where people meet to eat and drink. More than any other factor, it seems that food is used to define the identity of so many cities. Simply say any of the following words and a particular place immediately leaps to mind: bagel, cheesesteak, muffuletta, "chowda," and cioppino in the United States. Or think of the deep food associations with cities around the world, Naples and pizza, Hong Kong and dim sum, apple streudel with Vienna. Natives, of course, have many more associations—their favorite restaurants and markets, bakeries and donut shops, pizza parlors, and hot dog stands. Even the restaurants seem to have their own unique vibe wherever you go. Some American cities boast great steakhouses or barbecue pits; others, their ethnic enclaves and more elusive specialties like Frito pie in Santa Fe, Cincinnati chili, and the Chicago deep dish pizza. Tourists might find snippets of information about such hidden gems in guidebooks; the inveterate flaneur naturally seeks them out personally. For the rest of us, this is practically unchartered territory.

These urban food biographies are meant to be not guidebooks but rather real biographies, explaining the urban infrastructure, the natural resources that make each city unique, and most importantly the history, people, and neighborhoods. Each volume is meant to introduce you to the city or reacquaint you with an old friend in ways you may never have considered. Each biography also looks at the historic restaurants, signature dishes, and great cookbooks that reflect each city's unique gastronomic makeup. We have also begun looking at cities around the world and the historic food cultures they embrace.

These food biographies also come at a crucial juncture in our culinary history as a people. Not only do chain restaurants and fast food threaten the existence of our gastronomic heritage, but also we are increasingly mobile as a people, losing our deep connections to place and the cooking that happens in cities over the generations with a rooted population. Moreover, signature dishes associated with individual cities become popularized and bastardized and are often in danger of becoming caricatures of themselves. Ersatz versions of so many classics, catering to the lowest common denominator of taste, are now available everywhere. Our gastronomic sensibilities are in danger of becoming entirely homogenized. The intent here is not, however, to simply stop the clock or make museum pieces of classic cuisines. Cooking must and will evolve, but understanding the history of each city's food will help us make better choices, will make us more discerning customers, and perhaps will make us more respectful of the wonderful variety that exists across the globe.

Ken Albala
University of the Pacific

Acknowledgments

Most memorable moments around the table sharing a meal are such because we are surrounded by people we love and cherish. We enjoy thinking about food, cooking, and eating because these are activities that gather dear friends and family near us and create spaces where we share laughter and stories while nourishing our bodies and minds. Writing this book has also opened a valuable space for us to share our love for food and learn about different cultures and eating practices with our colleagues, friends, and family. As a collaborative effort that took place across the Atlantic, in addition to multiple crossings, we received much help and support on both sides of the big pond. Generous colleagues and friends supplied us with sources when we looked for information, provided contacts when we needed to ask questions or receive permissions, read and corrected drafts, generously prepared Catalan dishes, and tried our own when we were researching recipes. Above all, it was a joyful process because everyone helping us was excited to think and talk about food and Barcelona, and so were we.

We would like to thank Ken Albala, who generously read our proposal and gave it the go for the Big City Food Biography series, and María Paz Moreno, who not only wrote the excellent book on Madrid for the series but also had the brilliant idea that we should write the one on Barcelona. We learned so much from their work, and we hope our work contributes a little more knowledge on Catalan food while furthering interest in the exciting field of food studies. Special thanks to Kate Thomas and Shiamin Kwa, who, as part of Bryn Mawr College's 360°: Food and

Communication program, had much to do with a trip to Barcelona that planted the seed for this project.

Rosi thanks her colleagues and friends who share her love for cooking and travel, and who are always there to indulge her when ordering extra food just to try or to make that special trip to see what's being cooked. Food adventures shared with María Fernanda Lander, Kate Thomas, Bethany Schneider, Sharon Ullman, Camilla MacKay, and Homay King are always memorable. Cooking and texting about food and drinks with Bob Davidson and Fran Fernández de Alba bring daily laughter and joy. To Wadda Ríos-Font, who started all things Barcelona with an invitation to visit, and who since then has been a trusted guide to the city and its culinary secrets. To Kim, Rosa, and Xènia Coromines-Rizvi, who over the years have become her "Catalan" family and taught her so much about Catalan cooking. Special thanks to Montse, Aitor, and Leire Zuloaga-Gil, always on the lookout for places to try together in the city. To Maria Llera, Josep Gelonch i Solé, and their new daughter Sara, who from Lleida make sure that her supply of superb olive oil does not run dry. To Enric Bou, who taught her about food markets, advised her to ask lady vendors for recipes, and taught her about Catalan culture and history. To Mary Ann Newman for her kindness and for answering questions about translations from Catalan to English. To Joan Matabosch and his mother Caterina Grifoll Oliva for their charming and generous hospitality. To friends and colleagues who are always happy to share a meal: Elly Truitt, Tick Ahearn, Imke Meyer, Heidi Schlipphacke, Robert Ignacio Díaz, Eric Song, Sara Bryant, Tim McCall, Farid Azfar, Saïd Gahia, Michelle Mancini, Ted Wong, Jennifer Harford-Vargas, Manny López, Oliva and Juan Cardona, María Cristina Quintero, Roland Wedgwood, Martín Gaspar, Julia Rossi, Verónica Montes, Alberto Mira, Leigh Mercer, William J. Nichols, Juan Pablo Ortega Wert, and Malcolm Compitello.

Anna thanks her mother for cooking so much and so well, and also her large family for preparing the delicious recipes that played such an important role in her family reunions (most of them cooked by her uncle, Enric Arderiu), and which today are her best gastronomic memories. To her grandfather Martí Pi for teaching her that the simplest dish can be the most delicious. To her grandmother Maria Maynau for teaching her the "value" of food. She remembers picking vegetables from the family garden and trying the stew she made from the boar hunted by the family in the mountains of Cassà de la Selva. And to her paternal grandmother Maria Vidal for serving her the most delectable *canelons* she has ever tried and for teaching her the secret of her béchamel sauce. To her father José María, from whom she has learned to enjoy good food, good wine, good cigars, and life itself. She feels lucky to have met Alberto, who, with his joy for cooking and eating, nourishes those who surround him. Thanks to Enrique Reyes, Luz Ovalle, Tomás McKay, Samantha Jurgens, Luis Morejón, Paola Ramírez, and Anna Smith for the culinary adventures shared in California during the writing of this book. Thanks to all the women cooks who are not mentioned by name in this book, those who cook every day, at homes or in restaurants, because their work has been fundamental in making the chefs and restaurants we mention in this book. Also, to Rosi for the experience of writing this book and sharing the opportunity to learn more about her own roots and Catalan food.

We want to thank Aitor Zuloaga for bringing us together, which began our working relationship on Catalan gastronomy. Our thanks to Jordi Quer for putting us in touch with Editorial Barcino and their superb editions of historical Catalan cookbooks. Our gratitude to Joan Santanach and Paco Soler for allowing us to translate and publish a recipe for royal peacock from their edition of the fourteenth-century manuscript *Llibre d'aparellar de menjar*. We thank Jordi Falgàs and Casa Rafael Masó in Girona for permission to print images of early twentieth-century menus from their collection. Many thanks to chef Fina Puigdevall and her team for their generous reception during our visit to the restaurant Les Cols in Olot and for the recipe she gave us for this book. To chef Joan Roca, Josep Roca, and Jordi Roca, along with their team, for talking with us about their experience and view on Catalan gastronomy and its future. Our special gratitude to chef Ferran Adrià, who graciously met with Anna to talk about the experience of elBulli and shared with us his vast culinary library, helping us understand his philosophy of cooking. Thanks to chef Carme Ruscalleda for sharing her culinary knowledge and experience. To chefs Albert Raurich and Albert Adrià for their version of the traditional Catalan *allioli* and *sofregit*. To the press offices of these chefs who gave us permission to print images from their collections. To Inés Butrón, who kindly shared her knowledge on the history of modern cuisine in Catalonia and the nineteenth-century *ultramarinos*. To our friend Ferran Centelles for his invaluable assistance. To Lluís Tolosa for the inspiring conversations on Catalan wine and its future. To Angie Romero, Oscar Martín, and their communication team at the Institut Municipal de Mercats de Barcelona and the Ajuntament de Barcelona for providing printed and visual material for this book. To all the businesses and restaurants that kindly provided us with images for the book: Chocolates Simón Coll, Queviures Múrria, Can Lluís, Quimet i Quimet, and Can Culleretes.

Special thanks to Emily McBride for reading and correcting early drafts of the manuscript and to Erin McGarvey for the superb job of making this book readable. To Suzanne Staszak-Silva and Patricia Stevenson from Rowman & Littlefield for shepherding this project from manuscript to print.

As already mentioned, we could not have written it without the love for food and cooking that our parents instilled in us, the many travels to and from Spain that we made in our lives pursuing culinary adventures and embracing opportunities to try new flavors and dishes and, in the process, being always lucky to meet interesting people and to make new lasting friends. *A Taste of Barcelona* is what the title indicates: a taste that we hope our readers will enjoy and will travel to fully taste it in the future. Finally, and most important, we would like to thank our spouses, Duncan Black and Alberto Villalobos, for their unfailing patience, enthusiasm, and support for the project and everything else. We also want to welcome Noa, who was born to Anna as we were finishing writing this book, and we look forward to the day when she will be able to find and read her grandmother's recipe in these pages.

Introduction

L ocated in northeast Spain, Barcelona is the country's second largest city and the capital of the autonomous region called Catalonia. This region has its own language, Catalan, and a distinct culture with a literary tradition that goes back to the Middle Ages. The city has been in the news in recent years because of clashes between the Catalan independence movement and the Spanish central government in 2017 over the right of Catalans to hold a vote to decide their political fate on the Iberian Peninsula. The buildup to this referendum and the fallout are complicated to recount in neutral terms, but these events demonstrate that the region is culturally and linguistically distinct enough that its citizens desire political sovereignty. Nationalistic emotions are always messy, convoluted, and difficult to recount, especially ones that clash with others that are felt equally strongly. The current tense political situation between Spain and Catalonia makes this book on Barcelona more significant, highlighting how intertwined and complex their stories are while providing a historical background to understand both positions. As the second largest and most important metropolitan area of Spain and the capital of Catalonia, Barcelona holds a vital significance for both entities. Tracing Barcelona's distinct history and culture as manifested through its traditional cuisine draws an interesting map of the intricate politics that characterize the Iberian Peninsula. It is a political complexity that is fully reflected in its many regional cuisines, which are gaining international prestige precisely because of their wonderful variety and the many culinary delights that each has preserved throughout their history.

For the past several decades, Barcelona has become widely associated with avant-garde cuisine, lavish food markets, and beautiful architecture that have made it a favorite travel destination in Europe. The international prestige of many of its haute cuisine restaurants has transformed Barcelona into a gateway to a very special culinary world. The city continues to be known for its famous chefs and innovative restaurants, and food journalists and industry professionals write about the region's culinary traditions and publish cookbooks on Catalan cuisine both in Spain and abroad. In this book we take a close look at the gastronomic and political history of Barcelona that supports its current culinary boom. Offering a historical view of the city, we explore its urban and culinary development from the Middle Ages to the present. We examine how its food tradition has played an increasingly important role in determining the identity of the residents of Barcelona and, by extension, those living in the region of Catalonia.

To read and write about Catalan cooking is to learn to recognize its distinguishing features when compared to that of other areas of the Iberian Peninsula. There are also differences to be found when it is likened to the cooking of the Mediterranean region, with which it is often closely identified. The great connoisseur of Catalan cuisine and food critic Néstor Luján wrote extensively about the "personality" and "peculiarity" of its dishes in the past century.[1] Jaume Fàbrega, a food historian whose work is closer to our time, refers to the "language" of Catalan cooking.[2] Learning to recognize these characteristics, though, does not mean focusing on the uniqueness or the originality of each Catalan dish or its recipe. Instead, it translates into building an understanding that traces the many different influences that Catalan cooking has absorbed during its long history. We should not forget that Catalonia received many ingredients from faraway lands and adapted many recipes from different culinary traditions, making them its own. Barcelona traded and received spices and food products from around the world and welcomed migrants who continued to cook the dishes of their homeland in their new city. The capital of Catalonia was also fortunate to be bordered by fertile land to grow produce and the bountiful Mediterranean from which to extract other riches. These conditions shaped a cuisine that over the years developed its own practices, such as the use of lard in combination with olive oil or the mix of land and sea ingredients. Although lard has gone out of vogue in favor of the more Mediterranean olive oil, the combination of these two fats in cooking has been identified as unique when compared to other European cuisines. Throughout its history, Catalan cookery has retained a strong taste for aromatic herbs such as thyme, rosemary, savory, marjoram, mint, and oregano, which are probably remnants of its Provençal influences. What's more, the proximity of Catalonia to the central plains of Aragon facilitated the inclusion of the latter's hearty stews into Catalan cuisine. All of these characteristics, sustained by a strong tradition of medieval cooking, produced the roots of what we today recognize as Catalan cuisine.

Luján offered these observations not only to outline the development of Catalan cuisine but also to explain how Barcelona always managed to stay at the forefront of its evolution. As the capital of the (now-defunct) Principality of Catalonia, Barcelona's cooking and eating practices were consistently influenced by the many immigrants who arrived in the area looking for work and life opportunities.[3] A look around the city today confirms that the trend is still very much alive. Part of what makes Barcelona vibrant and exciting to explore is its ever-changing food landscape. These transformations take place because the city continues to develop and innovate, both as an urban center and as a culinary one. Interestingly, the city has been able to boast about its gastronomic culture to the world only relatively recently after achieving a greater sense of its own cooking tradition in the late twentieth century. Perhaps, as the well-known gourmet, cook, and popular writer Manuel Vázquez Montalbán teasingly pointed out, the Catalans needed the worldly accolades for their cuisine in order to finally start believing in the region's gastronomic prowess.[4]

Today, the value of Catalan cuisine is acknowledged by professionals working in the food industry as well as home cooks. Collectively, they also understand the importance of preserving their culinary practices for future generations. But part of what makes this love for traditional cooking remarkable is a willingness to "converse" with other food cultures without fear of losing one's own culinary identity. From that perspective, this new dynamic is quite different from legendary author and essayist Josep Pla's perspective on Catalan cuisine. For him, writing about Catalan cuisine was an expression of loss.[5] The memory of its cookery represented a disappearing way of life, a recollection of dishes imbued with nostalgia for gastronomic practices belonging to an irretrievable past. As our book demonstrates, this loss is only a matter of perception. Though much has changed since Pla reminisced about the Catalan way of life, in culinary terms, there has been a strong revival of its most traditional cuisine. The history of Barcelona and its culinary success reflects a return to culinary roots that propels innovation without forgetting its origins. Pla's fears have been shown to be unfounded.

The first chapter of this book offers a review of the gastronomic accomplishments of Barcelona from the late twentieth century until the present. It traces the story of how the modern Spanish cooking revolution began after nouvelle cuisine crossed the border from France in the 1970s. It shows the context from which the culinary creativity of internationally recognized chef Ferran Adrià originated and the consequences that his gastronomic adventure has had for the rest of Spain. It also points to the moment at which Catalan cuisine became political and why recovering the culinary tradition of the region came to be linked to the survival of its culture.

After surveying the current culinary landscape of the city, the second chapter of this book examines the history of the culinary tradition of Catalonia, including the medieval recipe books that survive today. Chapter 2 follows the founding of the city of Barcelona, its trade and its customs, and how it grew to become the center of the Catalan empire until its demise in the fifteenth century. This chapter also examines what the feudal system that organized Catalan society meant in terms of food production and consumption. It ends with a discussion of some of the medieval recipes that were popular during the Middle Ages.

Chapter 3 follows the political disappearance of Catalonia as a separate entity from Spain and the rebuilding of Barcelona after the 1714 siege that brought the city under the rule of the Bourbons. It then focuses on the nineteenth century, when the city underwent the period of great wealth and urban transformation that built the Barcelona that we recognize today. The chapter reviews the history of the city's beautiful cafés and the preparations for the World's Fair of 1888. The political tension that characterized the late 1800s is discussed in terms of food scarcity and the subsequent political radicalization of its residents. Chapter 3 also discusses the first Catalanist movements that sought to restore the regional culture and language to its society and how food and cooking played an important part in this political endeavor. Finally, we examine the important cookbooks published at the end of the 1800s and offer a review of the city's most iconic café, which remains (fully restored) today.

Chapter 4 examines the history of the fresh food markets of Barcelona, providing the story behind the construction of the market halls in the late 1800s and the social and political reasons that motivated these urban projects. It also describes the social role that these spaces of commerce played in the daily functioning of the city and how they were connected to the social life of each neighborhood. Interestingly, although market halls have mostly disappeared in other European countries, they continue to thrive in Barcelona (and in the rest of Spain, to an extent). Chapter 4 explains the stories of these markets, how they function, the types of goods they sell, and the increasing connection between the market and the food culture of the city.

Chapter 5 follows the trail of the internationally popular detective Pepe Carvalho to review the city's restaurant scene. Known as a gourmand, an accomplished cook, and a savvy sleuth, Carvalho's perspective is useful in examining the culinary phenomenon of Barcelona and its urban transformation starting in the late 1970s. This chapter offers a description of the city's most emblematic and traditional restaurants. We also discuss the careful balance needed to be attentive to Catalan culinary tradition while remaining at the forefront of a culinary revolution.

Finally, in the last chapter of the book, we offer a selection of traditional recipes. Chapter 6 is organized to provide the basis for understanding the "language" of Catalan cooking, starting with its most basic sauces and connecting them to how they work to build its most traditional dishes. In this book we maintain the Catalan spelling, especially for culinary terms as they are employed in Barcelona, although sometimes we also turn to Spanish, always offering respective translations when appropriate, as well as an English version. Sometimes the lack of consistency in the spelling reflects the reality of living between two languages that are very much alive.

A Taste of Barcelona: The History of Catalan Cooking and Eating is a collaborative work about the culinary history of Barcelona. We believe that we have achieved a good balance between "insider" and "outsider" views of the city. Whereas one of us is a native of the region and grew up as part of a large family connected to local eating traditions, the other has had the opportunity to become familiar with the area and its culinary practices through multiple visits over almost two decades. One worked as a food journalist during the exciting period when Spanish gastronomy was gaining media attention at home and abroad and is familiar with the latest food trends of the city, while the other, a specialist in contemporary Spanish culture and politics, has written widely about the social and cultural transformations of modern Spain. Both of us have traveled extensively and lived abroad, and our shared experience and perspectives helped us identify the ways in which Catalan cooking can be explained to an audience that is not always familiar with Spain or its different cuisines. Together we have sought to provide a clear understanding of the way Catalan cooking has evolved and adapted new practices while preserving others. Above all, our shared love for eating, cooking, and traveling has allowed us to find enticing stories to offer our readers so that they, too, become enchanted by this city and the food experiences it offers. We hope that through our general but comprehensive history of Barcelona, future and return visitors to the city can better appreciate and enjoy a culture centered around food and its deep connection to the culinary traditions that define its regional and urban identity.

1

At the Top of the Gastronomic World

Nature, Science, Foam

At the turn of the twenty-first century, Barcelona and the geographical region where is located, Catalonia, became a must-visit destination for foodies and chefs around the world. News of the avant-garde restaurants and their creative chefs was quickly spreading, and people were reading and hearing about "tasting" menus and small dishes served to diners that defied culinary expectations. Suddenly food journalists and chefs were talking about foams on plates and "deconstructed" dishes, like the classic Spanish potato (and onion) omelet that was served in a glass wherein the texture and flavor of the ingredients contrasted, enhancing the overall traditional taste of the dish. Familiar dishes were served in unrecognizable forms that diners could identify only when they tasted the food. Eating was no longer about satiating hunger but an opportunity to experience new sensations, like eating popcorn in a powder form or "olives" that explode into a liquid form in one's mouth, offering intense olive flavor in a totally different textural experience.[1] Or to be presented with six mussels in a row, each one prepared slightly differently, to allow the diner decide which one had the most authentic or pleasant mussel taste, taking into account different textures and flavors.[2] The description of these dishes were new, intriguing, and exciting to other chefs, journalists, and food lovers around the world. Terms like "spherification," emulsifiers, warm jellies, dry-freeze, and dehydrated food entered the vocabulary of haute cuisine, and those who were interested in trying this original way of cooking had to travel to Barcelona, the gateway to a revolutionary culinary world. But how did it all begin? How has the city become synonymous with cutting-edge gastronomy? What role did chefs,

Exploding olives from the restaurant Tickets. *Image provided by elBullifoundation.*

restaurants, journalists, and the local government play in making Barcelona into a culinary capital? We trace the story through the professional and media coverage of Ferran Adrià, Spain and Catalonia's most famous chef.

When Ferran Adrià was named as one of the hundred most influential people in 2004 by *Time* magazine, he was described as the person most closely connected to Spain's emergence as a pacesetter in international haute cuisine.[3] The chef had already been featured in other important international publications, and whatever was happening in his restaurant, elBulli, located near the town of Roses outside of Barcelona on the Catalan Costa Brava, everybody wanted to be part of it. At the height of its success, the restaurant received more than a million requests for tables, of which only about eight thousand could be honored. Adrià's tasting menus became legendary, comprising more than thirty dishes, including small snacks that could be eaten with fingers and larger dishes alternating between savory and sweet. The entire experience lasted an average of six hours. He served dishes that challenged diners' tastes in all directions, from unexpected flavors and textures to alternating from sweet to savory or from hot to cold.

Almost every dish he served was considered a work of art. His techniques and use of technology were so innovative that he was invited to the 2007 quinquennial contemporary art exhibition *Documenta 12* held in Kassel, Germany. Vicent

Todolí, former director of London's Tate Modern, was in charge of Adrià's partici-pation. It was the first time the prestigious international art event included a profes-sional chef. Afterward, Todolí, in collaboration with pop artist Richard Hamilton, published a catalog (with an index) of all the dishes the chef created and served in his restaurant from 1987 to 2007, which by then consisted of around fifteen hundred different items.[4] The addition of a chef to the event marked a significant moment not only in Adrià's career but also in art and culinary history. Despite the ephemeral nature of his cooking work, Ferran's dishes were considered art. As the title of the catalog of his work suggested, it was food that made you think. The intellectual element in his cooking set him apart from other chefs. Thanks to him, food was no longer only about sustenance, but it could also be considered science or conceptual play. It made a statement about what we eat, how we eat it, and how expectations about this process could be pushed to their limits.

When elBulli closed in 2011, it marked the end of an exceptional culinary period in Spain. However, Adrià's adventure was only part of a bigger story. His rise in the culinary world happened because he had a talented and highly motivated cohort of chefs and other professionals in the industry working hard to transform Spanish and Catalan cuisine. While he was diligently experimenting with food, the other chefs were busy evaluating the foundations and traditions of Spanish cuisine and updating it to modern sensibilities. What will remain as culinary legacy of Adrià's mix of food, science, and creativity remains to be seen, but what is certain is that the closing of his restaurant did not end Spain's prestige in the cooking world. For Barcelona, a city that served as a gateway to Adrià's culinary universe, the end of elBulli marked the beginning of its quest to become the best culinary city in the world. In addition to Adrià's cohort still active in Barcelona's gastronomic scene, a generation of chefs came of age during elBulli's culinary revolution. If we add to this list the many apprentices that all these seasoned chefs have trained over the years, the Catalan capital is poised to enjoy its status as a food destination for many years to come. How these kitchen professionals came to rule the city, with Adrià spearheading a gastronomic movement of his own, tells a fascinating story in which food, politics, and regional identity intersect to transform Barcelona into a culinary giant of the twenty-first century.

A CONSTELLATION OF STAR CHEFS

Barcelona today is a city with a surplus of exceptional chefs. A few of them have turned themselves into gifted restaurateurs. In addition to the highly trained professionals who have passed through Adrià's kitchen, the city enjoys a long line of talented chefs who have been working for decades to bring innovation and creativity to Catalan cooking. It is important to note that part of this culinary development took place in hotel restaurants. Hotels had invested heavily in these culinary talents; many of the tourists who visit the city are interested in the region's cuisine. Even today, many hotels continue to work in partnership with chefs. Their restaurants in the hotels are not intended to earn a profit. As long as they do not run at a loss, their presence is valuable for their business brand.[5] The continued collaboration between these establishments and the local chefs is part of Barcelona's history of haute cuisine. To illustrate the city's active professional culinary field, we highlight some of its more prestigious chefs and their acclaimed restaurants. We then turn to the origins of the culinary revolution that took place in modern Spain, first in the Basque Country and later in Catalonia.

Albert Adrià is perhaps the most illustrative example of a successful cook and entrepreneur to have come out of elBulli's experience. Today he is considered one of the most important chefs in Spain. Brother of the more famous Ferran, Albert is an accomplished chef in his own right. He was part of his brother's culinary adventure from the beginning, and he continues the legacy of his brother's creativity after the closing of the mythical restaurant in Roses. It has been said that Albert was the more creative and business minded of the two brothers, and the success of his current culinary enterprises seems to prove the point. He currently runs six restaurants in Barcelona, each with a unique identity. He is fully involved with the concept behind each establishment; collectively they encompass his own gastronomic vision.[6] The restaurants offer different cuisines and styles, foraying into non-Spanish cuisines as well. Perhaps the most well known is Tickets, a creative tapas restaurant that strongly resembles elBulli. It is supposed to be informal and more fun while offering some of Ferran's more emblematic creations, like the exploding olives. It is extremely popular among visitors to the city, and obtaining a reservation requires effort and patience. Others include Hoja Santa, a high-end gastronomic Mexican restaurant, and Niño Viejo, an informal cantina that offers tacos and other small Mexican dishes prepared by Mexican chef Paco Méndez. Pakta is a Nikkei-style taberna run by chef Jorge Muñoz. Bodega 1900 was created to recall a classic *vermuteria*, a place where locals would take *vermut* (a drink) and perhaps a small dish before going to a sit-down meal with friends or family. It serves more traditional tapas, and the quality of the products used is outstanding. Albert's latest restaurant, which was awaited with much anticipation, opened in 2017. His most "Bullinian" restaurant, Enigma, was created as a culinary amusement park with the purpose of reinventing the way people go to restaurants.[7] Ferran Adrià himself describes this restaurant as a "return" of elBulli, this time in the city of Barcelona.[8] Guests making reservations are given secret codes to access the eating venue. The restaurant, which also has a cocktail and snack bar called 41°, offers what can be described as modernist cuisine based on its tasting menus. Despite the innovative and creative air of his establishments, it is noteworthy that they are close to the chef's working-class neighborhood of Avenida Paral·lel. The mix of the culinary avant-garde and the everyday dynamic of a working-class neighborhood captures the basic elements of modern Catalan culinary history, which moves harmoniously between tradition and innovation.

Other chefs who have emerged from Ferran's kitchen include Oriol Castro, Eduard Xatruc, and Mateu Casañas, who currently run the restaurant Disfrutar. They earned their second Michelin star in 2018. After opening in 2014, they won the Miele One to Watch Award, and in 2017 they entered the extended the *World's 50 Best* list at number fifty-five, moving up to number eighteen a year later.[9] Despite the controversy surrounding restaurant lists and rankings, they cannot be ignored, as they bring publicity and prestige to these venues. Another "Bullinian" chef, Albert Raurich, opened Dos Palillos, an original tapas restaurant inspired by Asian cuisine with Mediterranean touches, and Dos Pebrots, a restaurant dedicated to exploring the origins of dishes and utilizing ancient recipes and ingredients, like the ancient Roman fish sauce, *garum*.

As noted, hotel restaurants played an important role in developing modern Catalan cuisine and bringing international culinary attention to the area. We could trace the beginning of this story to the 1960s in the restaurant of the Hotel Empordà in Figueres, under the leadership and vision of chef Josep Mercader, a close friend of writer Josep Pla, author of *El que hem menjat* (1972), a collection of essays about Catalan food practices. Influenced by nouvelle cuisine, Mercader was one of the first chefs who paid attention to the quality of ingredients and to local products that he could incorporate in his cooking. But the history really extends to the nineteenth century, when most of Barcelona's prestigious eating establishments were housed in hotels. The partnership continues strongly today. The city's two Michelin three-star restaurants are in hotels: Lasarte, by Martín Berasategui with head chef Paolo Casagrande, is in the hotel Monument, and Ábac, by Jordi Cruz with head chef David Andrés, one of the most promising young chefs in the city, is in the Hotel Ábac.[10]

The woman chef with the most Michelin stars is Carme Ruscalleda. Her fame as chef began in San Pol de Mar in her restaurant Sant Pau, which closed in October 2018.[11] She now runs the restaurant Moments with her son Raül Balam, also a chef, at the Hotel Mandarin Oriental, a singularly luxurious space, which specializes

Chefs Fina Puigdevall and Carme Ruscalleda (left to right). *Photograph by Alba Danés Boix.*

in reinterpreting traditional Mediterranean cuisine for their creative dishes. Fina Puigdevall, another important woman chef, built her reputation in the renowned restaurant Les Cols in Olot, a town in the province of Girona, about two hours from Barcelona. From 2016 to 2018, she managed the restaurant at the National Museum of Contemporary Art in Barcelona, where she often offered dishes inspired by the works of art exhibited at the institution. More recently, she received Spain's 2019 National Award for Gastronomy. Her three daughters are following in her steps: the oldest, Martina, working in the kitchen in Les Cols; Clara working the dining room; and the youngest, Carlota, finishing her culinary training in CETT, the Universitat de Barcelona's tourism, hospitality, and gastronomy program. Fina Puigdevall's cuisine uses autochthonous ingredients like black radish, buckwheat, and beans grown in the volcanic soil of Santa Pau. Her cooking focuses on connecting her kitchen to traditional gardens, farms, river, or forest products.[12] In her upscale restaurant in Olot, the view from the tables includes a green area where chickens roam freely, pecking the soil. They are locally bred animals, and the chef is committed to serving only local products to her guests.

Another important woman chef in Barcelona is Ada Parellada, who comes from a long line of professionals working in the hospitality business in the city. Her restaurant Semproniana recently celebrated its twenty-fifth anniversary. Artistically decorated, the restaurant organizes and hosts literary events, cooking classes, fundraisers, and other activities that interest the chef.[13] Chef Iolanda Bustos from the restaurant La Caléndula is also an important cook in the contemporary culinary scene of Catalonia. In her restaurant at the Hotel del Teatre, located in Regencós in the Empordà region, about ninety minutes from the city, she cooks in a style she describes as "biodynamic," focusing on flowers, plants, and other vegetation that grows in the area surrounding her restaurant.

Another famous chef currently working in Barcelona is Carles Abellán, who, along with Ferran Adrià, was the author of the previously mentioned "deconstructed" Spanish potato omelet, the *tortilla de patatas*. His first restaurant, Comerç 24 (now closed), could be considered among the first innovative restaurants of Barcelona. He brought to the city the format of the tasting menu and conceptually designed dishes that suggested what was going on up north on the Catalonian coast. He is expanding his own brand of restaurants specializing in gourmet and classic tapas, Tapas 24.[14] Together with his son, Tomás Abellán, he also runs the restaurant La Barra at the W Hotel, which specializes in gourmet seafood. A unique setting in Barceloneta, La Barra has a long bar counter where customers can see the chefs preparing dishes on the *robata*, a Japanese-style grill that is currently favored by chefs in many gourmet restaurants in Barcelona. The restaurant focuses on quality products from the sea and rice dishes and won its first Michelin star in 2018.

Paco Pérez is the Catalan chef with the most Michelin stars, currently at six. He is the brain behind the two-starred restaurant Miramar in the town of Llançà, about two hours from Barcelona. He is also the head of the restaurant Enoteca, housed in the five-star Hotel Arts. The restaurant has two Michelin stars, and the chef keeps busy consulting for three other restaurants in the city: L'Eggs, La Royale, and Bao. He received his most recent Michelin star for his work at Terra de S'Agaró, in the Costa Brava, a restaurant he served as a consultant.[15]

Romain Fornell is another prolific restauranteur in the city. He recently moved his Michelin-starred restaurant Caelis to the Hotel Ohla, offering a high cuisine inspired by the French tradition in a stunning space with an open kitchen facing diners. His cooking team was in the news recently as his head chef, Juan Manuel Salgado, was selected to represent Spain in the 2018 Bocuse d'Or competition with Adrià Viladomat, a personal chef.[16] Fornell runs seven more restaurants; one, Casa Leopoldo, which he operates with the entrepreneur and chef Oscar Manresa, is one of the most emblematic restaurants in the city and is described later in this book. There is another sibling duo among the star chefs: Sergio and Javier Torres, who run the restaurant Dos Cielos, located on the twenty-fourth floor of the hotel Meliá Sky. Their dream of running their own restaurant became a reality when they opened Cocina Hermanos Torres in the summer of 2018. They spent more than two million euros building a spectacular space with a kitchen with three separate cooking stations, one for meat, another for fish, and the main one without a heat source. Part of their restaurant project is educational, as they plan to train students in their kitchen and the dessert lab.

An important chef with a long history in Barcelona is Carles Gaig, who during the writing of this book announced that he was moving his Restaurant Gaig to the hotel Torre del Remei, in Bolvir de Cerdanya, about two hours outside of the city. His cooking is steeped in Catalan gastronomic tradition while still emphasizing innovation and creativity. Another chef who works from the same culinary perspective in his three restaurants—Pur Impur, Can Jubany, and Petit Comité—is Nandu Jubany, who also consults for the emblematic Majestic Hotel & Spa. Carles Tejedor is another chef who works in the luxury restaurant Sofia Beso (located in the Hotel Sofia). Chefs running multiple venues in the city is nothing out of the ordinary, but they have created a new trend for the management of more than one restaurant at a time, using two different spaces in the same location joined or separated by the kitchen. Jordi Vilà, for instance, offers a spectacular view of his kitchen and staff in both of his restaurants, Alkimia and Al Kostat, located side by side in the modernist building by the Ronda Sant Antoni. Both spaces display stunning, critically recognized design. In 2017, Alkimia was recognized by the SBID International Design Excellence Awards.[17] Vilà also runs the more informal neighborly restaurant Vivanda. Another double setup with two dining rooms, Rafa Peña's Gresca provides a formal space with thick tablecloths offering tasting menus and à la carte dishes and an informal space with a bar serving tapas and creative small dishes.

One more chef with a long family tradition in cooking is Marc Gascons and his sister Helena, third-generation owners of El Tinars, a Michelin-starred restaurant situated in Llagostera, along the highway that connects Barcelona to Costa Brava. A promising chef, Marc is behind the restaurant El Informal in The Serras Hotel in Barcelona, one of the ten best restaurants of 2016, according to *CNN Travel*.[18] Finally, we should mention neurologist and chef Miquel Sánchez Romera, who for two decades has been applying his training as a neurologist to haute cuisine, playing with the composition of taste and colors to please diners. After consulting for many restaurants, he returned to Barcelona and opened the restaurant Rice!, in which the grain is a key ingredient of many of the dishes.

The chefs we mention here are but a selection from a long list, but together they are representative of a professional collective that has made Barcelona a special city in gastronomic terms during the last thirty years or so. Each one of them reflects a specific way of understanding cooking, and through their different approaches we can trace Barcelona and Catalonia's modern culinary history. Their individual and collaborative work has shaped the city into a place known for its passion and dedication to creative cooking. Given current conversations and developments in the food industry in the city, future culinary trends probably will include more focus on plant-based cuisine, a return to traditional comfort foods, and budget-friendly menus that maintain a high cooking standard. Finally, we should not forget that the wine industry was a great partner in the Catalan culinary revolution.[19] With a history that extends more than 2,500 years, Catalan winemakers slowly worked to bring innovation to their craft. The biggest change took place during the 1980s and 1990s with the use of stainless steel containers, which allowed temperature control during the winemaking process. This modification greatly improved the quality of the wine and augmented the quantity of wine produced. In addition, the creation of a regulatory classification system for Spanish wines, *Denominación de origen* (designation of origin; similar to the French *appellation*), recognized twelve quality Catalan winemaking regions such as Penedès, Terra Alta, Conca de Barberà, Priorat, and Costers del Segre, among others, and helped to promote Catalan wine in Spain and beyond. In the past two decades, the Catalan wine industry has worked to produce organic wines using fewer chemicals and also making wine without sulfites. Winemakers have been working to recover and grow autochthonal grape varietals to the area. Barcelona is closely connected to winemaking. The city is surrounded by vineyards, and only twelve miles away, there is the winemaking region of Alella, where most of the wine production is organic. The region of Penedès is less than forty miles away from the Catalan capital, where the *xarel·lo* grape is grown and used in the production of *cava*, Catalan sparkling wine. Catalonia's vineyards cover more than 212 square miles and export around 230 million liters of wine and grape must.[20]

THE BEGINNINGS OF A CULINARY REVOLUTION

It is well known that the culinary change in modern Spain began as French nouvelle cuisine crossed the border into the Iberian Peninsula. By 1976, a year after the death of Francisco Franco and the end of a dictatorship that lasted more than three decades, Spanish cuisine was considered to have hit rock bottom.[21] This perception was not surprising after years of repression, isolation, and a conservative ideology that ruled by censorship and fear. It was a moment when Spanish society was in need of change, but, tainted by the country's problematic past, there was no clear guidance about how to proceed—politically, socially, culturally, even gastronomically. Meanwhile, the peripheral regions, always more alert to what was going on in their neighboring country, were more open to new ideas and foreign influences, especially in the Basque Country, in the north of Spain, where chefs were showing interest in the new culinary trends in France. They paid attention to how their colleagues across the border spoke of good eating, the need to simplify recipes, and their efforts to rediscover the cooking *du terroir*, which was accompanied by an impeccable culinary technique. Beautifully presented, elegant, and executed with perfection using seasonal and good-quality ingredients, the French dishes offered diners a new culinary experience.[22] Néstor Luján, the well-known Catalan food critic, closely followed the trend and spoke about the development of this French style of cooking parodying Picasso's artistic periods. He said, for instance, "we are entering the pink period of the grilled meats: the fish as well as the white meats are served when they are barely pink."[23] In Spain, nouvelle cuisine was described by its admirers at the time as honest cooking, intellectual and whimsical, even if slightly snobbish. To its detractors, it was provisional and perhaps even limited, as the star ingredients of French cuisine were only four: *foie gras*, truffles, lobster, and small game. The vegetables played minor roles in their cooking, appearing as decorations to the main ingredients of the dish.[24]

But the interest in what was happening in France was genuine, and the magazine *Club de Gourmets* and its editor, Francisco López Canis, sponsored the first Spanish roundtable on gastronomy. On November 29, 1976, I Mesa Redonda de Gastronomía was attended by French chefs Paul Bocuse (whose restaurant had three Michelin stars), Raymond Oliver, and Michel Guérard. The event was also attended by the top food critics of Spain: Luis Bettonica, Néstor Luján, the Count of the Andes, Eurico Guagnini, Rafael Ansón, and Llano Gorostiza. The moderator of the table was Víctor de la Serna. Juan Mari Arzak, already a well-known chef and practitioner of New Basque Cuisine, served as respondent.[25] Inés Butrón notes that the event's location, Guipúzcoa, was not surprising. Chefs in the region were already revolutionizing their own traditional cuisine.[26] The Basque Country had always been known for its cooking and the quality of its local ingredients. Its cooking was clearly influenced by the French, given their geographical proximity. The Basque Country already had cooking schools, and its people were accustomed to enjoying quality food. They were known for their gastronomic societies (groups formed by men around cooking and eating) and the discerning culinary taste of their upper class.[27] It was also during this time that chefs were working to educate people about their own culinary traditions. Juan Mari Arzak, of the famed Arzak restaurant in San Sebastian, tells of a time when, between his working hours in the restaurant, he would load his van with a wooden table and a couple of benches and drive to villages in the region, setting up an open-air kitchen in the main square to teach residents how to prepare traditional Basque dishes.[28]

The roundtable that took place in 1976 was significant for various reasons. Participants came to the realization that they shared many commonalities regarding culinary issues. They all agreed on the importance of regional cuisine. They valued simplicity in the process of preparing dishes. All shared the view that Spanish wine and olive oils should be promoted domestically and internationally. Finally, they were all wary of trends such as serving raw food to appear innovative or masking bad cooking by simply labeling it "modern." Butrón explains that it was during this encounter when the basis for understanding modern Spanish cooking was laid down. Soon after the roundtable, chefs Juan Mari Arzak and Pedro Subijana packed their bags and showed up in Chez Bocuse with the intention of learning in fifteen days everything that Bocuse had articulated in his book about French cooking.[29] Later, Arzak acknowledged that the time spent in Bocuse's kitchen provided him with the foundation necessary to start working on what was later identified as New Basque Cuisine. He was grateful to his French colleague and talked about how Bocuse took his visitors to the market every day or to visit farms and to learn about products. The French chef shared with Arzak and Subijana the latest culinary theories and explained how they inspired his own creations. Those two weeks were useful for the Spanish chefs to internalize this new way of cooking. When they returned, they were able to translate it to their own regional culinary practices.[30]

In Catalonia, a similar revolution took place in the early 1960s, also in proximity to the French border and in the kitchen of a hotel restaurant. Josep Mercader, the chef of the Hotel Empordà (or the Motel, as people from Girona called it), began experimenting with Catalan cuisine. He crossed borders, harmonizing French culinary influence with the local cooking traditions. He was also the first chef to add a creative spin to his dishes. Some see in the creations of the chef the real beginning of avant-garde cooking in Catalonia. One day, toward the end of the winter in 1973, he boiled a fistful of beans in salted water with some mint sprigs. He stopped cooking them while they were still crunchy and rinsed them in cold water. He boiled a few pig trotters, deboning and finely julienning them, along with a little bit of Spanish ibérico cured ham, fresh mint, and lettuce. Then he made a mustard vinaigrette with mint, processing it until smooth. Finally, he mixed the beans with the julienned lettuce, the mint, the Spanish ham, the pig trotters, and the vinaigrette. That day Mercader "deconstructed" a traditional dish, *faves a la cata-lana* (Catalan-style beans), and began the innovation of regional Catalan cooking.[31] His highly personal style of cooking influenced other Catalan chefs, among them the well-known Carme Ruscalleda and the late Santi Santamaria, whose Can Fabes outside Barcelona earned its third Michelin star before Juan Mari's Arzak in San Sebastian.[32] In celebration of the hotel's fiftieth anniversary in 2011, a book about it was published containing essays by chefs Ferran Adrià, Juan Mari Arzak, Joan Roca, Narcís Comadira, and Colman Andrews.

After the successful roundtable of 1976, more culinary meetings and conventions followed with the hope that they would help promote Spanish cuisine. In 1984, I Congreso de Cocina de Autor (Conference on Auteur Cuisine) was held in the restaurant Zaldarián in Vitoria, the Basque Country. The conference was attended by a young Ferran Adrià, known only to a few by then.[33] It was his first appearance at a cooking-related event, which, twenty-five years later, was considered the origin of the Spanish cooking revolution.[34] The next event, Lo Mejor de la Gastronomía (The Best in Gastronomy), took place in 1999 in San Sebastian. The meeting's name was later changed to San Sebastian Gastronomika. The new name signaled that the leaders of the new cooking revolution were the Basque chefs. Madrid also started organizing its own food events, starting its own international convention, Madrid Fusión, in 2003. In Catalonia, the most important culinary meeting for chefs and food producers was the 1999 Fórum Gastronómic in the town of Vic, which later alternated between the cities of Girona and Barcelona each year.

It is important to remember that the early work by Juan Mari Arzak provided the orientation that the rest of the Spanish chefs needed. The Basque chef's experience and cooking allowed his colleagues to see the potential in the gastronomic cultures of Spain. They also learned that they could perhaps one day compete with other more prestigious cuisines or at least make their cooking comparable to others.[35] What no one could have guessed then is how this collective work would evolve and how a generation of Basque and Catalan chefs would turn the culinary world upside down. The culinary revolution undertaken by the French in the 1970s eventually came to an end, and, as with countless collective enterprises, it was taken to extremes that left many longing for the return of traditional classic dishes. For Francisco de Sert, it was Adrià who catalyzed the movement, revealing the two roads open to the modern chef: the avant-garde way, global, making use of the latest technologies and new ingredients to take taste to its limits, or the neoclassical way, reviving the recipes of times past, mostly European, and adapting them to the present.[36] If we look back at what has taken place in Catalonia during the past thirty years or so, it is clear that both of these routes were followed—albeit with some modifications. The first one was taken by Adrià and his team and the second by other Catalan chefs who were discovering the rich culinary tradition of their region and finding ways in which to embrace them in the present and preserve them for the future.

COOKING WITHOUT LIMITS: THE MAKING OF FERRAN ADRIÀ

The cuisine of elBulli during its first years was purely French. It was during the early 1980s and Ferran Adrià described his classic French cooking in this way:

At the beginning I would copy what others did. In elBulli, in that first period, what we did was French cuisine, straight and simple. Until one day when I heard Jacques Maximin, the chef of the Hotel Negresco [in Nice, France], say that "creating was not copying." That sentence changed my life. I discovered that one could think on one's own. And in 1986 I deboned a pheasant in *escabeche* [a vinegar marinade]. That dish was something we prepared all the time and it was great but ugly looking. I simply deboned it. There wasn't much creativity in that, but there was some, because no one had done it before. Like the way there is creativity in making an omelet, mayonnaise, or phyllo dough, because they are all very weird dishes. The first ones who made them were authentic geniuses. . . . From then on we entered a period we called "Mediterranization" in the kitchen: it was an approach and adaptation of our traditional [Catalan] cooking to our restaurant. It was a move considered scandalous at the time because it was simply not done. Despite having good ingredients, there wasn't really a modern Spanish cuisine. Serving a good fish or some grilled asparagus with a bit of oil was unthinkable. . . . It was my own answer to the so-called international cuisine.[37]

His little experiment marked the beginning of a culinary adventure based on his desire to go beyond what was known. He also worked with the conviction that creativity was the outcome of hard work and not divine inspiration. Adrià put the staff of elBulli to work by focusing on all five senses, not only on taste.[38]

The publication in 1993 of Adrià's first cookbook, *elBulli: El sabor del Mediterráneo*, marked an important moment for the restaurant and for the chef. He was able to offer a compilation of the restaurant dishes and also to put his culinary philosophy in writing.[39] It was rare for star chefs to publish their own cookbooks, so the work in itself represented an important moment in Spanish gastronomic history.[40] Ferran himself recognized the importance of this cookbook, as he thought that it put elBulli on the Spanish map, even if the restaurant was still unknown everywhere else.[41] The book shed light on the way Adrià would keep evolving gastronomically. Xavier Moret points to a rather simple recipe of this period that proved to be significant: grilled vegetables with black truffle and Spanish ham.[42] It was noteworthy because until then a grill had not been used in haute cuisine. Adrià added to a familiar dish of grilled vegetables—onions, leeks, peppers, eggplant, zucchini, carrots, or asparagus—slices of fresh truffle, ham, and, poured over the plate, a purée of dried fruit with truffle juice. Ferran expressed his divergence from traditional haute cuisine by refusing to be limited to the classical ingredients it used. He said that high-end restaurants do not always have to serve lobster and caviar. If the sardines are good and well cooked, why not serve them?[43]

His next book, written in collaboration with Josep Maria Pinto in 2007, *Los secretos de elBulli*, presented a clear methodology behind his cooking. In it he insisted on the importance of not only the standard five senses but also the sixth, the one that allowed a person to experience emotion through food. It was his belief that diners could experience irony, provocation, humor, childhood memories, and other feelings through food.[44] Sight was essential in this cooking, as the presentation of the dish—shape, color, and identification—formed part of the experience for the diner, who also would notice the smell of the ingredients and the condiments used. In this mix of senses, taste played the most basic role, which was the recognition of the flavors of the food and the harmony among its components. Touch and hearing also would become part of the eating process as the guest experienced the different textures presented in the dish. Adrià emphasized the importance of texture in his cooking, which he described as the explosion of the sense of touch in one's mouth.[45] Another emblematic dish of elBulli featured the play in texture: the *Menestra de verduras en textura* (mixed or stewed vegetables with different textures), which consisted of almond sorbet, beet foam, tomato purée, an iced peach, basil gel, corn mousse, cauliflower mousse, avocado, and tender almonds. The dish also represented a new phase of the technique achieved in elBulli's kitchen. By 1994, the restaurant's chefs had developed the ability to achieve new textures and flavors, like savory ice creams, foams, and gels.[46]

In conversations with Moret, Adrià says that it was between the end of 1991 and January 1992 that he started creating his dishes outside the restaurant. He went to the studio of Xavier Medina Campeny, a sculptor in Poblenou, every day for two months to work on his creative menus. While his friend sculpted, he cooked. Some days, the sculptor would say, "Today I'm not inspired," and he would not do anything. Adrià learned that too. He would respond, "Me neither," and they would both go out to eat. It was the true beginning of his cooking experimentation, which, in 1994, was formalized into a process called *Desarrollo* (Development) by Ferran, his brother Albert, Andoni Luis Adúriz, and Bixente Arrieta.[47] When elBulli started consulting and working for the restaurant Talaia in the Port Olympic de Barcelona (the area built for the 1992 Olympics), Ferran and his team started spending many hours testing new dishes. After the team was joined by Oriol Castro, another creative cook, in 1997, they moved into some offices elBulli had in the Barcelona Aquarium. By then, they decided to create elBullitaller, a cooking workshop, which would be developed into a space for culinary experimentation. The team would be working on the menu items for the following season without having to pay attention to the daily running of a restaurant. The first workshop space consisted of a table, a chair, and ten books. In 2000, they moved into a larger space on Portaferrisa Street, where they still run what could be called their "food laboratory." Ferran remembers that the idea to separate the restaurant from the creative process occurred after the French chef, Jöel Robuchon, warned him about the changes elBulli would soon experience. He told Adrià that as his restaurant became more famous, he and his team would be expected to do more promotional work, giving interviews and engaging in other activities that would leave them with no time to create new dishes.[48] His decision to keep a workspace dedicated only to thinking up new dishes reflected his privileging of the experimental and creative side of cooking above all. ElBullitaller was an important contribution of elBulli to the cooking industry: it suggested how to streamline the creative process, and it was quickly replicated in other parts of Spain and other countries as well.[49]

STARDOM, LABELS, AND COOKING WITH SCIENCE

Once Adrià started combining experimentation with gastronomy for his restaurant elBulli, the accolades began. As he himself told CNN, "If you know nothing about what to expect, it's like magic."[50] Food critic Rafael García Santos from *Lo mejor de la gastronomía* (The Best in Gastronomy) awarded elBulli a 9.75, the highest score a restaurant ever received. The legendary Gault & Millau, the guide that helped launch nouvelle cuisine, declared the restaurant, situated in the small village of Roses near the city of Girona, comparable to the best French establishments. Suddenly the rest of the world turned to elBulli. By the time the restaurant earned its third Michelin star, everyone was talking about it. Adrià's restaurant was only the third restaurant in Spain to hold all three of the coveted stars (the other two were Arzak in San Sebastian headed by Juan Mari Arzak and El Racó de Can Fabes in Sant Celoni, a town outside of Barcelona, by the late Santi Santamaria). In 2002, the *World's 50 Best*, published by *Restaurant Magazine*, put Adrià on its throne. His restaurant would rank number one five times from 2002 to 2009.

Some of the iconic dishes he served during his reign show the creativity and innovation that critics and other chefs were fawning over. Here we review some of the twelve iconic dishes chosen by the *World's 50 Best* to remember elBulli.[51] The *Gazpacho de Bogavante* (lobster gazpacho) from 1989 was an example of an innovative dish made from a traditional recipe with tomatoes. What made it special was the way it was served: called *sopa emplatada*, the soup is finished at the table. The diner was served a salad garnish prepared in the kitchen, and the waiter would later serve the gazpacho over the garnish. Another key dish was *Espuma de judías blancas con erizos: la primera espuma* (white bean foam with sea urchins: the first

White bean foam with sea urchins: the first foam (2014). *Photograph by Francesc Guillamet; image provided by elBullifoundation.*

foam) from 1994. Foams were created with a texture lighter than mousse, but they were also able to carry stronger flavors and could be prepared using a cream whipper. *Sopa de guisantes 60°/4°* (pea soup 60°/4°), served in 1999, embodied Adrià's quest to make his food multisensory. In this case, the pea soup played with the sensation of hot and cold, as the soup was served at two different temperatures, in the same vessel, simultaneously. A much-talked-about dish was his *Caviar esférico de melón* (spherical melon caviar) from 2003. Adrià and his team learned that sodium alginate could aid them in the "spherification" process, basically a controlled jellifying process in which a substance encounters calcium salts, producing spheres with different textures and consistencies. He used these to create some of its signature dishes, like the melon caviar and the exploding olive. Finally, perhaps his most science- and technology-driven dish, *Pistacho-LYO con consomé gelé de trufa negra y aire de mandarina* (pistacho-LYO with black truffle jellied consommé and mandarin air), served in 2005, clearly represents a dialogue between science, gastronomy, and technology. Adrià made use of freeze-drying to prepare this dish.

But the most important coverage that Adrià received, which propelled him to the top of the gastronomic world and, along with him, Spanish cuisine, was Arthur Lubow's in-depth essay in *New York Times Magazine* published in 2003. Lubow declared French cuisine stagnant and complacent, and he set his sights on Spain as the new epicenter for creative gastronomy.[52] He described it as cooking that knew how to learn from its tradition without being trapped by it, one that merged the new and the old to produce dishes that were surprising and delectable. The journalist traced the journey of nouvelle cuisine, concluding that the movement had reached its limit but that Spain was only getting started.[53] Ferran Adrià, on the cover of the *New York Times Magazine* and featured in a fourteen-page article that extensively discussed Spanish gastronomy, became a national celebrity. A few months later, it was the French newspaper *Le Monde*'s turn. Ferran made the cover in 2004. Soon after, he made *Time* magazine's list of the one hundred most influential people of the year. With the international exposure from these three high-impact publications, it became clear that the chef had become a public persona who would need to negotiate the complications of international limelight.

As the chef's fame increased, so too did scrutiny of the type of cooking Ferran did with his team. Each day meals were created following a remarkably elaborate process, in which a team of sixty (forty were cooks) created dishes for fifty customers. The restaurant purchased an average of seven thousand grams of food products per customer, delivering just seven hundred grams of prepared food in their dishes. The kitchen used nearly two hundred ingredients for each menu, resulting in around fifteen hundred different types of cocktails, tapas, dishes, and desserts.[54] Journalists and other professionals in the service industry scrambled to find ways to describe it. During the 1990s, Adrià and his team had developed a large number of unique elaborations, including the previously mentioned foam and savory ice creams; what they called the new pastas and the new ravioli, the latter "stuffed" with liquid; new caramelization techniques; and other cooking methods that could no longer simply be described as "creative." What to name the new culinary trend that originated in elBulli became a topic of a heated debate, especially between 2004 and 2008. In fact, the discussion is ongoing. Most labels connect his cooking with science and art. In the end, the term selected by the national press to describe it—which was quickly picked up by the media outside of Spain—was "molecular gastronomy." Other names used include "creative cuisine," "auteur cuisine," "artistic cuisine," and "modern cooking." Another descriptive label used was *cocina técnico-conceptual* (technical-conceptual cuisine). It was understood as a cooking that searched for new methods to prepare or execute recipes. Meanwhile, the journalist Pau Arenós, in his *La cocina de los valientes* (The Cooking of the Bold), argued that the best way to describe this type of cooking was the term "techno-emotional cuisine." For him, chefs turned into scientists and their kitchen into labs where they prepared dishes with a different purpose:

> The goal of these dishes is to elicit emotion from the diner. In order to achieve this effect, they use new concepts, techniques, and technology, discovering or interpreting ideas and systems developed by others. They pay attention to the five senses and not only to the ones relevant to taste or smell. Instead of challenging tradition, they acknowledge their legacy and show their respect for it. They are socially committed and collaborate with foundations, universities, and nonprofit organizations. In order to build their knowledge, they maintain dialogue with scientists as well as with artists, architects, playwrights, novelists, musicians, winemakers, artisans, perfumers, poets, journalists, historians, anthropologists, psychologists, philosophers, designers. . . . They collaborate with them to ensure the survival of the product that is raised by farmers and livestock breeders or caught by fishermen.[55]

According to Colman Andrews, Ferran Adrià rejected most of these terms, wanting nothing to do with the whole idea of molecular gastronomy. He preferred to sidestep the labels applied to his cuisine and simply called it elBulli.[56] Nonetheless, during our interview with the chef, he expressed the opinion that a better label for this culinary movement would have been "the *nueva* nouvelle cuisine."[57] Currently he feels that the term "techno-emotional cuisine" might be appropriate to describe his cooking philosophy. One thing is certain: Adrià created his own culinary language. When we consider his cuisine, we are confronted with cooking that deploys scientific methodology and has clear intellectual and artistic aspirations. What Ferran provided was an experimental pleasure, one that needed the complicity of the diner:

his dishes were an invitation to play, and the guest had to be willing to go along. Another way in which his cuisine was explained was in linguistic terms. Adrià manipulated food as if it were a language. He shaped and revived it to metamorphose it into other artistic forms. Some believe that his genius consisted in seeing food as a medium that he then could redefine and develop into something else. His culinary evolution started with the creation of culinary syllables that evolved into a full and complex language with its own lexicon, syntax, grammar, and rhythm.[58]

Adrià's fondness for science and scientific method led to a period of fruitful collaboration between the chef and the Alícia Foundation, created in 2003 as a nonprofit center devoted to research and technological innovation in cuisine. The foundation, supported by the Catalan government and the Fundació Catalunya–La Pedrera, was established to gather specialists to study the application of technology in cooking. Part of the goal of the team of researchers is to improve eating habits in future generations and to study the region's food heritage.[59] In 2007, the center worked closely with Ferran to scientifically explain what he did or accomplished with his dishes by following his own intuition. The foundation continues to work to better understand the scientific and technical side of cooking and food. It also researches the growing and preservation of different species of vegetables and fruits. Part of its yearly programming includes outreach with diverse educational, social, and cultural communities to address dietary needs or nutritional concerns. Some of the projects the foundation has worked on include creating recipes for children with rare food allergies and finding ways to improve the quality and nutritive value of food served to patients in hospitals. The researchers at the center also work in close collaboration with the best chefs and scientists in Catalonia.

Another development following Adrià's international coverage was the creation in 2005 of the Ferran Adrià Chair at the Universidad Camilo José Cela in Madrid. It began with a program centered in gastronomic culture and nutritional science. It marked the moment when food studies began to be taken seriously as an area of study in Spanish academia. In 2009, the Basque Culinary Center opened, and a few years later the Universitat Abat Oliba in Barcelona started its postgraduate program in gastronomic communication. As Adrià's fame was rising around the globe, the "revolution" in Spanish cooking was well under way. Even though the focus continued to be on the Catalan chef, whom business schools like ESADE in Spain and Harvard University in the United States studied, there were other culinary developments taking place on the Iberian Peninsula.[60] Although it is true that the international attention directed at Ferran helped to propel other Spanish chefs professionally, it is also true that it would be impossible to imagine Adrià's culinary achievement without taking into account the work of an important cohort of professionals dedicated to bringing innovation to their country's cuisine. On

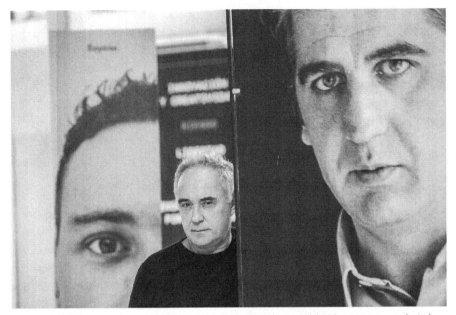

Ferran Adrià between portraits of brother Albert Adrià and his late partner Juli Soler. *Photograph by Marta Bacardit.*

the one hand, the attention that Spanish gastronomy received during the years of elBulli propelled its cooking to unprecedented levels. But it is also true that Adrià's success luckily coincided with a period during which a group of gifted chefs were toiling away individually and collectively from their own restaurants and other organizations. Together, Ferran included, they were able to transform Spain's culinary world in the late twentieth century. Their work had international repercussions, impacting the way that chefs and diners thought about creative or haute cuisine. Spanish chefs examined their own culinary traditions and how they were transmitted, adapted, and reinterpreted throughout the centuries. In doing so, they developed a specific culinary aesthetic and gastronomic knowledge and worked to link them to the history of their own geographical and cultural regions.

IN SEARCH OF A NATIONAL CUISINE:
REGIONAL IDENTITY AND FOOD

Going back to the year 1976 and Spain's first gastronomic roundtable, we should remember that one of the conclusions reached by its participants was the importance of regional cooking. The interest in this topic intersected with one of the most important political periods of modern Spain. It marked the beginning of the country's transition to democracy after the end of the Franco dictatorship known as the *Transición*. Although the nature of the true democratic changes achieved during this period continues to be debated in Spain, one of the most important transformations experienced by its people was the cessation of the official persecution of regional cultures and their languages. Regions of the peninsula that were considered historically different, with their own languages and customs— like the Basque Country, Catalonia, and Galicia—were officially acknowledged through a new political organization. The country was divided into seventeen autonomous communities, some recognized by historical precedence and others for new administrative reasons. In culinary terms, this political organization began a process of identifying gastronomically not what united Spain, but rather what made each region distinct.[61] Historically, however, this focus on diversity was not something new. In what could be considered the first gastronomic map of Spain, writer Ramón Gómez de la Serna, after spending months traveling the country and tasting its food, published an account that illustrated its variety rather than its unity.[62] If the map from the 1920s was done with irony and a sharp sense of humor, the focus on regional cooking took clear political connotations later at the end of the century.

In Catalonia, the effort to link political autonomy with cooking had an early precedent. In 1928, Ferran Agulló, a journalist, gastronome, and politician linked to the first Catalanist political party, the Lliga Regionalista (Regionalist League),[63] wrote a cookbook connecting sovereignty with the idea of a national cuisine:

> Catalonia, the same way it has a language, rights, customs, its own history, and its own political ideal, has its own cuisine. There are regions, nationalities, and people who have a special or characteristic dish, but not their own cuisine. Catalonia has one, and something more: it has the power of assimilating dishes from other cuisines, like the French and Italian, making them its own, changing them to its own style and palate.[64]

Many decades later, Manuel Vázquez Montalbán, another writer, would revisit this connection and work toward the recovery of traditional Catalan cooking. In 1979, he wrote in *L'art de menjar a Catalaunya* (The Art of Eating in Catalonia) about his difficulty in identifying the region's cuisine. He compared it to an archaeological endeavor (with the noted exception of the region of the Empordà, which preserved its cooking traditions magnificently).[65] But this deficiency would be remedied quickly, as the Catalan government put into action a program to revive its regional cuisine.

In the early 1980s, soon after the recognition of the new autonomies in Spain, there was a conscientious effort to connect gastronomy to Barcelona's history and, by extension, to that of Catalonia. Although the initiative should be understood in the context of the city's preparation to host the 1992 Olympics, geared toward attracting tourists during the international sporting event, it also implied an explicit effort to assert its regional identity. In addition to the economic incentive to make Barcelona into a gastronomic destination, the Catalan government understood that part of establishing its regional identity was through culture and language. From this perspective, Catalan food and traditions became an important aspect of investment for the Generalitat in the 1980s. The local government organized its first convention on Catalan cooking and gastronomy between 1981 and 1982 over the course of an entire year.[66] The year-long event consisted of food festivals and meetings in different parts of Catalonia to highlight local food products or food-related traditions, such as *calçotada*, the grilling and eating of a local variety of spring onions in the town of Valls;[67] *matança*, pig slaughtering in Solsona; or the practice of cooking with *cava* in Sant Sadurní d'Anoia. A detailed report of all these events and essays penned by food critics and journalists were later published in *Congrés català de la cuina* (Catalan Convention of Cooking).[68] The goal behind this project was, according to Frances Sanuy, Conseller de Comerç i Turisme (regional minister of commerce and tourism), to demonstrate the depth and reach of Catalan culture through its gastronomic practices across the region.[69] Talking to cooks and collecting oral food traditions was part of a political effort to vindicate Catalan identity after the many decades of repression. In the process, this effort put in motion a swift development of its traditional cuisine.

Inés Butrón, for instance, notes that by the time Vázquez Montalbán published the second edition of his book on Catalan food, his attitude was much more positive.[70] He wrote in this later introduction:

> I can say that the outlook of Catalan cooking has changed dramatically. Catalan cuisine has been restarted; it is recovering, a fact that is reflected in the opening of restaurants, in the qualification of the restauranteurs, in the reissuing of the copious culinary works of the past (from Ignasi Domènech's cookbook to Ferran Agulló's and to the classic *La cuynera catalana*). What was most important was the positive public opinion about Catalan cooking that also made diners more demanding and the appearance of a young generation of amateur cooks.[71]

Néstor Luján, who prefaced the second edition of the book, agreed with the author's emphasis on the role played by a young generation of Catalan cooks. For the food critic, the reason behind the success of modern Catalan cuisine was the young chefs' eagerness to learn about their own gastronomic traditions.[72] They worked to identify and to value them, teaching other chefs how to preserve these culinary practices while drawing inspiration from them to create new dishes. Butrón agrees with this assessment, arguing that Catalan cooking today—along with its prestige around the world—comes from the work of this early generation of cooks. They took charge of the kitchen stoves, and, after preparing and trying hundreds of *allioli* sauces and many versions of the Catalan stew *escudella i carn d'olla*, they learned to cook and to create. They were able to produce an innovative cuisine that eventually changed the culinary world. Butrón concludes that the most fervent spokesperson for Catalan cooking who did the most to achieve its international recognition was the son of an immigrant family of modest means. When Ferran Adrià started cooking in the 1980s, he probably knew nothing beyond the conspicuous Spanish potato omelet; yet later he revolutionized Catalan gastronomy and cooking in general driven by his only desire: to create.[73]

THE CHEF MAKES HIS EXIT

Adrià tells the story of working as a dishwasher in 1979 at a restaurant in Castelldefels, where the head chef would make him study one page of Auguste Escoffier's *Le guide culinaire* (1903) every night. In a year he had memorized most of Escoffier's recipes. His fascination with the French chef and haute cuisine comes from the experience of his first job. Adrià has said repeatedly that Escoffier was elBulli's reference and that his work would not be understood without knowledge of the cuisine of his culinary predecessors.[74] Perhaps this is the reason why Ferran dedicated his last creation on the last day of his restaurant, July 30, 2011, to a dish inspired by a classic Escoffier recipe. He served his last dish, a dessert called *Melocotón Melba Deconstruido* (deconstructed Melba peach), to the lucky fifty guests who dined that evening at the restaurant.

Philippe Regol wrote in his food blog *Observación Gastronómica* that creating a last dish inspired by Auguste Escoffier meant that Adrià was placing himself in the culinary history of the world. It was his way of saying, "I am also a link in the illustrious chain that goes from Carême to Guérard."[75] In addition to Adrià's fondness for Escoffier, the Foundation Auguste Escoffier in Nice, France, held special meaning for Adrià. It was there that he met chef Jacques Maximin and heard the adage that creating was not copying, which would later guide his professional career.

The famous dessert that Escoffier invented in 1893 in honor of the Australian soprano Nellie Melba consists of peaches poached in simple syrup served with vanilla ice cream and raspberry sauce. Adrià interpreted *la pêche Melba* by deconstructing it and playing with texture. The list of ingredients is long and technical, but Ferran's dish presented a waffle cone made of raspberry caramel with peach shots, bitter almond oil, and crème anglaise.[76] It is meaningful that with his last dish Adrià paid homage to the world's most prestigious French chef. Escoffier, with his organizational charts and codification of cooking, enabled the creation of a culinary language. He was also the inventor of a mode of culinary organization that could be exported to other kitchens. Finally, he transformed cooking and being a chef into a dignified profession. Regol suggests that Adrià sees a parallel between the French chef and himself, as they both achieved great things and received recognition in countries where the work of a chef was not traditionally well regarded.[77]

As Adrià was at the height of his culinary prestige, and perhaps already thinking about how to conclude his culinary adventure, criticisms of his cooking started surfacing. Chef Santi Santamaria started the most public feud in 2008 when he published his book *La cocina al desnudo* (Naked Cooking).[78] In this award-winning volume, he attacked the type of cooking done by Ferran and his followers. He criticized how they were abandoning traditional forms of cooking and incorporating chemicals into their food to achieve an effect without much care for health or nutrition.[79] The Spanish press jumped on this attack, and criticism shot back and forth between the chefs, mostly in defense of Adrià. Santamaria himself came under attack, as his own dishes were shown to utilize the same chemicals that he denounced as being harmful to one's health. His unexpected death ended the feud, but criticism of Ferran and elBulli kept resurfacing over the years.[80] Most express concern about the many non-food ingredients (food coloring, flavor enhancers, stabilizers) necessary to produce the spectacular dishes that seduce diners and other chefs; such is the case of Jörg Zipprick's *¡No quiero volver al restaurante!* (Don't Want to Go Back to the Restaurant!) (2009).[81] Books by Miguel Sen (2007) and José Berasaluce (2018) examine the culinary boom around elBulli and question its true innovative or creative achievements.[82] Berasaluce sees in Adrià and his cooking a temporary fad, a marketing ploy that enables gastronomic snobbery and has little to do with actual culinary talent. Other critics, like Almudena Villegas, lament a larger phenomenon caused by star chefs like Adrià. The popularity of gastronomic events, financed by large companies and publicized by the media, is shifting the training of young chefs. Many of them prefer to pay attention to the promotional and business aspects of their trade, training to become entrepreneurs rather than cooks. Instead of gaining culinary experience through hard work in front of the kitchen stove, they choose to think in terms of innovation, creation, and imagination[83]—qualities that they know are marketable but that unfortunately say little about their true culinary skills or knowledge.

Yet despite the criticism—and there is no doubt that there will be further detractors of the elBulli phenomenon—it is important to remember that more than two thousand cooks passed through its kitchen during the course of its operation. The restaurant worked as a culinary network, and the experience and knowledge shared by these *stagiaires* reached all five continents. Although it could be argued that Spain's influence might be limited given the number of Spanish chefs working in kitchens around the globe, it is undeniable that Spanish cuisine, and Adrià in particular, has had a significant impact in the culinary world. Regol and Andrews have argued that perhaps a better way to understand Adrià's significance is in terms of his culinary ideology.[84] It is difficult to say what will happen to this legacy, but his name continues to be linked to the international prestige that Spanish (and Catalan) restaurants and their chefs enjoy today. In the controversial but still popular San Pellegrino list of the best one hundred restaurants of 2018,[85] Spain has as many restaurants on the list as France: ten. In the 2018 edition of the *Michelin Guide*, there were eleven three-star Spanish restaurants, illustrating how far Spanish cuisine has come. Ultimately, the current popularity that gastronomy enjoys in Spain cannot be explained without the Adrià phenomenon.

A CHANGE IN PARADIGM?

In this chapter we have intentionally excluded—until now—some important names in today's Catalan cuisine: the brothers Roca (Joan, Josep, and Jordi) and their world-famous El Celler de Can Roca. Joan is the chef, Josep the sommelier, and Jordi the magician of sweets. Together, they represent a new culinary paradigm that has garnered much respect from the gastronomic world. They have occupied the number one position on the list of the world's best restaurants a few times and are consistently among the top names. Yet what seems to distinguish them from the others is their keen awareness and dedication to their local roots. Joan's cooking, which started in the kitchen of his parents' neighborhood restaurant alongside his mother and grandmother, maintains its connection to that humble origin. The family bar, still open today, is located next to the prestigious restaurant. Locals continue to eat the daily lunch menus there as they have done for the last five decades or so. The cooks and waitstaff of the Michelin three-star restaurant take their meals at the bar to promote and to preserve the local and family connection. The

The Roca brothers in the kitchen of El Celler de Can Roca. *Image provided by El Celler de Can Roca.*

brothers have openly talked about moving away from the harsh kitchen culture in which staff expect to be overworked or held to impossible standards. They strive to treat their kitchen and service staff kindly and with respect. They also believe in offering educational opportunities to train young professionals.

The dishes they serve in their restaurant are firmly rooted not only in the practices of avant-garde and modernist cooking but also in Catalan cooking and their own family history. In the presentation of their tasting menu in June 2017, the initial "snacks" served to the guests represented both their own beginnings working in their family restaurant and their later world traveling. The latter was a dish in the shape of a world globe with protruding arms carrying four small bites that captured the flavors of the places the brothers had traveled. The "game" was to guess the origin of each snack; if guessed correctly, the globe opened to reveal a final snack "gift." The Thailand snack contained chicken, coriander, coconut, curry, and lime; the Turkish one, lamb, yogurt, cucumber, onions, and mint; and so on. Having showcased their travels, the Rocas brought the diners back to their local origins with the second set of snacks. The dish was called *Memories of a Bar in the Suburbs of Girona* and featured a cardboard construction of their parents' bar and the neighborhood, with each of the brothers doing what he enjoyed most: one in the kitchen, another riding the bike, and another standing by the bar. The snacks were made of breaded squid, kidneys with sherry, Campari bonbon, Montse's meat cannelloni, and pigeon bonbon. Once the connection between

ℛ

EL CELLER DE CAN ROCA

Menu

The world:
Thailand: thai, chicken, coriander, coconut, curry and lime
Japan: miso cream with nyinyonyaki
Turquia: lamb, yourt, cucumber, onions with mint
Peru: "Causa limeña"
Korea: panco fried bread, bacon with soya sauce, kimchi and sesame oil
Memories of a bar in the suburbs of Girona: breaded squid, kidneys with Sherry,
Campari bonbon, Montse's meat cannelloni, pigeon bonbon
Green olive's ice cream
Starfish
Coral: *escabeche* mussels. Pesto razor clam
St. Georges mushroom bonbon
Truffled brioche

Green chickpeas hummus

Consommé gelée of chickpeas, yogurt, cucumber, garlic, cumin, hummus powder and
green chickpeas

Oyster fennel sauce, black garlic, apple, seaweed, mushrooms, distilled earth and sea anemone

Langoustine with sagebrush, vanilla oil and toasted butter

Mackerel with tempeh of "ganxet" beans

Prawn marinated with rice vinegar

Prawn's head sauce, crispy prawn legs, seaweed velouté and phytoplankton

Cuttlefish with sake lees and black rice sauce

Turbot with vegetables fermented in brine

Iberian suckling pig with salad of green papaya, Thai grapefruit, apple, coriander, chilli pepper, lime
and cashew

Duck with corn and cherries

Charcoal-grilled lamb consommé

lamb's tongue, vinaigrette and lamb scratching with lamb brain and tripe

Squab civet and its parfait

A fragrance adapted: Miracle by Lancôme

ginger cream, grapefruit granita, a sorbet of lychee, roses, violets and pink pepper

Orange colourology

Old book

Puffed pastry of butter cookies, cream of Darjeeling tea and old book essence

Menu from El Celler de Can Roca from June 23, 2017.
Photograph by H. Rosi Song.

the world and their home was made, the tasting menu began. Each dish could be identified as Catalan cooking, such as the coral made with mussel *escabeche* and pesto razor clam, or as dishes influenced by other culinary traditions, such as prawn marinated with rice vinegar.

What is clear is that the culinary vision that the brothers try to communicate encompasses values that balance the business aspect of their projects. They embrace the commercial side of their enterprise in order to expand the knowledge and experience of their team. In recent years, they accepted financing from the multinational banking group BBVA to close their restaurant and travel with their entire staff to different parts of the world, including Peru, the United States, and Mexico.[86] Although these tours were planned to bring their cooking to carefully chosen cities and clearly accessible only to a privileged few, the Roca brothers thought of them as opportunities for their team to learn and experience new flavors, ingredients, and techniques that they could bring back to their own kitchen. Most of their partnerships seem to progress organically and harmoniously. Another event that showcased the collaborative nature of their work, as well as their innovation and creativity, was *El Somni* (The Dream) in 2013. The project, conceived as a gastronomic opera, was the result of the teamwork of more than sixty artists (poets, philosophers, artisans, musicians, and goldsmiths). Directed by Franc Aleu, it took place in the art center in Barcelona, the Centre d'Arts Santa Mònica. The Roca brothers demonstrated their artistic sensibility through their food and wine selection, offering the guests a twelve-course meal that lasted three hours and made use of the five senses. They used a special montage of music and images projected over the tables and the room where the diners gathered.[87]

Although the spectacle quality of the event recalls the practices of elBulli, the intention of the brothers seems to set them apart. These projects are designed to be mobile, to be exported to other cities, and the experiences re-created for others rather than keeping them in one location where diners need to make a pilgrimage. The business opportunity that these mobile projects create are obviously clear. It is also true that these events will continue to be accessible only to a selected crowd. But the brothers are intent on achieving balance and trying to give back to the communities with which they come in contact through scholarships, internships, and other collaborative opportunities. The comparison between the business and promotional aspect of El Celler de Can Roca and its human side might not be satisfactory, but there is a conscientious effort to achieve balance between their gastronomic fame and their commitment to do good work. In our conversation with Joan, the chef expressed appreciation for what their privileged gastronomic status allowed them to experience, the doors it opened for them, and the people with whom they were able to connect.[88] But more important is how these experiences made them value their own roots. Part of their culinary work today is to find ways to invest locally the knowledge they acquired through their travels. They work on projects with local farmers and producers to explore varietals of different produce to grow in Catalonia or traditional methods of distilling alcohol with nearby artisans. At the 2016 exhibit at the Palau Robert in Barcelona, *From the Earth to the Moon*, a retrospective of their thirty years at El Celler de Can Roca, the message was clear: what makes them special is how the culinary adventure never lost its local flavor.[89] The implications of this commitment are narrated in terms of human and ethical values, harmonizing cooking, drinking, and enjoying a meal with raising awareness for sustainability, creating professional opportunities for new generations of chefs, and preserving traditional cuisine. After the meteoric rise of Spanish cuisine and the attention that some Catalan chefs received during those years, what the Roca brothers embody seems to point to a new, equally creative, but gentler chapter in Catalan gastronomy.

The Roca brothers' journey into the culinary world of their homeland and the many international connections they made parallels the development of the region's cuisine. In the following chapters, we trace this evolution through the long history of the area and the many transformations its cookery has undergone while always holding on to a few basic cooking principles that define the identity of Catalan cooking.

2

Medieval Cooking in Catalonia

Catalonia has not one but two culinary treatises that have survived from medieval times to the present. One of them, which has received much critical attention, is *The Book of Sent Soví* dated back to 1324. This text survives in two manuscript forms: one in the library of the city of Valencia and the other in the national library of Catalonia in Barcelona. Like other medieval cookbooks, it consists of recipes compiled by an anonymous author and amended, adapted, and expanded by later hands.[1] The other book, the *Llibre del coch*, was written around 1490 by Rubert de Nola, known as Mestre Robert. The latter may well be considered the first recipe book published in the Iberian Peninsula, given that it had a clear author and boasted multiple editions in the years following its original publication in 1520. Mestre Robert was known for being the cook of King Ferdinand I of Naples (1458–1494); through his work, we are provided with an explanation of Catalan cooking in the true Renaissance spirit and its implementation years later in the refined Italian court of the fifteenth century.[2] From both compilations of recipes we can delineate the long tradition of a distinct Catalan cuisine, as some of these earlier dishes are still present in modern day cooking in the northeast region of Spain.

Before delving into the particularities of both early manuscripts, we should trace their historical context and the way they are tied to the fortunes of the city of Barcelona. Far from being widely available, cookbooks in the Middle Ages were used mostly by professional cooks. When cookbooks were part of a library, they were more a testament to the wealth and position of the owner than to gastronomic capacity or culinary interest. In other words, recipe collections tied to the city of Barcelona and their survival in manuscript form should be seen as evidence of its flourishing into an important urban center during the period spanning from the thirteenth century to the late fifteenth century, when the peninsular power shifted toward Castile. At the same time, these cookbooks and other written works from the period also capture the particularities of the region's cuisine. Rudolf Grewe, the first to publish the *Sent Soví* manuscript in 1979, expounded on the characteristics unique to Catalan cuisine, which were identifiable by specific culinary techniques, favored ingredients, and typical dishes. It is from this perspective that Grewe outlines the history of Catalan cuisine, intrinsically tied to the history of its people, with a "definite set of culinary traditions and an internal evolution."[3] The Catalan region, as he defines it, includes Catalonia, Valencia, the Balearic Islands, and Rousillon. Its language, Catalan, evolved from Latin, akin to Provençal and the Langue d'Oc. Barcelona, as the center of Catalonian power, also developed over time, gradually becoming an intrinsic part of the region's history and sense of identity.[4]

THE ORIGINS OF BARCELONA

Although it may be tempting to paint an illustrious ancestry for the city of Barcelona going back to Roman times, the fact is that it was hardly a settlement of interest in comparison to the prominence of the larger port of Tarragona (Tarraco). It was but a hick town until its transformation into a medieval metropolis.[5] The Latin name probably originates from an indigenous population by the name of Bàrkeno near the mountain Montjuïc.[6] It is important to remember that for Rome, southern Spain mattered more in economic terms than the northern region of the peninsula, as the former had more strategic significance.[7] Nevertheless, roads from the Empordà region that are recognized today as part of Catalonia went through Tarraco, which was then the chief coastal port. The later success of Barcelona as a city, after many more centuries and a few more invasions, hinged on the economic development of the region linked by roads and organized by small plots of land that solidified into minor settlements and households, which later evolved into larger villages or *poblets*. Robert Hughes identifies this well-connected area as the foundation of a "deep" Catalonia.[8] Along these routes Romans exported olive oil, cereals, wine, and goats.[9] Pigs were probably also traded along these routes, as they were already popular in Roman times and the consumption of pork well established.[10] The area of Tarragona was famous for its oysters, but the bountiful oyster beds were lost with the arrival of the Visigoth to the area.[11] Grewe theorizes that Rome laid the foundations for what would become Catalan cuisine, even if earlier colonizers introduced staple items into their diet. Some of the basic foods consumed by the Romans in the Iberian Peninsula—bread, cheese, olives and olive oil, wine, and roasted meats—were actually brought by Greeks and Phoenicians.[12] The earliest settlers already had been producing olive oil along the coast; the Malvasia grape that the Greeks brought to the area laid the foundation for what would later become their wine industry.[13] Nevertheless, the Catalan region was not known for its exports, and compared to other Roman settlements in the Peninsula, it remained isolated; farmers consumed what they produced and any surplus would go to sale locally or nearby. Hughes also theorizes that the Roman settlement pattern in Catalonia explains the region's linguistic development. As the different trade routes from Hispania Ulterior and Hispania Citerior evolved, so, too, did their languages—Spanish and Catalan, which developed separately from their common Latin root.[14]

Barcelona's role in the Roman settlement was useful as a small harbor where ships beached looking for provisions or trade. What began as a collection of huts was formalized much later when Roman authorities in Tarraco decided to make it an administrative center to control the local surplus goods that started making their way to the ships like wheat, woolen goods, wine, oil, and *garum*, the fermented sauce made from anchovies or tuna.[15] In Hispania, this sauce was made from the viscera and blood of tuna or mackerel, and other small fish like anchovies could be added during the process and left for fermentation. According to Néstor Luján, the well-known specialist in Catalan food history, the thick sauce was much appreciated by the Romans, who used it in all sorts of meat and fish dishes.[16] Rafael Chabrán also notes that *garum hispanum* was among the best and most expensive.[17] Reading from texts of the Roman period, Luján points to the frequent praise that food products from the Catalan region received: in addition to *garum*, its golden wheat, opulent wines, green and thick olive oils, delicate oysters and clams, and fragrant saffron were renowned.[18] During the Roman settlement in the area of Catalonia, Barcelona remained a ceremonial and administrative center but not a residential one; its people lived outside the city walls, remaining closely connected to their farms and villages. The Roman influence in the kitchen can be seen in the beehive-type oven, which greatly improved the quality of the bread eaten on the peninsula at that time and is still used to this day.[19] The mortar, another important kitchen implement of Roman origin, remains essential in Catalan cooking. In addition to the bread, wine, and olive oil that were considered staples of the Roman diet, pork and pork products should also be mentioned. Lard was already being used in cooking. Among the dishes that could be traced to this time are porridges made of wheat, barley, or oats.[20] Legumes that were popular included fava beans, chickpeas, and lentils, which were typically consumed by poor Catalans throughout the region's history. In terms of spices, mustard seed and pepper were also in use during Roman times.

With the decline of the Roman Empire, the rich turned to the protection of their own properties: self-contained and self-defended *finques* that can be identified as the origins of feudal countships that later dominated Catalan politics during the Middle Ages.[21] When these fortified farms populated with refugees from the city started to barter directly with each other, it had an adverse effect on Barcelona, which, as a market, was bypassed. The city, once known for its *garum* and olive oil, by the fifth century was importing these same products from North Africa.[22] Furthermore, Roman Spain was an important producer of salt fish and its derivatives such as *garum*, but by the early Middle Ages this sauce had fallen out of favor with European cooks.[23]

The collapse of the Roman Empire led to invasion of Germanic tribes, as Vandals, Suevians, and Alani began charging south to the peninsula circa 490. The Romans allied with the Visigoths to stop the invading armies from the north, and it was the Visigoths who marched to Barcino and set up their court.[24] The settling process was a gradual one, a process of absorbing and merging. Rather than killing off the Hispano-Roman aristocrats, the Visigoths built their own baronies by marrying into local noble families and simultaneously reinforcing the path toward the creation of a feudal society in Catalonia. The strengthening of the nobility eliminated the free peasantry. The arrival of the Arabs on the peninsula in the eighth century meant the end of the Gothic baronies. Peasants fled to the north, seeking shelter between the passes and granite formations of the Pyrenean foothills, forming settlements in the deep northern valleys around the Ter River, winding down from the mountains and growing into an isolated, independent, and, most important, free existence. In these isolated peasants hacking a subsistence out of small patches of soil between rocks, Hughes sees the authentic Catalan character: hard, resistant, sharp eyed, and "suspicious peasants whose social horizons were bounded by their valleys and who were, above all, free."[25] In terms of the cuisine of the time, Grewe describes some of the important changes that took place during the Visigoth settlement: The charcoal fires atop mason tables were replaced by large open fires, first in the center of the kitchen and later against a wall and with hoods on top to control smoke.[26] The *llar*, as it is known in Catalan, became an important way to cook in medieval Catalonia and clearly shaped its cuisine as well.[27] The open wood fire was good for roasting meats and slowly boiling meals in cauldrons hanging over the fire. These two modes of cooking set the course of the meal as well: first the "roast" course and then the "boiled" one.[28] The meats were usually served with sauces that were not cooked, but rather prepared cold using the mortar and pestle. Herbs and spices were pounded and nuts and bread added as thickening elements. The mortar, *el morter*, was made of marble and the pestle of wood, and they rested on pedestals for easier use. The utensil was essential in Catalan cooking and widely used in the medieval period throughout the region.[29] Grewe adds to the dishes of this period the *panada* (the Castilian *empanada*), a dough filled with meat, fish, and spices and cooked in an oven, which became another important kitchen implement in medieval Catalonia.[30] Another dish of the time was soup served in a bowl lined with slices of bread. The eating and cooking utensils used during this period were the spoon and knife, or *ganivet* in Catalan, a diminutive of the Frankish *knif*.[31]

DIVERSIFYING CATALAN CUISINE

When Visigothic Spain was overrun by Muslims from North Africa in the eighth century, their cuisine left a strong mark on Spanish gastronomy. For Chabrán, this contact is what makes Spanish cooking so distinct from other regions in Europe.[32] Although the influence and amalgamation of Christian and Muslim cultures are much stronger in the southern part of Spain, their gastronomic and cultural influence is present all over the peninsula. The Arabs brought the use of glass goblets to Spain, which eventually expanded throughout Europe, and also established the serving order of the different dishes still used today, progressing from soup to meat dishes and ending with sweets.[33] The list of gastronomic dishes and food products introduced to the peninsula by the Arabs is quite substantial, and in Catalan cuisine in particular specific traits can be traced to Muslim recipes, such as the mix of sweet and savory flavors and sweet and sour.[34] They used sour grape, tamarind, and bitter orange to flavor their dishes.[35] Another influence is the use of ground almonds as thickeners in some of the medieval recipes that are discussed later in this chapter. Dishes influenced by Arabic culture in the Iberian Peninsula include rice dishes, stuffed vegetables, savory pastries, and sweets such as cooked meats with fruit. Though there is debate, especially on the Iberian Peninsula, regarding what European cuisine owes to the Arabs, their influence is undeniably present due to constant contact between Christians and Muslims. By the eleventh century, Christian kingdoms had already begun the *Reconquista* in the northern region of the country and counted Mozarabs (conquered Muslims) among their population. For example, it is generally agreed among specialists that Arabs introduced to Europe the following tropical plants: rice, sorghum, sugarcane, spinach, artichoke, shallot, eggplant, watermelon, apricot, lemon, and bitter orange.[36] Among the seasonings they introduced were cinnamon, cumin, ginger, turmeric, saffron, sumac, caraway, sesame, mint, orange blossom, and rose water. In Arab cuisine, beans played an important role when grain was in short supply, as did lentils, fava beans, chickpeas, and peas. Other fruits and vegetables introduced included carrots, beets, turnips, radishes, cauliflower, cabbage, lettuce, onions, garlic, leeks, squash (the Old World species, gourd and calabash), cardoons, cucumbers, melon, fennel, celery root, wild celery, and parsley. Some types of mushroom were eaten, too, including black and white truffles, although the "*muhtasib* of Seville tried to forbid the sale of truffles in the vicinity of mosques on the grounds that they were a food for debauchery."[37]

Their gastronomic legacy is also identifiable in the Arabic-influenced words in Spanish and Catalan: for example, eggplant (*berenjena*/*alberginia*), artichoke (*alcachofa*/*carxofa*), rice (*arroz*/*arròs*), saffron (*azafrán*/*safrà*), oranges (*naranja*/*taronja*), almonds (*almendra*/*ametlla*), spinach (*espinaca*/*espinac*), and meatballs (*albóndiga*/*mandonguilla*), among many others. An important culinary technique that was introduced in Spain was the preservation of cooked meat and vegetables using vinegar. The term *escabeche* in Spanish (*escabetx* in Catalan) refers to a marinade made with vinegar and other ingredients. Some of the most common forms are for fried fish in cookbooks used in the Iberian Peninsula from early on.[38] Perhaps more significantly, the Moors introduced pasta to the Catalans. Although the first pasta makers of southern Europe were probably the Greeks (*itria* is the oldest recorded word for noodles in the Mediterranean), the dish was adopted by the Arabs, who brought it to southern Spain, where it came to be known as *alatria*, which appears in two of the recipes in the *Llibre de Sent Soví*. That name has all but disappeared in the *Països Catalans*, but another pasta term from the Moors has survived: *fideus*, a short, thin pasta, one or two inches long, which may be as thick as Italian spaghetti, although typically it is preferred thinner.[39] The other pasta dish popular in Catalonia is the *canelon*, which is similar to Italian cannelloni. The Arabic word *fāḍa* seems to have entered the Romance languages (*fideos* in Castilian) by way of Mozarabic, the dialect of Spain's Arabicized Christians. Andrews notes that the word first appeared in Catalan in 1429, more than 150 years before the word *fedelini* appeared in Italian.[40] The influential 1520 cookbook *Llibre del Coch* mentions *fideus*, as well as its preparation and how to serve it, depending on the taste of the master.[41]

The connection between Arabic and Spain cuisine, however, was not something that drew critical or popular attention for a long time. Manuela Marín offers a two-part explanation, arguing first that food studies did not receive serious academic attention as a field of study until recently. The second, and perhaps most important, reason was to distance Spain from the African continent: acknowledging any Arab influence in Spanish culture would negate its efforts to be seen as part of Europe.[42] Despite recent interest in recovering the Arab-influenced Andalusi part of Spain's history and identity, this European bias is key to understanding Spanish Arab studies. Another version of this past that has received critical attention (albeit serious contestation) is the idealized society wherein three cultures—Christian, Muslim, and Jewish—lived in paradisiacal heaven.[43] Historical contestations aside, what becomes clear is that in analyzing food, there is ample documentary evidence of cultural exchange ranging from philological influences as well as dishes, ingredients, and preparation techniques. Merely listing food products does not reflect the intense cultural contact that likely took place during the period. We know, for example, that the food practices of the Jewish community in Catalonia accompanied and formed a part of life's major rites of passage. When a child was born in Spain, the new mother was regaled with gifts and special dishes were prepared. In Catalonia, they ate wafers and doughnuts and rice with oil and honey.[44] Other dietary habits included dishes that were consumed on both feast and ordinary days, such as stews. *Hamín* was omnipresent and was mainly made of legumes (chickpeas) and seasonal green vegetables such as cabbage and leeks. Its composition varied according to geography; for instance, in Catalonia, *hamín* was made of spinach, chickpeas, mutton, salt meat, and eggs; in Toledo, it comprised chickpeas, beans, meat, coriander, caraway, cumin, pepper, and onion, and in the Canary Islands they used goat's meat.[45] The daily diet for a typical middle-class Jewish family during the fourteenth and fifteenth century included bread, cooked cabbage, salad, olive oil, and wine.[46] Marín argues that if Arabic loanwords are accepted as evidence of cultural transmission, it can also be argued that Andalusi cooking had its major impact in the realm of sweets. Nevertheless, it should be noted that sweets were consumed only minimally, since they required expensive ingredients (i.e., sugar, almonds, pistachios, etc.) and "denote a process of adoption of 'exotic' food for the well-off."[47]

EVERY GREAT CITY NEEDS A GOOD ORIGINS STORY

Given the tendency to minimize the Muslim influence on the Iberian Peninsula, it is common to see their territorial presence limited and their cultural expansion downplayed. This view ignores the fact that there were entire communities of Mozarabs living on the peninsula. One sector they could not penetrate was the remote Catalan villages. When Charlemagne came to power on the Frankish frontier, the Holy Roman Empire stretched across the Pyrenees. Charlemagne wanted to extend his rule as far as the river Ebro, but his expedition failed. However, he was able to hold on to the northern part of the Iberian Peninsula because its inhabitants placed themselves under his protection. Girona gave itself over to Charlemagne in 785, and soon the nearby *comarques* (small districts) followed suit. Barcelona, as previously mentioned, was merely a town by the end of the eighth century. In 801, Louis the Pious, the son of Charlemagne, conquered the city and installed a French regent there, but it did not become the capital of the region until a much-mythologized warrior, Guifré el Pelós (Wilfred the Hairy), conquered all of the *comarques*. Born in the mid-ninth century and dead by 808, little is known of Guifré, but his legend still fuels the spirit of Catalan independence. He endowed many monasteries and churches and built most of the earliest churches remaining in Catalonia, such as the Santa Maria de Formiguera in 873, the Santa Maria de la Grassa in 878, and the San Joan de Ripoll in 885.[48] Guifré's power resulted from wresting control from a Frankish nobleman whom Charlemagne had exiled to Spain; therefore his land usurpation was not seen as an affront to the Carolingian rule.[49] However, his takeover of the region did eventually signal the end of emperor rule, and Catalonia was transformed into a self-generating countship tied to the city of Barcelona, with Guifré its first count.[50] The city is still known as the City of Counts (Ciutat Comtal in Catalan and Ciudad Condal in Spanish). When Guifré moved to Barcelona, the little town became an administrative capital, a title that it has retained to this day.[51] The myth surrounding the hero of Catalonia, whose blood is represented in the national flag, is nothing but foundational lore. The four stripes of red across the yellow background supposedly refer to Guifré's blood when he was wounded in battle by the Saracens in the siege of Barcelona. It is said that Louis the Pious rewarded his warrior by dipping his fingers in his wound and dragging them down his shield, which did not yet have a blazon. The gesture, no matter how many times revisited and celebrated in literature and in paintings, cannot be true, as Hughes points out: "Louis died before Guifré was born, and Barcelona was conquered long before that. However, in terms of heraldry, politics, and myth, the idea of Catalan independence begins with Guifré el Pelós."[52]

Guifré's presence in Barcelona and other vestiges of Carolingian architecture cannot be found in the city. Historians have blamed the Moors, led by the vizier of Cordoba, al-Mansur, who retook Barcelona in 985.[53] The city recovered well despite the upheaval and its economic life continued. Most of its architectural destruction was owed to early Catalan "developers" rather than the invading troops. Later, any surviving remains were razed off in the 1880s when the city prepared for Barcelona's 1888 World's Fair. Remains of early Christian structures are abundant not in the city but in the countryside.[54] There is, however, an early Gothic building in Barcelona, the Sant Pau del Camp, in the neighborhood of El Raval, which resembles a countryside church because it was built outside the walls of the city before they were torn down. A noteworthy Romanesque legacy in Spain is evident in the carved façade of the previously mentioned Santa Maria de Ripoll, located in the town of Ripoll. It is interesting for us because of its representation of quotidian life in Catalonia, showing local people going about their lives throughout the calendar year: "casting bronze in January, tilling in March, picking fruit in May, pruning in June, harvesting in July, butchering a deer in November, and so on."[55]

Understanding Guifré's lineage as count-king of Barcelona makes it easier to understand how the city was built as much as by contract as by force. The fierceness and independence of the Catalan villages from absolute order became part of their local identity. Hughes refers to this unbending character to explain the area's litigiousness with Castile later on, as the organization of feudal Catalonia encouraged a social order of its own that respected rights and obligations between nobles, clerics, peasants, burghers, and workmen.[56] The changes that took place during the Middle Ages transformed the region of Catalonia and also shaped the way that Barcelona was made into its urban center. Antoni Riera-Melis describes these changes in terms of rural transformations affecting the city, as when small settlements were being established in the countryside and the infrastructure that sustained them rebuilt, which in turned expanded the circulation of money and stimulated economic renewal.[57] What allowed these transformations was the slow but steady rise in population that continued until the end of the thirteenth century. From the eleventh century on, the warrior aristocracy took advantage of the growing population to parcel out and lease their lands to peasants for growing crops and pasturing farm animals.[58] The increase in manpower meant that more fields were cultivated while marshes and swamps were drained to allow for more land for farming and settlements connected by roads. However, this growth also meant that forests were being cut down for wood and to expand land for cultivation. Soon, lords would closely regulate the use of forests to preserve their hunting territories, construction materials, and fuel. The increasingly limited access to these lands also meant that hunting and the resulting supply of meat was then reserved for the privileged class.[59] The feudal lord had the right to yield, sell, or reserve the right to hunt. In addition to rabbits, hunted animals included grouse, hare, bears, wild boar, and deer. Bears were supposedly numerous in the Pyrenees in the twelfth century, and when hunted, one or two thighs and the four feet of the animal were presented to the lord as they were considered the most valuable part of the beast.[60] The expanded fields were used to cultivate cereals that were used to make bread: barley, rye, millet, wheat, and spelt. These were times when vineyards were on the rise, too, and lords gave peasants more autonomy in order to feed the demand for the consistent production of high-quality wine. The growing of vegetables and greens that used to be done in monastic kitchen gardens, around seigniorial establishments, or in peripheral spaces around fields was now carried out around the peasant household, where the work of women and children made these spaces more fertile for growing broad beans, leeks, cabbage, onions, and spinach.[61]

The feudal society that was supported by the agricultural work of the peasants also created a surplus market, in which goods that were not consumed could be sold or traded. This augmented production led to the expansion of the use of money, road travel, and the growth of urban centers with a variety of tradespeople.[62] The rise in agricultural production stimulated the development of cities in addition to enriching the aristocracy. The "agriculturization" of the rural economy also had nutritional consequences shaped by the restrictions on the use of woodlands by the feudal aristocracy, the increase in rural markets, and the connection between these markets and their urban counterparts. Riera-Melis observes that foods of vegetable origin started to become more prevalent than meat among the poorer classes and that the variety of foods consumed across the different social classes between 1050 and 1280 decreased when compared to the earlier Middle Ages.[63] Bread and wine were consumed more than meats or vegetables, which were almost relegated to accompaniments. Gathering and hunting as a means of obtaining food was no longer normal practice, but rather marginal activities that were engaged by the poor (gathering) and the rich (hunting). Each social class played a particular role in the medieval agricultural economy, either taking care of animals by pasturing or hunting them. It is clear from studying the dietary habits of this time that the food consumed, in addition to the types of dwelling and clothing people owned, was a clear indicator of social status.[64]

The ugly side of the feudal system was that the privilege of noblemen allowed them to virtually hold peasants as their slaves. The property of free small landholders was taken over by warlords and strongmen, turning them into serfs whose work and profit had to be shared with the lord and his manor.[65] The social class that ruled over Catalonia was a group of the older patrician families with new lineages of counts and viscounts, and under them, the lesser nobles, castle keepers, and knights. The nobility had the peasants under their control and offered military protection in exchange for taxes, known as *feu*, which were collected by the military or the minor nobles, who kept their own portion before offering them to the lords.[66] The greed of the *noblesa castral* created a power vacuum that plunged the region into violence and chaos in the eleventh century. When Ramon Berenguer I emerged as the first feudal monarch of Catalonia, he had to construct a political space—a legal framework—that would maintain the balance among the throne, the court aristocracy, the *noblesa castral*, the emerging merchant class, the tradesmen, and the peasants. Berenguer was behind the first written bill of rights in Europe, the *Usatges* (Usages), which was completed in the early twelfth century (almost a century before its English counterpart, the Magna Carta), initiating a period that could be described as responsible feudalism.[67] This bill of rights recognized that all burghers or "honored citizens" (*ciutadans honrats*—that is, anyone not reduced to serfdom) stood on equal legal footing with the nobility: "when rights were in dispute, issues were not to be settled by rulings from above: they had to be thrashed out before an adjudicator, as between equals, on level ground."[68] The resolution was then often reached in terms of a "pact," a negotiated agreement between interested parties. Although these practices did not guarantee a perfect coexistence, they did create an atmosphere in which peasants and traders could defend their interests.

The Catalan peasantry strengthened from the rights they enjoyed in medieval times and it showed in the way the peasants farmed, consumed, and traded their goods: always fiercely protective of their own but acting within measure and fairness. Their autonomy in the work they carried out, protected by a "lease," meant that even if the land they cultivated did not belong to them, land tenure made it almost impossible for the landlord to revoke it. Growing vines for wine making illustrates this relationship clearly. Riera-Melis explains that the contracts of *complantatio* guaranteed the vine-growing leaseholders (*rabassaires*) almost half of the resulting vines in addition to the usufruct of the other half in exchange for assuming all the costs of preparing and cultivating the soil, which resulted in a greater expansion of vineyards during the Middle Ages.[69] Interestingly, the length of the lease was geared toward the life of the *ceps* (vines). When three-quarters of the vines had died, the owner could decide whether to renew the lease. The situation known as *rabassa mort* ensured that the Catalan *rabassaires* became very good at keeping vines alive; their stocks survived fifty years, longer than a man's working life.[70]

BUILDING THE CATALAN EMPIRE

The start of the royal lineage of Catalonia, the House of Barcelona, and the reign of King Jaume I turned the small port of Barcelona into the center of a newly formed Mediterranean empire. The king was determined to capture the island of Majorca and take over its trade routes. Achieved swiftly, the *Reconquista* in the Catalan region was over by the thirteenth century. The kingdom of Aragon and Catalonia (or

Catalonia and Aragon, according to Catalan history) was eager to build an empire. However, using Barcelona as a foundation for this new empire proved difficult for two reasons. First, the shallowness of the harbor was a big problem for the pot-bellied caravels used for Mediterranean commercial transport at the time.[71] The second, and more threatening, obstacle was the Moors. Having been driven out the Catalan mainland, the Moors were installed in the Balearic Islands (Majorca, Mi-norca, and Ibiza), which meant that large medieval vessels could not avoid these is-lands and the danger of being captured or plundered when sailing from Barcelona. Blaming the Arab "pirates" for threatening Barcelona's sea trade, and in the name of Christianity, Jaume I launched an attack to capture a series of islands that would open the Mediterranean to the Catalans from the Balearic Islands to Sicily. The "threat" was an economic one, as the Moorish occupation of Majorca clearly meant that Arab traders benefited from the connections that reached to Venice, Genoa, Sicily, and Tunis.[72] Jaume I launched a successful invasion in 1229 by amassing an

Jaume I, portrait from the series *Retrats dels reis d'Aragó* by Jaume Mateu and Gonçal Peris Sarrià. *Printed with permission from the Museu Nacional d'Art de Catalunya.*

impressive number of vessels. The shallow coast was well suited for the small ships that were used to quickly sail to the islands.[73] The conquest of Majorca was the first step in the kingdom's growing expansion into the Mediterranean Sea, making Barcelona not only where the royal crown of Aragon and Catalonia resided but also where the nobility that sustained its imperial ambition lived and prospered. Jaume I himself wrote about the conquest in his thirteenth-century autobiography (the only one written by a medieval king): the *Llibre dels fets* (Book of Deeds).

After King Jaume I received help from the Aragonese to conquer Majorca, they in turn wanted Valencia. The conquest was much bloodier and took much longer than the six years Jaume I spent consolidating his power in the Balearic Islands. It took sixteen years, from 1232 to 1248, for the Aragonese to impose their feudal system, reorganizing their cultivated areas into serf-worked lands, while Barcelona took the coastal provinces. From Lleida on, the region was completely Catalanized, and by the end of the fifteenth century, Catalan likely was spoken more around the Mediterranean ports than any other Romance language with the exception of Arabic.[74] Later, Jaume's son Pere II (1240–1285), or Pere el Gran (the Great), expanded the empire to Sicily by marrying its princess, Constanza. The island was still considered the granary of southern Europe and operated as a doorway to the Levant—that is, to Greece, Egypt, and Constantinople.[75] Part of this expansion included the massacre of Sardinia, not a proud chapter in the history of the Catalan empire.[76] For the next two centuries or so, Catalan, along with Sicilian, was the official language of the region with a royal presence in Palermo and Messina.

These military expeditions meant that Barcelona (and Catalonia) quickly grew into a commercial empire. By the end of the thirteenth century, the kingdom had consulates in more than one hundred cities across the Mediterranean, including Constantinople, Venice, Malta, and Tripoli. The expansion of the Catalan empire also influenced Barcelona's trade with cities like Beirut and Alexandria in the Levant area, which became very profitable, as was evident in the growing luxury trade. Barcelona exported woolen goods and sheepskin, dried fruit, olive oil, coral, tin, iron, imported pepper, incense, cinnamon, and ginger.[77] Catalans also imported alum and slaves, and to other areas of the empire, such as the Balearic Islands, Sardinia, Naples, and Sicily, they exported cloth, leather goods, saffron, and arms in exchange for wheat, cotton, coral, and salted fish. When they were not at war, Catalans also traded by treaty. They were sending dried figs, Valencian rice, cheese, and nuts to the middle and western coastal regions of North Africa and returning in their Barcelona caravels with raw cotton, dyes, and, most important, gold. The main dealers in North Africa were Catalan Jews, who were esteemed as useful trading agents in the thirteenth and fourteenth centuries, setting up businesses in North African cities where Christians could not. Barcelona flourished during this time and was flush with money like Venice.[78]

The wealthy Catalans of this time came to represent a strong middle class, praised for their *seny*, the Catalan belief of virtue by excellence, and the spirit embodied by their merchants. What was good for business was good for Catalonia, according to Francesc de Eiximenis (ca. 1130–1409), a theologian who wrote a monumental thirteen-volume encyclopedia explaining Christian principles and practices. The high esteem enjoyed by the Barcelonese merchants meant that they were highly conscious of their rank, which played an important role in shaping and maintaining a prosperous city and empire.[79] Testament to their position and work in the city is the Llotja (Lodge), which served as a stock exchange. This building, facing the water that brought so much business to town, was built in 1350 by Pere Llobet, the architect who built the Saló de Cent (Hall of the Hundred). During this time, the government of the city of Barcelona was administered under the rule of the Consell de Cent (the Council of One Hundred). A democratic, more populist organization created by Jaume I in 1249, the Consell was a committee of "peers," twenty high-ranking citizens (*probi homines*—honest "men"; *prohoms* in Catalan) who advised on city management. The men also had the power to convene a larger citizens' meeting. In 1258, the count-king appointed an electoral college of two hundred men representing different interests, professions, and trades to appoint the council of twenty.[80]

The economic boom of this time shaped the construction of the city of Barcelona, as the merchants and the medieval nobility built palaces and other monuments that reflected their power and status. The city was organized by types of workshops, which could be found by their sounds and smells.[81] Today, the street names in Barcelona's Gòtic neighborhood reflect those past trades: Agullers (needle makers), Boters (cask makers), Corders (rope spinners), Dagueria (knife grinders), Semoleres (pasta makers), and so forth. Some of these constructions are still maintained in the old part of the city. Montcada Street is noteworthy for having been built from scratch. Arguably, it could be seen as one of the early efforts to "urbanize" the city. Although the structures that line this street are so well preserved (they were built at a later time and renovated in recent years), they nonetheless demonstrate the wealth of that time. The nearby Santa Maria del Mar, a beautiful example of a Catalan Gothic church, was built by the city's guild of fishermen and was also the subject of a popular novel written in 2006 by Ildefonso Falcones: *Cathedral of the Sea*.[82] The growth of trade shaped Barcelona's political framework rather than the other way around. Interestingly, as the city became the epicenter of the Catalan world, it was built not from the inside out, but rather from the outside in, thanks to its strong relationship with the hinterland. The noble houses of Catalonia resided in the mountainous regions, where they were protected and able to prosper. These noble families also built residences in the city but moved into the area only when they could tie their futures to the fate of the crown of the House of Barcelona.

The era of the expansion of the Catalan empire until 1443 proved to be economically and culturally enriching. Catalan vessels visited and traded in most of the ports in the Mediterranean. Culturally it produced two exceptional figures: Arnau de Vilanova (ca. 1240–1311), one of the most renowned physicians and religious reformers of the Middle Ages, and Ramon Llull (ca. 1235–1316), a philosopher and logician who is considered the creator of Catalan as a literary language. He wrote some 256 texts in Catalan, Latin, and Arabic. Both men are frequently mentioned when illustrating the importance and influence of Catalonia in the medieval period. As personal physician to popes and kings, de Vilanova was deeply influenced by Muslim and Jewish religious and scientific beliefs, and his treatise on dietetics, *Regimen sanitatis ad regem Aragonum*, was written for King James II of Aragon. His dietetic work dates to the ancient Greek and Arab periods and it was influential in later cookbooks like Rupert de Nola's *Llibre del coch*. De Vilanova's instructions on how to maintain good health and hygiene were tailored to his audience, from the general population to professionals to kings and the nobility.[83] An important contribution was his introduction of distilled spirits to Spain. The process of distilling, whereby substances are vaporized and then condensed by cooling, is said to have been invented by Zosimus, an Alexandrian Greek alchemist. The descriptions of the process are found in Muslim texts and given Arnau's knowledge of Arab medicine, he was familiar with texts dealing with the distillation of rose water, vinegar, and wine. His expertise in the distillation of alcohol as it appears in the treatise *De vinis (sive de confectione vinorum)* quickly spread across medieval Christian Spain. He wrote that "from the distillation of the wine . . . we get *vino ardiente* (burning wine), which is called the 'water of life' and which is the most useful part of the wine."[84] As Chabrán notes, in medieval Spain "distillation was central to the production of alcoholic drinks, medicines, and perfumes, and signifies the beginnings of modern chemistry."[85]

The cultivation of grapes and production of wine was important during this time. Barcelona had vineyards that were mostly produced by the monasteries in the city. In fact, the clergy was by far the largest producer of wine, even more than the land-owning aristocracy. Clerics were large land lenders for vine growers, and they consumed large amounts of wine during their meals and also used it for liturgy. From the thirteenth century on, wine became even more important as the Pia Almoina, the eleventh-century Gothic "House of Pious Alms" serving the Order of St. Augustine, provided food for the city's poor. Wine was a major component of this meal, and it constituted one of the largest expenses: 16.6 percent of the total expense for feeding the poor.[86] Of the 340 days of the year when the detailed expenses were annotated, wine appears on all but two days, the Thursday and Friday of Easter Week (likely because of religious reasons).[87] Drinking wine, beer, or any fermented beverage was attractive not only because of its high caloric content but also because it was a way to avoid contaminated water and therefore undesired ailments. As sanitary conditions deteriorated in the city because of poor sewer and drainage conditions, drinking wine became a necessity. According to the archives of the Pia Almoina, the wine distributed to the poor was brought from the surrounding vineyards and was of the lowest quality.

In terms of culinary tradition, thanks to the preservation of the *Sent Soví* cookbook, we have an idea of the sophistication and complexity of this period's cuisine. Before delving into the particularities of the manuscript, it may be useful to define some cooking terminology and ingredients of the time. In terms of the kitchen equipment, this period was in many ways a continuation of earlier times, as the open hearth, or *llar*, remained the main source of heating in cooking. The *bresquet*, a type of brazier that stood on legs, was used to burn coal and had a built-in rack for pots and pans. It was used to make more delicate dishes or sauces that required constant heat to avoid curdling.[88] A new cooking utensil used during this time was the *cassola* (a word of Arabic origin), which was flat and low rimmed and usually a type of earthenware dish used to sauté meats and fish. Grewe highlights the following culinary techniques from the period that continue to be part of Catalan cooking today: *Picada*, a sauce prepared in a mortar to finish other dishes, is a highly adaptable recipe. It consists of pounding aromatic ingredients such as herbs, spices, and garlic in a mortar with a thickening agent such as bread, almonds, or hard-boiled egg yolks and is used to finish or thicken soups or stews. Luján notes that in the medieval *picada*, chicken or duck liver was also used.[89] The resulting paste was diluted with water, broth, vinegar, or wine before being added to the final dish. *Sofregit* is the foundation for many dishes and sauces. It is usually based on minced onions that are slowly fried. After tomatoes were introduced from the New World, they also were included. A Catalan thickening technique uses raw egg yolks in broths or sauces. The resulting sauces are creamy and often tart, as the recipes call for the addition of *verjus*, or vinegar, to prevent curdling. Finally, because almonds grew abundantly in the Catalan region, they were used in many different and creative ways in the kitchen. Almond milk is perhaps the most common by-product and a key ingredient in the popular *menjar blanc* and other sauces. Almonds were also used in confectionary in the preparation of marzipan (*mersepa*, old Catalan) and nougats (*torrons*).[90] As for ingredients, the recipes of the time called for a great variety of animals, both domestic and wild, and especially fowl for the nobility. Naturally, much of the locally grown produce was also utilized in the recipes of that time: eggplant, rice, spinach, sugar, bitter orange, onions, garlic, leeks, fava beans, chickpeas, lentils, parsley, wheat, barley, oats, almonds, walnuts, hazelnuts, pine nuts, pistachios, raisins, figs, and dates. Sour and bitter juices made from lemon, pomegranate, and unripe grapes were used in cooking, as well as flower waters. The spices mentioned include pepper, ginger, cardamom, cinnamon (in both sweet and savory dishes), cloves, and nutmeg.[91]

CATALAN MEDIEVAL COOKBOOKS

One may identify the thirteenth and fourteenth centuries as the highlight of Catalan gastronomy given the culinary manuscripts that have survived until today. The previously mentioned *Llibre de Sent Soví* and the *Llibre del coch* reflect a well-established way of cooking with ingredients and dishes common to the upper class and therefore reflect a period of wealth and heightened commercial activity. Eliana Thibaut i Comalada argues that by this time, Catalan cooking was recognized in the Mediterranean region and regarded highly by intellectuals, such as the humanist Bartolomeo Sacchi, who was known as Platina after his birthplace (1421–1481).[92] The prestige continued throughout history; centuries later the Frenchman Grimod de La Reynière (1758–1837) wrote that while Parisians were novices in cooking, the Catalans and Basques were masters in the culinary arts. Indeed, many of the traits distinctive to Catalan cooking of that time can still be found in the region's culinary practices today, such as the previously mentioned *picada* and *sofregit* and the combination of sweet and sour or sweet and savory flavors.[93] Medieval cooking techniques that are still used include cooking on embers (*escalivada*), mixing lard and olive oil for frying, and the use of eggs in a *truita* (omelet).[94]

In the preface of the most recent edition of *The Book of Sent Soví*, Joan Santanach describes it as a text that was widely circulated well into the sixteenth century. Only one manuscript has survived, and it is now in the library of the University of Valencia.[95] As the author of the individual recipes and the collection as a whole is unknown, it is hard to deduce exactly how it was assembled and to what end. Santanach suggests that, in accordance with other medieval text and manuscript compiling practices of the time, the book was derived from an original text that was amended, adapted, and extended by others, including the professional cooks who used it. It was seen as a practical text, a tool for cooks that could be adapted as needed. What survived is likely a version that had gone through many interventions; therefore it can be said that "we are dealing with a text that reflects a great swathe of the culinary traditions and the tastes of a whole period of history."[96] The influence of this text can be seen in the way its recipes appeared in later texts in Italy and in Castile, far from Catalonia. The recipes also appear in other texts such as *Llibre d'aparellar de menjar* (Book of food preparation), *Llibre de totes maneres de potages* (Book of every kind of dish), the famed *Llibre del coc* (or *coch*—both spellings are common—of which Catalan and Spanish printed versions survive), and the Italian treatise *Cuoco Napoletano*.[97]

Part of understanding a medieval text like the *Sent Soví* is acknowledging the many changes it has undergone and the variations that exist between copies. The inherently changing nature of all medieval texts was characteristic until the advent of the printing press, especially with practical texts like cookbooks. Santanach insists on this point, reminding the reader that the medieval cookbooks we see today "are not only some distance removed both from the hypothetical 'original' text but also include annotations resulting of [*sic*] actual hands-on experience in the kitchen."[98] These recipes are not meant to be followed step by step; they are guidelines for those with cooking expertise. Specific quantities, times, and temperatures are omitted from these stripped-down recipes. It was the job of the cook to "interpret" the recipe based on the ingredients at hand and prepare the dish. During this process, the cook might add notes or his own instructions. Recipes were also simply copied and made into new collections, as there was no real authorial ownership during this period. From these practices, it can be surmised that the Catalan text was probably also used by professional cooks who worked for the richer privileged class. Some of the recipes in the *Sent Soví* are clearly designed for banquets. Based on his study of other Catalan medieval cookbooks such as the *Llibre del coc*, Santanach has no doubt that the Valencian copy is quite different from the original. An important clue is the discrepancies in the index, which suggest earlier versions of the book. Of the ninety-one recipes listed, only seventy-two are included in the surviving version. Santanach speculates that of the hundred or so recipes that were included in the manuscript at the time the index was compiled, some thirty have been lost. Copyists may have dropped recipes and added others over time. The fourteen chapters added at the end of the manuscript are among the most remarkable entries: none seems to follow the tradition of the *Sent Soví*.[99] Freely compiled recipes that clearly belong to other manuscripts point to the complexity in recipe transmission during this period.

What is important about the *Sent Soví* is that it can be read as a homogenous cookbook that is both practical and useful despite its many variations. The book's prologue emphasizes its gastronomic credentials, no doubt important to those who served the *senyor grans* (great lords) and *bons hòmens* (gentlemen). The matter of gastronomic authority is important, as it demonstrates that the book was composed by a good cook who had experience cooking for the king of England. However, Santanach points out that the mention of the English royalty has to do with propaganda rather than historical accuracy.[100] Grewe has a similar outlook, as the manuscript does not contain any English dishes, is written purely in Catalan, and uses Mediterranean ingredients.[101] That the compilation is "approved" in the introduction of the manuscript is also important: "And all the squires of the land, and the cooks, ministers, servants, and subjects of their lords commend, accept, and approve it, that it was all composed and true."[102]

The cookbook opens with a recipe for "peacock sauce," a two-part procedure that includes the preparation of the sauce that accompanies the dish and the instructions for preparing the bird. From the description we know it is an elaborate and spectacular medieval dish in which the fowl is presented perfectly roasted, with the feathers of the head, neck, and tail still intact.[103] As Grewe states, this is one of the more lavish medieval dishes, which explains its prominent placement in the compilation.[104] This recipe was likely the combination of two separate recipes. An important practice to remember about medieval cuisine is that sauces were prepared and served separately from the meats. Meats were usually roasted on an open spit—the previously mentioned *llar*—and served on flat plates. Many types of meats and sauces were served, and the diner could choose what to eat, which often depended on his (or her) social status. Hughes refers to this recipe in one of the anecdotes he tells about the relationship between literature and cookery: when Joan I of Catalonia and Aragon married his fourth wife, Sibilla de Fortià, in 1381, at their wedding feast a roast peacock with all its feathers was set before the bride with a poem printed on a card tied to its neck that read "A vós me dò, senyora de valor (I give myself to you, lady of bravery)."[105]

Sauces seem to have played an important role in banquets—of the first fifty-eight recipes in *Sent Soví*, around twenty deal specifically with the preparation of popular sauces of the time, some cold and others hot. There are recipes for camel sauce (named for its color), lemon sauce, meat sauce, goose sauce, sauce for any kind of meat, parsley sauce, and so forth. The book likewise offers recipes geared toward food preservation, such as fish in vinegar and gelatin, vinegar sauce (the previously mentioned *escabetx*), or vinegar dressings (*sols*). There are also recipes for broth, which Santanach links to the close relationship between food and medicine during the Middle Ages.[106] There is ample documentation from the period that discusses the curative properties of different food items and the conditions for which they are prescribed. A few of the recipes in *Sent Soví* contain explanations

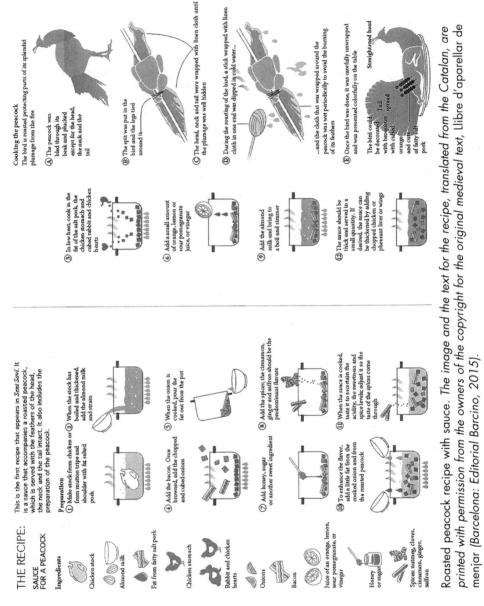

Roasted peacock recipe with sauce. The image and the text for the recipe, translated from the Catalan, are printed with permission from the owners of the copyright for the original medieval text, Llibre d'aparellar de menjar (Barcelona: Editorial Barcino, 2015).

about the virtues of the dish for certain ailments. The interest in the relationship between health and food is not surprising, considering the dietetic treatises of the time, such as the texts by Arnau de Vilanova mentioned earlier. The humor theories put forward by the Greek physician Galen of Pergamon (129–ca. 216) were still influential in the Middle Ages, and dishes and specific food ingredients were recommended or warned against to address humor imbalance. For instance, the chicken broth recipe from chapter XV is suggested for someone in need of "strength." On the other hand, "almond broth"—made from chicken and salt pork but named for the white, almond-like color of the salt—from chapter XVI can be adapted for a variety of conditions, from "delicate health" to fever or "liver heat":

> If you are preparing these chickens for someone who has an acute fever, you can add cold seeds, such as melon or squash, and purslane, and you can add chickpeas. And if it was someone who has liver heat, put in a little sow thistle or endive. In this way you can make any kind of broth. For someone who is feverish you can add some parsley leaves and a little sour grape juice to the almond broth. In this way you can make any kind of broth for the sick, as with kid meat or other kinds of meat, for anyone who is sick, as has been said before.[107]

Thibaut i Comalada points to the many medicinal uses for the food items known and used during the medieval period in Catalonia, such as lemon trees (gout), strawberries (nerves, indigestion, menstruation), garlic (arthritis, hypertension), onion (asthma, headache), nettle (lack of appetite, diabetes), ginger (headaches, rheumatism), chicory (indigestion), and so on.[108]

Francesc Eiximinis, in his famed multivolume treaty on Christianity—of which the third volume, *Terç del Cretià*, deals with sins and remedies—categorized dishes as *cuines* or *pietances*: those one eats from bowls with bread or a spoon or those—usually meat or fish—that are roasted, grilled, boiled, poached, or breaded and fried. The *Sent Soví* recipes also are categorized by these two ways of preparation, though there are no instructions for *pietances*, except for one recipe for roast fowl with a particular sauce.[109] Other recipes, including *sosenga* (fried meat sauce), could be described as a *cuines* dish, although others do not fall into either category, such as the clearly Arab-influenced dish of stuffed and baked eggplant. There are also recipes that are served in bowls that are not sauces or broths, such as *genestada* (broom pudding), a yellow-colored sweet cream that is similar to the well-known medieval dish *menjar blanc* (white dish). The difference between them was the use of chicken; therefore, the *genestada* was suited for fasting days since it did not contained meat. Interestingly, there is no recipe for *menjar blanc* in the *Sent Soví*; instead, there is a cheese sauce, *almadroc*.[110] The *sosenga* from Santanach's edition is a good example of a sauce recipe using proteins, produce, and spices, as well as the techniques of the period:

> To make meat sauce of rabbits, hare, or whichever meat you want, and of mutton, veal, kid meat, or partridge, cut the raw meat into small pieces, and fry them in salt pork grease, oil, or animal fat. Then take onion cut into large pieces, and fry it with parsley, herbs, honey, vinegar, and toasted bread, and the broth of other meat. Fry them raw, as said above, in pork grease mixed with fresh oil or some salt pork. When this is fried, take a found onion cut in large pieces and fried, and put it in the pot or a casserole, according to the quantity there will be. After that put in some thick broth, verjuice, and sweetening, and minced livers of other meats, and some whiter meat; boil it until it is well cooked. Flavor it with salt, spices, and sweet and sour sauce. And when you take it off the fire, if it is not thickened to your liking, put in beaten eggs.
>
> And if you want to make it more delicate, instead of another ground substance, put in almonds, and for verjuice put in pomegranate wine or orange juice, and for sweetening put in honey or sugar. In this sauce there should be more cinnamon than any other spice, and any spice may be added. Generally it can be made with any type of meat, and it can be served in the morning or in the evening.[111]

Another dish that was popular beyond the borders of Catalonia, according to Grewe, was *mig-raust*, literally "half roasted," which is finished in a sweet and sour sauce of almond and spices.[112] In this recipe, the chicken is roasted on a spit, while a broth is made of parts of other chickens or the innards of the fowl being roasted and blended with almond milk. To this mix verjuice, sugar, and spices like pepper, ginger, cloves, cinnamon are added and boiled into a sauce for a long time. The dish was finished by cooking the sauce with the quartered meat taken from the spit.[113] Interestingly, although many recipes clearly mark this as a Mediterranean cookbook, there are few seafood recipes and no shellfish recipes. The fish recipes, for both saltwater and freshwater fish, specify whether they should be consumed fresh or salted. The salted and dried fish mentioned are dried eel (*congrio seco*) and dried and salted tuna (*sorra*).[114]

Another important recipe book from the period is the aforementioned *Llibre de coch*, written around 1490 by Rupert de Nola, which quickly spread throughout Europe in multiple editions. It was first published in 1520 in Barcelona, and in the title the author is identified as "Mestre Robert," chef to King Ferdinand of the Kingdom of Naples. In the book, the author explains Catalan cooking and its implementation in the refined court of Naples.[115] Although dating to the late fifteenth century, many of the recipes can be traced to much earlier periods. Colman Andrews dates the book prior to its first known printing in Barcelona, since it contains recipes that refer to Lenten dietary restrictions that were abandoned in 1491. He calls it more

Cover of the *Llibre de doctrina para ben servir, de tallar y del art de coch, ço es de qualsevolmanera de potages y salses* (ca. 1520). *Public domain image from Biblioteca Patrimonial Digital, Universitat de Barcelona.*

"international" than *Sent Soví* because it includes dishes that are clearly Provençal and Italian and some that appear to be from Istria or Dalmatia.[116] The dating of the cookbook is further complicated because it is known that Martino da Como drew from these recipes for his *Libro de arte coquinaria*, the most significant culinary work of fifteenth-century Italy.[117] Later, Bartolomeo Sacchi, known as Platina, used Martino's work in his *De honesta voluptate et valetudine*, which was published in the late fifteenth century.[118] What is known is that once the recipe book was published, it was an absolute success. Indeed, it was translated into Castilian and printed in Toledo in 1525, even though it contained no Castilian recipes. Catalan food historian Néstor Luján writes that the Castilian version was more popular than the Catalan one.[119] Isabel Moyano Andrés speculates that if the cookbook was printed thanks to the support of King Ferdinand of Naples, its translation into Castilian might have been inspired by another king, Charles V, who might have become familiar with the cooking and recipes of Nola during his stay in Barcelona in February 1520.[120] She supports her theory by observing that the first edition in Castilian carries the imperial coat of arms, which occupies a large part of the cover. The Castilian edition does not quite match the Catalan edition, as it introduces some changes in the instructions for the preparation of dishes but retains the original recipes. It was reprinted at least fourteen times in the span of one century, which is surprising for a cookbook during this period and speaks to the importance of courtly cooking during the Italian Renaissance.[121]

The connection between the cookbook and Charles V produced an interesting reading of its cuisine a few centuries later by one of the earliest Spanish food journalists, Dionisio Pérez (1871–1931). In addition to politics, Pérez wrote extensively about food and was known to be quite the gourmand. He wrote about Spanish gastronomy under the pseudonym "Post-Thebussem," after the great Mariano Pardo de Figueroa, "Doctor Thebussem," who wrote about food with a great sense of humor. Pérez was motivated to prove that the origin of the cookbook was Castilian, once and for all, and that Spanish gastronomy was superior to French. Pérez believed that the French were frivolous and that their cooking was based on sauces stolen from other countries, like mayonnaise, or on dishes like the pheasants from Alcántara. He even argued that puff pastry and *foie gras* were the inventions of Spaniards. Néstor Luján took great joy in disproving the southern journalist (Pérez was born in Cádiz), arguing that *Llibre del coch* actually demonstrated the superiority of Catalan cuisine and its longer tradition compared to that of Spain and of other European countries. Luján speculated that the reason Pérez did not know about the Catalan roots of the recipe book was because he did not understand the unique characteristics of its cooking, such as the use of *picada*. Another clue about

Pérez's ignorance was his explanation of an ingredient that appears in the book: *aigua rosada* (rose water).[122] Luján noted that if Pérez had read any medieval recipe texts, he would have known that *aigua rosada* was the aromatic water made by infusing rose petals. This ingredient was widely used to prepare fish dishes like trout or grouper. It was also used with grape must and bitter orange to make a sweet and sour sauce that accompanied beef or pork dishes. The Catalan food writer traces a long list of words used in the *Llibre del coch* that reveal the Catalan roots of its cooking in an effort to differentiate it from Castilian cooking.[123] In the late nineteenth century, the gastronomic rivalry was due in part to the political relationship between Madrid and Barcelona, but the discussion about the differences between Catalan and Spanish cooking certainly has not ended.

The *Llibre del coch* consists of three parts. One addresses the cooking and serving staff and offers instructions for carving meat, setting the table, and for properly serving diners.[124] The second and the third part deals with dishes that can be served during non-Lent and Lent days. Among the non-Lent recipes are sauces, dishes that could be described as stews (*potatges* or prepared in *cassolas*), and fruit dishes. Recipes for Lent use fish and seafood in preparations like *escabetx*. Due to the many fish and seafood recipes in the book, Andrews deems the chef quite knowledgeable about them. The book mentions at least twenty-nine varieties of fish and shellfish, and aside from trout and barbell, they all can be found in the Mediterranean and continue to be eaten in Catalonia today: conger eel, tuna, dentex, hake, spiny lobster, squid, cuttlefish, octopus, and swordfish (called *emperador*—"emperor"—by Nola, a commonly used name for the fish).[125] There is also a clear Moorish influence in the cookbook, as several of its recipes call for the use of eggplant. Chabrán brings our attention to one of them, *Alberginia a la morisca* (Moorish eggplant), which calls for the vegetable to be cut in quarters, cooked, pressed to remove its water, chopped, and fried with good bacon fat. When well fried, the eggplant is cooked in a pot with broth, grated cheese, and ground coriander. Included in the recipe is the comment "Moors do not eat bacon" as evidence that the recipe adapted was from an Arabic one.[126]

A popular medieval dish present in all medieval cookbooks was what the Catalans called *menjar blanc*—literally "white food"—and despite being mentioned in the *Sent Soví*, it does not appear among its recipes. The *Llibre del coch* offers a version of this recipe that uses a hen, rice flour, rose water, fine sugar, and goat milk, which can be substituted with almond milk. The hen is cooked and finely shredded, sprinkled with rose water, then cooked with flour and milk and finished with fine sugar on top. Andrews explains that this popular dish is said to have been invented around Reus, near Tarragona, sometime during the eighth or ninth century, and he incorrectly states that, even if the French claim *blancmanger* as their own, it is of Catalan origin.[127] He links this particular version of the *menjar blanc* to Catalan monks who seem to have been quite clever when it came to outwitting the dietary obligations imposed by the Catholic Church. *Menjar blanc* appears to have been such a recipe, as the church forbade meat and milk during Lent. However, the "milk" of almonds was allowed, and Catalans began to use it to enrich a variety of savory dishes (as well as to replace meat ingredients). The dish could be considered one of the most famous and enduring of its time, although today, far from its medieval origins, it has become a dessert, "a mild, subtly delicious sweet pudding with a ghost of almond flavor."[128]

DIFFERENT DIETS FOR DIFFERENT PEOPLE

The surviving cookbooks give us an idea of what the privileged classes of Catalonia ate during the Middle Ages. Fewer details remain about what the peasant and lower-class Catalans ate during that time. Another source of information is the bookkeeping records from the period detailing the food expenses of the noble class and their servants. In feudal times, the castle (and estate) guard or administrator (*castlà*) housed the lordship of the estate. Rafael Conde traces the stay of the wife of Guillem Ramon de Montcada, Guillema, in the castle of Sentmenat in the twelfth century. By looking at the bookkeeping, he can identify the money she spent on food and other items, including alms to the church and shoes for her servant. Her spending provides a useful window into the dietary practices of the time, though it does not provide exhaustive details about quantities of goods or the number of people who consumed them. It offers an overview of the foodstuffs purchased to feed Guillema's servers and herself over the course of her stay in the castle from April to August 1189, with some interruptions in between. Conde describes a diet mostly composed of bread, wine, and meat seasoned with pepper, with the exception of Fridays, when they abstained from eating meat, consuming instead cheese, eggs, and, on one occasion, fish.[129] The difference reflected in the diet is measured primarily by how often they ate meat. For instance, April is considered a poor month since meat appears only three days during an eight-day stay. They have fresh and salt pork (with pepper) and lamb; for the rest of the stay, they eat bread, eggs, and cheese. In May the diet is richer, as meat consumption becomes more frequent and includes fresh and salt pork, chicken, and other meats, in addition to vegetables such as onion and cabbage. In June the diet is even richer and more diverse. In addition to the fresh and salt pork, there is beef, lamb, geese, and chicken.

Although the basic diet consists of meat (mostly pork) and bread, there is a notable increase in the variety of items consumed when Queen Petronila visits the castle. During her visit, the meats consumed include fresh pork, chicken, geese, capons, hens, ham, and salted meat, as well as vegetables, eggs, cheese, oil, and salt.[130] Other accounts of the time are similar and include food items such as rabbits, fresh and salted fish, spinach, lard, vinegar, and fruit. Teresa Vinyoles Vidal explains that in the thirteenth century, there was a decisive step toward an economy based on the cultivation of grains and a diet primarily reliant on bread.[131] The most cultivated grain was barley, which was used as a base for the bread eaten by the peasants. Other cereals grown were oat (mostly as horse feed), rye, millet, and spelt, which could be mixed and made into bread. In times of need, even acorns and legumes were used to make bread. It is clear that wheat was part of the diet of the seigniorial class, and white bread was a sign of luxury and privilege. As part of their dues, peasants could offer baked bread to their lords, in the form of either large, round breads (*fogasses*) or flat ones baked on a wood fire (*coques* or *placentes*).[132] Their dues were also paid in wine or even harvested grapes. Sometimes wines were made in the fields in which they were grown, but they were also carried into the cities and made in the cellars of houses. As mentioned, wine was a staple in the Middle Ages, though it tended to be low quality and was often mixed with water.

The peasant tenants offered meat products, especially ham, pork, chicken, capons, hens, and geese, as part of their rent, or dues, to the owners of the land. Poultry and other bird meat were not consumed by the lower classes; they were primarily reserved for the tables of the aristocracy. Pork was the meat most consumed, both fresh and salted (the latter especially by the poorer classes). They also ate lamb and mutton, and the wool was used to pay the land rent. Beef was not consumed widely, and game like pigeons was consumed mostly by the upper class. As for meals, people generally ate twice a day, lunch and dinner. The daily meal of a working-class family consisted of a vegetable- or legume-based stew using cabbage or broad beans with some kind of meat or eggs or cheese, always with bread and wine. Meals for the poor were provided through alms, such as the Pia Almoina referenced earlier, and consisted of mixed grains, wheat, barley, and spelt. They also received soup with cabbage and at times legumes and meat. On abstinence days they received cheese or fish. Meat consumption was greater among the wealthier class: the nobility, the clergy, and the bourgeoisie ate meat every day unless forbidden by the Catholic Church.[133] There were already professional cooks during these times. For instance, every day in 1267, the Order of Cardona had to pay its cook, Bernat de Torà, a pound of white bread, wine, and meat or fish, the same as the other members of the order, and when there were eggs, he received four and a pound of barley bread. As payment for his wardrobe, he received a measure of salt.[134] His duties were to prepare the meals for the members of the order and their guests; in turn, he received the necessary salt to cook and make bread, in addition to the pots that he used in the kitchen.

Olive trees were protected since the eleventh century, and their sale and purchase were regulated and documented. In many places, the trees were counted to ensure that there were enough to provide adequate oil to the religious orders, since olive oil was used to cook fish during abstinence days and to light the oil lamps. Fish consumption was important, as the church mandated 107 days per year in which meat couldn't be eaten. Archives from monasteries show that they received donations to purchase fish on Fridays and during Lent. It is important to remember that other meats were obtained as dues received from peasants, but fish had to be purchased, which required income. In cities, records indicate that people could purchase beef, veal, goat, mutton, game, and poultry in the markets. Honey was a valued sweetener, as there is no documentation of sugar during the thirteenth century. The condiments (spices) mentioned in documents of this time include saffron, pepper, ginger, nutmeg, cloves, cumin, anise, and mustard seed. The most popular spice was pepper.[135] According to a 1157–1158 report, the queen of Catalonia and Aragon ate wheat bread and drank wine every day, including during Lent.[136] The meat consumed by the nobles were hens, chickens, capons, geese, mutton, fresh and salt pork, and lamb. Spices (usually pepper) were used with ingredients like garlic and onion to offer a variety of dishes for the nobility. During this period there was a definite relationship between the food and one's social class, and the nobility engaged in excessive eating to exhibit their privilege.[137] The most powerful ate meat—and lots of it—as meat symbolized vitality and strength. Eating meat became more of a psychological need than a biological one.[138] It is no surprise that the church would restrict meat as a way to exercise its control and power over the nobility, often rivals when it came to influence and power. The place a guest occupied at the table was also an important indicator of social status. Eating alone was an act of penitence and of social marginalization. Excommunication was not only the expulsion from an order but also the expulsion from the table: no one could sit with someone who had been excommunicated without running the risk of being punished as well.[139]

Life during the medieval period was full of social activities but also tension and civil unrest. Court records of the time are filled with crimes that are common today, from wife beating to poisoning, from embezzlement to rape. According to Hughes, there is even a Catalan version of the legend of Sweeney Todd, the demon barber who baked his clients into pies. In the Catalan legend, it was a woman innkeeper with her two daughters who ran a meat shop:

> From those who came to drink there
> they killed some [sic] when they cut them up
> they made pies and tripe
> they made sausages and salamis
> the best in the world.[140]

Luján also tells stories about eating and lodging establishments in medieval Barcelona. Although few records remain, such establishments must have been numerous given the capital's popularity among merchants and travelers. In 1393, there was already a guild for hostel owners. Some were associated with horror stories like the Hostal de la Flor del Lliri (Hostel of Lily Flowers), which supposedly had a room with a diabolic bed. When the guest laid down, the bed slammed shut, trapping and killing the lodger, whose luggage was stolen and whose body was salted, cooked, and fed to the other guests. Another lodging, Hostal de les Dides, came to be known as a hostel for wet nurses. Aware of the need for breast milk, many women came to the city from the countryside, waiting at the hostel until their services were engaged. The wet nurse had to pass a test to prove the quality of her milk: she was expected to express milk into a glass, which was quickly emptied and then watched to determine how quickly the remaining milk ran down the side of the container. If it was thick and took a long time, the milk was considered of good quality. Wet nurses and nursemaids celebrated Saint Agatha's day, in honor of the martyr whose breasts were cut off as part of her torture. They ate *panellets*, a type of marzipan pastry made of almond paste and pine nuts, which they dipped in milk. They believed sweets would increase their milk production.[141]

An important area of interest during the medieval era was the education of the residents of the city, especially the newly rich ones, who belonged to the merchant class of Barcelona. Francesc de Eixeminis offered advice regarding table manners. For instance, one should not clean one's teeth or nails between courses or talk about disgusting things that might cause others nausea or vomiting while eating. He wrote about Catalan cuisine in his Christian treatise and deemed it exemplary for other Christians, given the honest eating and moderate drinking of the Catalans. In his treatise on how to eat and drink well, he wrote about the commendable eating behavior of a monk. The account is interesting for the options this cleric had in terms of dining and drinking. He ate alone to decrease his gluttony and forsook all banqueting and costly meats like fowl, the best fish (*peix de tall*, larger fishes

Detail from the fresco *Miracle dels peixos; Sant Sopar; Miracle de Billettes; Miracle antimulsumà; Miracle de la dona malalta que combrega per coll* by Jaume Serra. Printed with permission from the Museu Nacional d'Art de Catalunya.

that could be served in pieces), sauces, expensive wines, and exquisite breads. He tried to reduce the quantity of his eating, so he ate meat cooked on a spit; he did not partake of meat dishes cooked in a pot. He abstained from every fruit except raisins and those taken medicinally. He denied himself sweetmeats made with sugar or honey, all types of milk, clarified butter, cheese, sweet juices like those made from oranges and lemons, manmade confectionaries such as nougat, doughnuts, spiced wine, wafer rolls, white wine, and so forth. He showed such moderation in his drinking that at lunch he drank only three cups of heavily diluted wine and at dinner two. For dinner he ate half of his meal, which consisted of bread and two eggs.[142] His diet shows us the connection between health and food and the belief in the Christian value of moderation. His eating decisions also illustrate a culinary culture that is abundant and diverse but dependent on good harvests and wealth.

Toward the end of the Middle Ages, the frailty of a society dependent on agriculture became clear. Poor harvests were devastating, and even when grains could be purchased, the menace of famine was ever present during this period. The fourteenth century experienced two great famines—1315–1317 and 1346–1347—and the Black Death in 1348 decimated the population.[143] Barcelona as a city was not immune to scarcity and famine, and despite the enlightened culinary period of the Middle Ages, the lower classes were always vulnerable to hunger. In fact, the history of Barcelona's radical politics has always been tied to hunger, as we will see in the following chapter. Meanwhile, the fifteenth century marks the end of the Catalan empire, as the last member of the House of Barcelona, Martí I (Martin the Humane), died without an heir. During this period, the city and the region were gravely affected by deadly plague epidemics, the collapse of the rural economy, and the failure of the banks, while Castile enjoyed better fortune. By 1497, the population of Catalonia, about 600,000 before 1350, dropped to 278,000.[144] The Mediterranean empire was now but a faraway dream, and the region was immersed in political turmoil, including a civil war that broke out in 1462 and lasted ten years. Ferdinand II (the Catholic) inherited Barcelona, a stagnant capital in financial distress, from his father Joan II. By marrying Isabella I of Castile, Ferdinand II brought the region definitively under Castilian influence, ending a stretch of independence for the Catalan principality that had begun about six hundred years earlier.[145]

3

Cooking Up a Nation

In 1888, a tourist preparing to visit the city of Barcelona for the World's Fair would have read the following description in one of the popular guidebooks of the time: "This city, considered one of the best in Europe, has many promenades and gardens and public and private buildings of great artistic merit. Its Eixample [expansion], authorized in 1861, has received much attention for its straight and spacious roads and for its constructions where one can study the exquisite taste of their ornamentation, a valuable jewel that justifies the fame of the capital of this province."[1] Just as the city's architecture was renowned, so were its cafés, as other writers informed visitors:

> Barcelona is, perhaps, the only city of Europe that has so many luxurious cafés. And one should be advised that the price of the beverages served in them are excessively modest, and in many of them, the service unbeatable. Unlike other locations, the client is not under obligation to tip the server, as his salary gets paid by the owner of the establishment. The waiters of the Barcelona cafés also don't look ridiculous as the ones in Paris, Madrid, etcetera, who are made to serve with an apron, as if they were the cook waiting the tables. The ones in Barcelona serve like private house servants or from the inns.[2]

Though another writer laments the lack of high-quality lodging available in the city in which to host the city's distinguished visitors, more authors praise Barcelona for its many attractive establishments, like its numerous *xocolateries*.[3] They admire the milk shops (with milking cows in the back) and note that Barcelona's shops compare with shops found abroad. Finally, they also compliment the number of taverns and luxury shops in the city where travelers could find the best local and foreign wines.[4] The descriptions of the cafés, with their large banquet halls, tastefully decorated ladies' bathrooms with mirrors and marble, and the food service, are in part responsible for the fame that the city enjoyed not only in Spain in the late nineteenth century but also throughout Europe and the United States.

It could be argued that the fame that the city of Barcelona enjoys today—architecturally, artistically, politically—was achieved largely during the nineteenth century. But to comprehend this achievement, we must understand how Catalans view their past. The perception of Catalonia as a separate political and cultural entity stems from its medieval past, when it reached the zenith of what Michael A. Vargas calls its "territorial elaboration."[5] The region not only functioned under its own government for centuries but also had a separate legal system, customs, and culture, which, after the marriage of Ferdinand II of Aragon and Isabella I of Castile, began to be absorbed under the centralized rule of the latter. The loss of sovereignty by the Catalan principality, which had existed for about six centuries, characterizes the debate about the region's understanding of its own distinct identity and culture.[6] The imprint of the urban and cultural changes experienced during the nineteenth continues to make Barcelona one of most visually memorable destinations in Europe. The history that leads to this urban aesthetic, with its lavish and opulent cafés and restaurants, is complex and full of contradictions, but one that physically and psychologically shaped the city and Catalan identity. After the demise of its medieval principality, the city of Barcelona was chiefly associated with the arrival of industrialization in the Iberian Peninsula. Catalonia is considered the place where this process first took root and distinguished itself as being more technologically advanced and more developed than the rest of the nation. The opening in 1832 of a factory in Barcelona to manufacture woven cotton goods on mechanical looms, for instance, can be pinpointed as the start of the modernization of the textile sector and led the way for new factories to open in the city and its surrounding areas, making Barcelona a powerhouse in Spain's new industrial economy.[7]

The great wealth accumulated by a sector of the Catalan society, materialized in the beautiful and striking buildings and drinking and eating establishments that characterize the city, is part of this success story, but so are the social unrest and political radicalization that accompanied this economic boom as a growing workforce was forced to live and labor under appalling conditions. Perhaps this paradox explains nineteenth-century Barcelona, taken to the brink by the violence of civil and political unrest amid technological advancement, urban development, and a nascent nationalism that bred a lasting and highly influential literary and artistic movement. These political and social crises—such as succession wars and foreign invasion and occupation—stemmed from older conflicts going back to the seventeenth century and affected Spain as a whole. In addition, the ideological confrontations that divided the peninsula between liberal and conservative forces in the name of progress and modernity versus tradition and absolutism shaped the politics of the region through the early twentieth century. At the same time, radical movements seeking social and political change often incited violence. One could argue that the civil war of 1936 was a continuation of the same conflict, one that would create long-lasting consequences for Spain. The Franco dictatorship that followed the end of this struggle was particularly hard on Catalonia, as it was singled out and ruthlessly dealt with by forbidding its language and culture in favor of a unified Spanish culture and language. The nineteenth century highlighted the contradictions that characterized this convoluted period. For example, amid the great expansion of the city and the wealth of its booming bourgeoisie, Catalans were unable to muster any meaningful political influence in the country. Hidden behind Barcelona's great prosperity were its ties to the slave trade and the social injustice suffered by its working class, which manifested in bouts of violence that disrupted a seemingly pleasant bourgeois existence. Meanwhile, the revival that Catalan culture experienced during this period through the literary and aesthetic movements of the *Renaixença* and the *Modernisme* (and later the *Noucentisme*) was a manifestation of a deep-felt desire to assert its identity and cultural importance despite the existing anti-Catalan sentiments on the Iberian Peninsula. And although the literary works that articulated Catalan identity came from the urban-dwelling upper echelons of society, its nationalist sentiment was rooted across social classes, especially among people in the countryside. The popular sentiments regarding regional identity continue to play an important role in the present-day Catalan independence movement, despite being connected to the area's conservative political parties.

Given the contradictory nature of this period, it is perhaps unsurprising that Catalan culinary history is also complex. Although the growing number of opulent cafés and other drinking and dining establishments during this period speak to local prosperity, its gastronomic scene was nevertheless characterized by its strong foreign influence. The rich tradition of medieval Catalan cooking began to lose its influence on the Iberian Peninsula, and from the late fifteenth to the seventeenth century, the center of gastronomy moved to Castile and the court of the Habsburgs, which would influence other cuisines in Europe and the New World.[8] Later, with the arrival of the Bourbons to the Spanish court in the eighteenth century, the culinary reference for the country became France and Italy, as the court's inclinations dictated the gastronomic preferences of the nobility and the bourgeoisie. Barcelona (and, by extension, Catalonia) was able to reassert its culinary prestige in Spain in the nineteenth century when it witnessed once again the increased circulation of published cookbooks compared to other regions and its famed restaurants were regarded more favorably than the ones in Madrid. Yet even with the success of these publications and the city's renowned restaurants, it should be acknowledged that the cooking in Barcelona was shaped by French (and Italian) influences, imports from the American continent, and other trends considered "modern." There was, however, a striking gastronomic development, one that paralleled the general evolution of the city. As the prosperity of the Barcelona bourgeoisie physically transformed its urban landscape, it also created luxuriously decorated establishments such as extraordinarily beautiful modernist cafés, banquet halls, hotels, and beer and cocktail bars that populate the city. This abundance represented an outstanding period in which affluent locals and visitors enjoyed the gastronomy and hospitality offered by this European metropolis. The World's Fair of 1888 in Barcelona played a significant role in shaping this culinary culture as the city prepared for the international event. The further development of the hospitality and service industry during this time is also important to take into account, as it established a precedent for the thriving tourism that continued to transform the city from the late twentieth century until the present. The limelight enjoyed by Barcelona reflects how its industrialization intersected with gastronomy and cookery in particular ways, merging technology, convenience, and advertisement with food production and consumption. Finally, this culinary boom should be analyzed within the context of food crises and food insecurity, which were part of the daily experience of many of the city's residents and played a crucial role in the political radicalization of the period. To better understand the particularities of Barcelona and the region's culinary history during the nineteenth century, a quick overview of the long and convoluted history that shapes today's Catalan identity and culture is useful.

THE DEMISE OF THE CATALAN EMPIRE

The decline of medieval Catalonia described in chapter 2 was followed by at least three centuries of political conflict. Despite eventual absorption into Castile, Catalonia nevertheless was able to maintain a recognizable political entity with its own rights (*drets*), privileges (*furs*), and institutions, such as the Consell de Cent, which was mentioned in the previous chapter. Succession conflicts regarding the

Spanish crown and their aftermath eventually led to the complete loss of political sovereignty of the region. But amid the European wars that raged during this long period, business opportunities arose for Catalans. Under Castile's rule, the trade routes of the Atlantic eventually opened to Catalans, which had been closed to them until the eighteenth century. The loss of the northern European territories by the Spanish crown, and along with them their weaving mills, meant that Catalonia would become the center of textile production for Spain, which would allow it to position itself to develop into the first industrialized city in the Iberian Peninsula. The wealth that the *indianos*—the Catalans who went to the American colonies to engage in trade and other commercial activities—brought back to the region also spurred entrepreneurship and industrialization. But the continual political upheaval that characterized these changes in fortune also meant that Catalonia, and especially Barcelona, suffered heavy losses, both economic and human, in addition to being besieged by outside forces. The city had been surrounded by a wall since the Middle Ages—Jaume I started building the first wall atop the older Roman ones in the thirteenth century—and since then, the fortification built to protect the city played an important role in Barcelona's urban history, as it was also used by invading forces to control it. It is therefore not surprising that the concept of siege has acquired metaphorical and even methodological significance when studying the city. Robert Davidson, for instance, thinks of Barcelona as a captive city, one that learned to live under watchful eyes due to the military forces and restrictive centrist policies of the Spanish state during a large period of its modernization.[9] What is more, during the nineteenth century, when Catalonia was undergoing a foundational period in both cultural and political terms, it was experiencing brutal class warfare among its residents. This crucial moment of urban and economic growth undercut by street violence showed what it meant to exist under attack from the ruling and working classes, besieged by interests pulling in opposite directions.[10] The fact that the city survived this violence, which included a prolonged dictatorship during the twentieth century, is a testament to the survival instincts of this urban enclave and to the creativity and adaptability that characterizes its modern history.

Although the combative history that leads to the foundational nineteenth-century politics and culture of Barcelona is rich in detail, a brief overview is helpful in understanding the way that the culinary culture of the city and its surrounding areas evolved amid the ups and downs of warfare, politics, trade, and industry. It is a worthwhile review, as the cultural achievements of the nineteenth century sparked the current attraction to and international interest in Barcelona. An efficient narrator of this history is John Payne, who traces the major struggles that laid the path for Catalonia's modern history.[11] He starts with the Revolt of the Catalans of 1640 to explain the origins of the tension between the Spanish monarchy and Catalonia. The event is also significant because part of the underlying reason for the rebellion was lack of food. The Habsburgs at first paid little attention to Barcelona; Seville and Cádiz were the centers of the crown's monopoly on colonial trade with the New World. The Catalans were loyal to the crown as long as their rights were ensured. "If not, not" was the principle that regulated these relations until the reign of Philip IV and his chief minister and the most powerful man in Spain, the Count Duke of Olivares, who was intent on getting the Catalans to contribute men and money to finance the wider Habsburg interests in Europe.[12] When the authorities imprisoned several members of the Barcelona Council of One Hundred after they had endorsed the refusal of Catalan villages and towns to billet the troops, more than a thousand peasants entered the city and freed the local officials. The temporary capitulation to the peasants' demands had tragic consequences later when the confrontation erupted in the Catalan peasant uprising of 1688, in which the French aided the peasants. The royal troops quelled the rebellion and murdered one of the leaders of the uprising, displaying his head in a cage on the wall of the Generalitat.[13] The French, who first supported the peasants, signed a treaty with the Spanish crown that allowed it to keep the Catalan counties of Roselló (Rousillon), Conflent, Vallespir, and the upper half of Cerdanya.[14] Despite being a minor conflict, it is culturally significant because the peasants—*els segadors*—who started the uprising later inspired the national anthem of Catalonia in the nineteenth century.[15] An important reason that the peasants refused the billeting of soldiers was the locust invasion of 1684 onward and the bad harvest of 1687.[16] They suffered significant losses and could not afford to feed the soldiers, who were not happy about begging for food. Since the nobility, clergy, lawyers, and doctors were exempt from these contributions, the chancellor of Catalonia sided with the peasants, sympathetic to their hardship.[17]

Involving the French in the revolt was treasonous; by seeking foreign help, the Catalans expected harsh punishment from the Spanish crown, but to their surprise they were allowed to keep many of their separate institutions. The leniency of the Habsburgs and the memory of the betrayal by the French, who abandoned them during the fight, likely influenced the Catalans' decision in 1701, when the last Spanish Habsburg emperor-king, Carlos II, died without an heir. The Catalans supported Archduke Charles of Austria rather than the French Philip of Anjou, the first Spanish Bourbon who would rule as Felipe V (Felipe IV in Catalonia).[18] Historian Felipe Fernández-Armesto calls this decision the most interesting problem of this conflict. He speculates that the primary reason for backing the Austrian was to keep the war away from Catalonia to avoid disrupting the citizens' daily lives and businesses, even though the Bourbon king offered access to the trade routes of the New World.[19] The ensuing war was catastrophic for the Catalans. First backed and later betrayed by the English, they were abandoned and left to fend for themselves in a prolonged battle that ended with the siege of the city in 1714. The decisions leading to this outcome involved religious fanaticism and the portrayal of the battle as a war for freedom from despotism instead of one to protect the fiscal rights of the region.[20] The Bourbons entered Barcelona on September 11, 1714, and two centuries later, Catalans started celebrating a national holiday, *la Diada*, on that date.[21] Interestingly, the year 1714 has acquired more significance over time: it is recognized as the year during which Catalans lost their sovereignty and their culture was almost eradicated. In fact, recent works like the one by Albert Garcia Espuche about eighteenth-century Barcelona should be seen as a conscientious effort to establish the city's history and the legacy of its strong urban culture and vibrant economy.[22] Incidentally, the three-hundred-year-anniversary celebration of the siege in 2014 was marked by a gastronomic event that included a culinary tour of the region.[23] Barcelona is portrayed as a cosmopolitan city in 1714, with a number of *becos* (inns),[24] hostels, bars, Dutch and Catalan distilleries, cafés, and shops selling drugs, sweets, tobacco, and luxury items. These items, including products and spices imported from Europe, Asia, and the Americas, were arranged in lavish displays and sold by the doors of the shops. Before the siege, Barcelona was a city populated with migrants from diverse places and origins (unlike Castile, as Miguel de Cervantes observed in *Don Quijote*).[25]

With the Bourbons in power, Barcelona lost its courts and the *Diputació*, the symbol of Catalonia's ancient right to autonomy. However, the loss of liberties was felt most when it came to previously waived taxes and economic privileges. Fernández-Armesto suggests that these losses acquired nationalistic connotations later, when the concept of "nation" became more developed, especially in the nineteenth century.[26] A physical act of repression against the city was the building of a citadel to keep a watchful eye over its residents. A much-reviled construction, it was not demolished completely until the short-lived First Spanish Republic (1873–1874). At present, it is the site of the Parc de la Ciutadella, a park on the northeastern side of the city that includes a zoo, the Palau del Parlament de Catalunya (a meeting place for the Parliament of Catalonia), a fountain, and the museum of natural science. For many years it was the only green space in the city, and the use of the area as a site for the 1888 World's Fair aided in its development. Some constructions from that time remain, like the Castell dels Tres Dragons, which resembled a medieval castle and was used as a restaurant during the exhibition.

THE CULINARY PREFERENCES OF THE NEW KING

Life under the Bourbons quickly returned to normal, with a clear effort to forget the immediate past. It led to a period of great affluence that can be appreciated in the buildings that still stand today, like the remodeled Llotja (Barcelona's stock exchange); the house of the Baró de Castellet, which houses part of the Picasso Museum; and the Palau Moja on Las Ramblas boulevard.[27] The opening of this old waterway into a main urban artery was a sign of what Robert Hughes calls rational urbanism, a desire for clarity and order in a space's functionality.[28] Although the avenue of Las Ramblas nowadays has become a city landmark, it then carried a distinct message of power, one that reminded the city of its occupied status.[29] This new road, which ran through the middle of the labyrinthine streets of the medieval part of the city, was perceived as a form of invasion that would change the fate of the capital of Catalonia. Notwithstanding this sentiment, Barcelona enjoyed prosperity when it was annexed by Madrid, as its merchants gained access to the American trade. By 1778, Catalans were exporting primarily brandy and textiles but also spices, drugs, and paper.[30] It was during this time that Catalan vineyards first began to export, and since there was little interest then in Spanish wine on the continent except for Madeira, sherry, and port, Catalans were happy to export brandy to the American colonies, as it didn't occupy much space in their trading vessels. Textiles were also an important part of the trade, as Catalonia became the center of the textile industry after the Bourbons lost control of the weaving mills in northern Italy and the Netherlands.[31] Riding on the coattails of the Spanish economy, the city profited from its luxury trade, especially the import and production of chocolate, which developed an almost cult-like following in the region. The number of chocolatiers increased sixfold between 1729 and 1770, and the consumption of chocolate was surrounded with rituals that marked social differentiation and wealth.[32] Hughes reminds us that by the mid-eighteenth century, Spain had only two bourgeois centers; one was Cádiz, known for its buyers, sellers, agents, and traders, and the other was Barcelona, a city of makers and, above all, exporters.[33] A testament to this wealth from the viewpoint of the upper class exists in the detailed account of Rafael d'Amat i de Cortada (1746–1819), known as the Baró de Maldà (the Baron of Maldà), who kept a personal diary that grew to sixty volumes. He was known for his passion for food and was addicted to chocolate. In his *Calaix de sastre*, he kept a meticulous account of his gastronomic experiences, describing banquets, celebrations, special meals, and so forth. He also commented on the political events of the time, mostly through personal anecdotes. The volumes of his published writing show a rich cuisine with a heavily French influence and the culinary traditions and practices that spanned from the late eighteenth to the early nineteenth century.[34]

The royal kitchen played an important role in the creation of dishes and culinary trends in Spain. It is not surprising that the cooking was distinctively French under the Bourbons, since their cooking was highly esteemed in European courts by the nobility. This influence is apparent by the many French terms incorporated into the Spanish language, as well as in the menus of the nineteenth century and early twentieth century, when dishes were mostly French and written in that language. French food was popular in Castile and Catalonia, not only because of its culinary prestige but also because of the general Frenchification of the Iberian Peninsula, which identified its neighboring country as modern.[35] María Paz Moreno points to the difference between the diet of the Habsburgs and the Bourbons, the latter bringing more sophistication and refinement to the way dishes were cooked and served compared to the earlier, more straightforward and heavily spiced style of food preparation.[36] As the royal court was not physically in Barcelona, the city residents perhaps could not obsess over it as much as their Madrid counterparts. They did have an opportunity to do so, however, when the court of Carlos IV visited Barcelona in 1802 from September to November to celebrate the double wedding of his children, Ferdinand (the future king) and María Isabel, to Princess Maria Antonia of Naples and Francis I of the Two Sicilies. The social event was the result of a long and complicated political plot, but since the affair involved Naples and the Mediterranean, Barcelona, given its history, was chosen as the perfect site for the occasion.[37]

Preparations to receive the court show how complicated it was for a city to host more than 2,300 members of the court in addition to the other visitors it would receive for the celebrations. Barcelona then had a population of 160,000, with only about thirty or so lodgings and another thirty eating establishments.[38] Arrangements had to be made to ensure the proper supply of food during the court stay, including staples like wheat to make bread. The city government also had to ensure that prices would not rise due to high demand, although prices for items considered luxuries, such as snow from the mountains, were allowed to increase in order to guarantee their availability. Meat, oil, sugar, fish, and hay for the horses as well as wax for candles were also required. Availability of fresh water was very important, as was the continued supply of chocolate, not only for the court members but also for the population in general.[39] The Baró of Maldà, who, like other city nobility, had to offer lodging and serve as a host to members of the court, was not amused by the royal visit. He was charmed, however, by the desire of the king and queen to sample typical Catalan dishes prepared in the most popular and traditional

ways. They wanted to try the Catalan *guisats* (stews) and other recipes prepared
in terra-cotta dishes. The baron muses that it must have been enjoyable to see the
monarchs and their court members being served on these rustic dishes when they
were accustomed to the then-fashionable silver and gold plate settings and dishes
made of porcelain. He observes that since cooking on terra-cotta dishes is healthier,
others should adopt the trend. According to his sources, the king had a pheasant
dish with a lemon sauce and another Catalan stew. He notes that these dishes were
not known by the Castilians, who cooked everything with garlic and pepper and
without an understanding of what is considered good food. He also mentions that
the king and queen next wanted to try tripe cooked in the Catalan style and served
with *allioli*, a dish that goes well with alcoholic drinks. By enjoying these traditional dishes, the baron concludes that the royal couple showed their appreciation
for the Catalans.[40] The popular nineteenth-century cookbook, *La cuynera catalana*,
which is discussed later, contains recipes similar to the dishes served to the monarchs.[41] The recipes *Perdiu de altre manera* (pheasant in another way), *Estufat
de cuxa de moltò, cabrit, ò anyell* (leg of mutton, goat, or lamb stew), and *Tripes
de altre modo* (tripe in another way) provides an idea of the types of dishes that
the royal guests enjoyed during their visit. The first dish grills the pheasant then
slowly cooks it in a baking dish with parsley, salt, pepper, oil, bay leaves, chopped
garlic, lemon or orange peel, covered with water. An egg yolk finishes the sauce
after the dish is cooked and removed from the heat. The stew also grills the meat
first and then cooks it—along with salt, fatty salt pork, sausage, cloves, a head of
garlic, white wine and *aiguardent* (the distilled spirit mentioned in chapter 2), bay
leaves, oregano, savory, water, and cook—in a pot with the lid covered with brown
paper. After the tripe is boiled and cleaned, it is placed in a baking dish (*cassola* in
Catalan; *cazuela* in Spanish), covered by toasted bread, and topped with *allioli* and
other spices before repeating the layers. This dish can also be finished with eggs.
Afterward, a mix of pine nuts, saffron, parsley, and other spices is added to the tripe
and then cooked slowly over a long period of time.[42]

BARCELONA BECOMES WEALTHY

The capital accumulated by the Catalans through the American trade is said to
have later propelled the economic development and industrialization of Barcelona. The wealth also shaped the physical appearance of the city when the *indianos* or *americanos*—Catalans who had made their fortunes in America—returned
home and built handsome mansions along the main streets like Las Ramblas or

in their own villages in the region.[43] An interesting building from this time is the porticoed neoclassical block near the abovementioned Llotja, called Porxos d'en Xifré, which still houses one of the oldest restaurants in the city, Set Portes (Seven Doors). Josep Xifré was an *indiano* who made his fortune in Cuba exporting sugar grown on slave estates. When he returned in 1831, he went into banking and real estate, becoming the largest property owner in the city.[44] Noteworthy are the reliefs portrayed in the arcades that depict some of the sources of wealth during that period: slaves, bananas, and coffee. Xifré is not an isolated case of bourgeois Catalans using American-earned affluence to build more wealth back home. Some surnames should sound familiar to those visiting the city today, such as Güell, as in Eusebi Güell, the patron of famed architect Antoni Gaudí, whose father Joan was an *indiano*.[45]

The relationship between Cuba and Catalonia is rich in culinary terms. Prior to the nineteenth century, Spain had received new products from the New World such as tomatoes, green beans, potatoes, peppers, corn, and chocolate. Turkey is also an American addition to the Spanish diet. Some of these products were more quickly accepted than others. Peppers (and their ground form) and green beans, for example, were swiftly incorporated into cooking. Sweet potatoes gained quick reception, too, perhaps due to their sweet taste.[46] Turkeys became a staple for holiday meals, especially during Christmas time in Catalonia.[47] Also in Catalan cooking, chocolate started appearing in sauces to accompany rabbit, lamb, and even a lobster and chicken dish.[48] Tomatoes were not widely used until the eighteenth century, but then they are frequently present in sauces and salads and served with eggs. Meat and vegetable dishes that in the past were seasoned with mustard or cumin began incorporating tomatoes into them. Tomato sauce clearly becomes a staple in the Spanish diet, as it is referenced in many cookbooks, though instructions for its preparation often is omitted altogether because it is assumed to be common knowledge.[49] Sauce recipes indicate regional variation in names such as *salsa de tomates a la española* (Spanish-style tomato sauce). Potatoes, however, took longer to be accepted as a food product for human consumption; they were used primarily as feed for pigs. During poor harvests of wheat and other grains in the eighteenth century, there was an effort to convince farmers and the working-class of the nutritional value of potatoes and their benefits to human health. For a long time, they were identified as food for the poor. Given the importance of bread in the daily diet, potato flour was substituted many times over the years for wheat flour, with varying results. Its introduction to Catalonia was also mixed. Potatoes started to be cultivated around the city of Barcelona and sometimes sold in the El Born open-air market during the late eighteenth century, but they were considered to taste insipid (in comparison to the flavor of the potatoes grown in Ireland or, even better, in the Americas). Potatoes were more widely grown in the area of Camprodon, though they were mostly used for pig feed and grazing, proving that they were not enjoyed as much as radishes, parsnips and carrots.[50] But Baró de Maldà thought otherwise; he considered the potato a novelty worthy of consideration, especially by the local authorities whose job was to guarantee food provision for the people. He wrote of past failed wheat harvests and mentioned that potatoes, given their wide availability, ought to be explored as a substitute in breads. He offered his own experience of tasting bread made with potato flour, advising that potatoes first should be well baked in the oven and then mixed with wheat flour. The result was a white bread—tasty and, according to him, healthy, since potatoes aid in digestion—that served as a good accompaniment to heavier dishes.[51]

From the late eighteenth to the nineteenth century, the culinary exchange between Catalonia and Cuba became more regionally specific. Cocktails arrived in Barcelona from Cuba in the late 1800s, and bars serving them became very popular in the early 1900s. Recipes from the period frequently mention whether a dish is made in an American or Cuban style (*a l'americana* or *a la cubana*). Food historian Jaume Fàbrega highlights two examples of such recipes, *arròs a la cubana* (rice served with fried eggs and tomato sauce with optional fried plantains) and the drink *cremat* or *rom cremat* (burnt rum). The drink is now presented as an intrinsic part of Catalan culture.[52] Made with rum, sugar, spices (especially cinnamon), lemon peel, and coffee, it is today served ritually in towns along the Empordà during *havanera* concerts, a music born from the mix of Spanish country dance and indigenous and black music from Cuba that was popular in the region throughout the nineteenth century. The dance has enjoyed a revival as part of the recent interest in recovering Catalan traditions.[53] In addition to the trade of brandy and *aiguardent*, Catalans imported horse meat jerky, rum, sugar, and cigars. The invention of white rum was actually the work of a Catalan from the town of Sitges, Facund Bacardí i Massó, who, in collaboration with Joseph Léon Boutillier, developed a distilled rum in 1862 that was smooth, filtered from impurities with charcoal, and stored in wooden barrels. Since then, it has become the world's standard for rum and retains the Catalan's last name as its commercial trademark.[54] Fàbrega mentions that one of the first books on Cuban cuisine that was also one of the first Catalan cookbooks published in Spanish was written by an *indiano*, Joan Cabrisas, who in 1858 published the *Nuevo manual de la cocinera catalana y cubana. O sea, completísimo manual de cocina, repostería, pastelería, confitería y licorista, según el método práctico que se usa en Cataluña y en la isla de Cuba* (A new handbook on Catalan and Cuban cooking in Havana. That is, a complete handbook on cookery, sweets, pastry, confectionary, and beverages, using the practical methods of Catalonia and Cuba).[55] Reportedly an old cook from the well-known inn Fonda de los Tres Reyes, the author in his introduction urges readers to use the cookbook if they appreciate Catalonia, the country of good wines. He explains that the book contains instructions for seasoning and preparing typical Catalan dishes like *escudella* or the much-enjoyed *allioli*.[56] The commerce between the two sides of the Atlantic also influenced the food shops that were popular in the city during this time, which is discussed in the next chapter along with the fresh food markets of Barcelona.

GROWING PAINS

The Bourbon policies established to eradicate Catalan autonomy created the appropriate financial opportunities to make Barcelona a powerful industrial force. This fast-paced economic transformation exacerbated the disparity between the privileged and the lower working class. The tension produced by this inequality also created conflict between conservative values and modernizing trends that brought into view different political ideologies. Meanwhile, the Catholic Church was fighting to maintain its long-standing role as an arbiter of social and political values.[57] This social unrest fed into the political struggle between liberals and conservatives, who were fighting for the values espoused in the 1812 Constitution written in Cádiz when Ferdinand VII (who had celebrated his wedding in Barcelona) was dethroned by the French during the Napoleonic invasion of the peninsula. His return in 1814 marked the resurgence of an absolutist form of power that was resisted by liberals and later resulted in a series of wars when he died without a male heir and his brother Carlos claimed the throne in lieu of his three-year-old niece Isabella II. The Carlist wars, supported by rural Catalonia and other rural areas of Spain, came to represent a confrontation between traditional and absolutist interests against decentralization and modernization. Paradoxically, the wars forced many peasants to flee the countryside and move to Barcelona, increasing the population of the city and the number of factory workers, who, without housing or labor protection, lived in increasingly appalling conditions.[58]

The population increase during this time is striking: from 1840 to 1900, it grew from 121,815 to 533,000.[59] By the late 1800s, Barcelona was one of the most densely populated cities in Europe. It suffered a series of epidemics that paralyzed and emptied the city as residents with resources left in search of safety. The remaining inhabitants were the poor, who went hungry when shops, factories, and the port closed during these episodes. During these outbreaks, the city council distributed food to the poor and the hospitality industry was actively involved in this charity work.[60] A diet provided for the poor during an epidemic consisted of 600 grams of bread, some distilled spirit (*aiguardent*), soup with two ounces of meat and half an ounce of bacon for lunch, three ounces of chickpeas or beans at night, three ounces of salted cod, and half of a *porró* (glass wine jar with a long, tapered drinking spout) of wine per meal.[61] In 1885, an outbreak of cholera that lasted from July to November left 1,318 people dead. The bacteria that caused the illness was found in a well by Carrer de l'Hospital in the old part of town.[62] Residents used water obtained from wells and public fountains, and water salesmen also sold ten-liter water containers for 10 *cèntims*. As there was no sanitary control of these waters, people were in constant danger when drinking water or cooking. Water consumption was linked to typhus, dysentery, and other diseases.[63] According to Jaume Codina Aporta, from 1859 to 1875, the poor of Barcelona started dying of a new illness, tuberculosis, caused in part by a deficient diet.[64] Madrid approved the expansion of the city and the tearing down of the city walls in 1854 partially for sanitary reasons, as a measure to stop the spread of these illnesses and overcrowding.[65]

Another way in which the increase in population affected Barcelona was by reducing land where grapes could be grown for wine. Despite the extensive consumption of wine by the working class, the city was losing space to grow and manufacture a staple to its citizens' everyday diet. Grapes were still cultivated in the city; the varietals grown included *sumoll*, *garnatxa*, and *picapoll* for red and *xarel·lo*, *muscatel*, *joanenc*, and *picapoll* for white wine.[66] The wine produced in Barcelona was not very good and though most of the production was for local consumption, there were nonetheless a few wines—and especially distilled spirits and liquors from Badalona and Santa Coloma de Gramanet—that were valued abroad. In the early 1800s, the city had around 211 taverns and 104 shops for wines and liquors. Later, the industrialization of wine production meant that wine was made on a larger scale and small vineyards around the city disappeared. The industry expanded, creating factories for bottling and packaging wine. During the phylloxera epidemic, Barcelona and the surrounding areas became large exporters of wine, though the insect eventually arrived to the city by the early 1880s. Within a few decades, the infestation exterminated all vine crops in urban areas; however, it also resulted in the creation of agricultural institutions and labs to research and find solutions to the crisis, which later led to the early application of technology and the promotion of viticulture in Catalonia.[67]

Another manifestation of the political struggle and the discontent of the people was the strong anticlericalism that erupted, which led to the burning of convents and churches, including those around Las Ramblas. Significantly, these spaces were later used to build covered food markets. The vendors who worked alongside the walls of the church properties moved to these buildings in the late nineteenth century.[68] The Mendizábal decree of 1836 allowed the confiscation of church property and liberated much-needed urban space. The Catalan bourgeoisie quickly bought these lots and later used them in the expansion and reconstruction of the city. The author of the legislation, Juan Álvarez Mendizábal, an economist and politician with clear liberal sympathies, was the prime minister of Queen Regent Maria Cristina. His policies were an effort to modernize Spain and follow the steps of more liberal European countries. During this time the church lost many of its properties, and four-fifths of its land was sold off in Barcelona.[69] Interestingly, part of the struggle between liberal and conservative forces started to be channeled into a Catalan nationalistic discourse aligned with other nineteenth-century nationalisms, especially when Catalans became conscious of their cultural and political identity and began searching their past for traces of their history, traditions, and cultural heritage.[70] This effort could also be understood as a reaction to the anti-Catalan sentiment so prevalent and evident in the Madrid press of the period.[71] The resulting cultural movement, the *Renaixença* (the Renaissance), plays a crucial role in the rise of the literary and aesthetic movements that define modern Catalan culture. The close relationship between Catalan identity and the arts has been used to argue that the latter was mainly a product of the elite; yet historians have made a clear case for the continuity of a Catalan movement since the seventeenth century, evincing that the debate about its origins remains an ideological rather than a historiographic one.[72]

The social tension in the late 1800s that shakes Catalan society to its core originates from the disparity that exists between the bourgeoisie and the working class. Despite espousing progressive values when making claims for social and economic change in Spain (except when demanding protectionist policies to defend their businesses), the industrialists were reactionary when it came to their attitudes toward their workers and their wages, living and working conditions, and the employment of female and child labor.[73] Artisans and skilled workers tended to sympathize with the factory workers, even when the violence and destruction spread beyond the churches and affected factories and the machinery they needed for their work. The ongoing discontent also made Barcelona a fertile ground for anarchism and popular activism, practices that would later play important roles during the Spanish Civil War and the Franco dictatorship. At the height of the struggle, Barcelona experienced violent confrontations, including bombings in public gathering places. One of the most noted incidents was the 1893 bombing of the Barcelona opera house, the Liceu, by the anarchist Santiago Salvador. He threw two Orsini bombs, one

LA CAMPANA DE GRACIA

UN ENTRAN INESPERAT.

La noticia de la retirada de la escuadra de Cartagena ha caigut com una bomba en mitj del ministeri.

Political cartoon referring to the bombing and violence of the time: "Un entran inesperat" (An unexpected dish), published by *La campana de Gracia* (October 26, 1873). *Printed with permission from the Biblioteca de Catalunya.*

of which exploded, killing twenty-two people and injuring many others. Deeply shocking to the Catalan bourgeoisie of the time, the event was later referenced in the Sagrada Familia by Antoni Gaudí, who installed a sculpture depicting a demon tempting a worker with an Orsini bomb in the Chapel of the Rosary.[74]

The mobilization of workers eventually led to the founding of an anarcho-syndicalist trade union, the CNT, in 1907, but it could not avert the violent confrontation of 1909, which came to be known as the *Setmana Tràgica* (Tragic Week). Catalans who opposed sending reservists to fight in the colonial war in Morocco began a wave of violence that resulted in the destruction of eighty church properties, some containing schools, and more than eighty deaths.[75] The desperation felt by the working class is evident in the stark contrast between their food consumption compared to those of the privileged class. Their diet was based mostly on poor-quality bread, wine, and vegetables. As for animal protein, they had access to salt cod, pickled fish, and bacon, and the meat they could buy was usually offal and other animal extremities, which in the past were believed to be less nutritious and harder to digest.[76] Ironically, workers were criticized for their high alcohol consumption and their use of strong condiments that supposedly negatively affected their health and well-being, such as pepper, garlic, and raw onion.[77] Most texts of the time document that workers rarely consumed meat, except for important holidays. Otherwise, their diet consisted of mostly soups and stews with rice, pasta, and cabbage, some with boiled millet flour, bread made from buckwheat, and bruised fruit. Despite its poor quality and quantity, this diet represented 54.7 percent of a worker's salary according to the data gathered by Ildefons Cerdà, who designed the nineteenth-century expansion plan for the city of Barcelona that would later be approved by Madrid in 1860.[78]

AN URBAN EXPANSION FIT FOR A COSMOPOLITAN CITY

The plan by Ildefons Cerdà i Sunyer (1815–1876) allowed for a massive extension through a new proposed development called the Eixample (Expansion). The expansion was organized in a grid and divided by broad boulevards extending beyond the old walls, which would become the site for the most celebrated modernist buildings of the city.[79] As mentioned, part of the reason the Spanish government approved the plan was to stop the spread of illness among the working class and the overcrowding of buildings. The urban expansion dreamed by the socialist engineer reflected his optimistic view that technology—steam, gas, electricity—could be used to end human suffering.[80] His abstract plan garnered much criticism at the time, as it displaced the focus of the city away from its old center and therefore away from the prevalent interest in Catalonia's historical roots.[81] But his original plans were never fully realized and, in fact, mostly mangled by the greed of developers and landlords. The building of the area was slow, and it did not take off until the mid-1870s during the economic boom known as *febre d'or* (gold fever). Because there were no urban codes or regulations in place, the land was used to build more slums for the proletariat interspersed among the opulent and beautiful buildings for the new rich. In 1888, a doctor and sanitary engineer

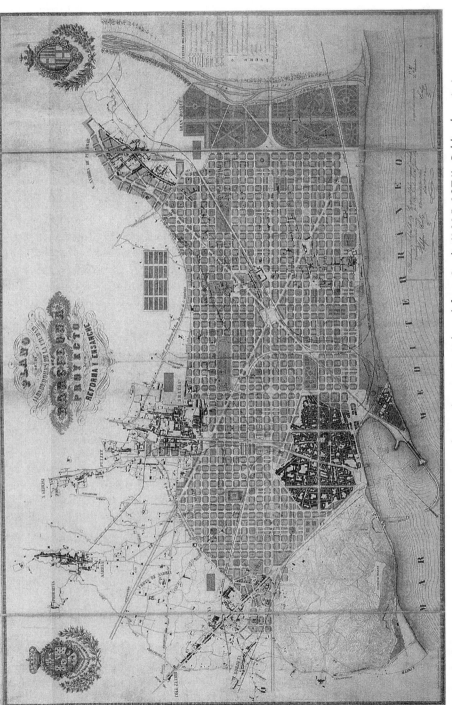

Original plan for the extension of the city of Barcelona (1859) by Ildefons Cerdà (1815–1876). *Public domain image.*

named Pere Garcia Fària wrote a report denouncing the living conditions in the Eixample, which were the antithesis of Cerdà's intention of providing the common people with light, space, gardens, and utopian hope. They had become as bad as the Old City: "veritable slums, in which the Barcelonan family is imprisoned."[82] But, as Hughes observes, the Eixample has since become one of the most interesting urban areas of Europe, "irreplaceable though mangled evidence of a social consciousness of a single, visionary designer" and, despite its monotony, "nowhere else can one see such a mass of the daring, generously overwrought, sublimely mannered structures of the Catalan *modernisme*."[83]

Buildings such as Casa Milà, Casa Batlló, Casa Amatller, and Antoni Gaudí's celebrated Sagrada Familia have become visual references of the city around the world. The aesthetic movement that gave rise to these constructions, the *Modernisme*, is linked to the *Renaixença* (Renaissance), a nineteenth-century literary and political movement that sparked a renewed sense of Catalan nationalism and accompanied the region's economic growth.[84] The origin of the movement is often associated with the publication of Carles Aribau's 1833 poem "Oda a la Pàtria" ("Ode to the Fatherland"), in which he equated language and homeland, emphasizing the crucial role Catalan language would play in creating a sense of shared identity.[85] The poem should be seen as part of the collective work to modernize and spread the use of Catalan not only as a colloquial language but also as a literary one.[86] The effort represents the beginning of the search for Catalan roots in its literary traditions. The interest in Catalan literary roots brings in 1859 the revival of past practices like the *Jocs Florals*, a medieval literary contest that was greatly celebrated in Barcelona.[87] There are also many references to Catalonia's glorious medieval past in the architecture of the time—for example, in the Cafè-Restaurant built by Lluís Domènech i Montaner for the World's Fair of 1888.[88] Yet the spread of writing and reading in Catalan was slow because Castilian was Spain's official language and people read newspapers and serialized novels published in this language. The *Modernisme*, the artistic movement that followed the *Renaixença*, recognized the need to modernize Catalan to meet the higher professional standards and ambitions of contemporary writers. The revival of the Catalan language continues to impact Spanish politics today. The struggle between Catalonia and Spain is closely connected to the region's linguistic policies after the end of the Franco dictatorship that mandated the teaching of Catalan and its use in education and the workplace.

The *Modernisme* was particularly successful in architecture and design. Thanks to the buildings created under its aesthetic influence, Barcelona became a famous European city. The nineteenth-century Catalan capital turned into the city of exceptional cafés celebrated for their beautiful design. The *modernistes* left historical revivalism behind and turned to original invention using traditional Catalan building materials like brick, iron, ceramic, and stained glass in daring ways. The work produced by famed architects like Domènech, Gaudí, and Josep Maria Jujol are associated with Art Nouveau from northern Europe for their preference for fantastic forms inspired by nature. But the comparison with this movement is superficial, as it ignores the way Catalan artists had already been working: their use of ceramic surfaces and iron fencing with palmetto motifs predates the invention of the northern style.[89] The European style did, however, have an important impact on Catalan graphic and decorative arts, which favored its natural forms and curved lines. The aesthetic of Art Nouveau was especially suited for ornamental pieces, which were in much demand to decorate the interiors of the beautiful new buildings and even more impressive cafés that were being built in the prosperous Barcelona. These famed and numerous establishments first began to appear around Las Ramblas and the Plaça Reial and later moved toward Plaça Catalunya and the Eixample. These lavish cafés—known for their salons with beautiful mirrors, frescoes, and paintings decorating the walls, gilded moldings, and marble tables and comfortable sofas and chairs, all brightly lit by numerous gas lamps—captivated locals and outsiders alike.[90] Although it is true that the World's Fair of 1888 brought many (some of them prominent) visitors to the city, Barcelona already had become a popular destination. The guidebook industry of this time shows that the city, despite being smaller than Madrid, had as many guides published as the capital. These books were useful for both natives and visitors because the city was changing rapidly. Business owners used them to advertise fashionable products for sale or to announce the opening of new establishments.[91] In the second half of the century, the guidebooks began expanding their focus from highlighting historical sites and monuments to including information about lodging, restaurants, and cafés.[92]

THE MOST BEAUTIFUL CAFÉS

One of the famous visitors to the city was Hans Christian Andersen, who arrived in 1862 and was enchanted by its cafés. He wrote that he had never seen cafés as luxurious and tasteful as the ones in Barcelona. He mentioned a café on Las Ramblas where he met with his friends every day. He described its hundreds of gas lamps, the painted ceiling supported by tall and svelte columns in the main salon, and the valuable paintings and magnificent mirrors on its walls. The café had an upper floor with other rooms including billiard rooms, and the garden was covered by an awning that was retracted during the late afternoon so customers could enjoy the blue skies. The people who frequented the establishment belonged to all social classes, from elegant gentlemen and ladies to high- and low-ranking officers and rich farmers dressed in velvety suits carrying colorful throws on their shoulders. As an anecdote, he recounted a time when he saw a modest-looking man enter the establishment with his four small daughters, who looked around with curiosity at the luxury and the exquisiteness of their surroundings. Andersen speculated that for the girls, this visit was comparable to the experience of seeing a theater play for the first time.[93] Although he does not mention the name of the café, we know he was referring to Cafè Cuyàs (also known as Café de las Siete Puertas, owned by Josep Cuyàs), which was considered the pearl of the Barcelona cafés in the 1866 Barcelona city guide by Cornet i Mas.[94] The café was noteworthy for its large rooms, the Gran Saló on the main floor and the room known as the Sala de les Mil Columnes (the salon of a thousand columns), a garden patio that was used as an open-air café during the summer, an elegant confectionery with a separate entrance, and a room that served as a restaurant. Underground, there was a cellar and two large salons where beverages could be served that contained two grand pianos. This was during a period in which an opening or a remodeling of a café was a great city event. Before opening to the public, the owners hosted large soirées with buffets flowing with French champagne to which city officials, politicians, businessmen, and other important residents of the city were invited.[95]

The large number of cafés in the late 1800s and their popularity reflected not only the hobbies and the taste of the Barcelona bourgeoisie but also those of the general public. Many of these establishments, as already noted, were well established around Las Ramblas and slowly, in the later part of the century, moved toward Plaça Catalunya and then the Eixample area. Each café had its own regular customers and served as the site for different group gatherings. Paco Villar, in his detailed book about Barcelona as a city of dazzling cafés, describes the scene in these establishments as so popular that they were full of people and chatter from the afternoon into the evening. Each locale had its own *penya* (a social group formed around an activity like playing cards, following a sports team, or some other hobby) or *tertúlia* (a social gathering that could be culturally or politically inclined depending on the composition of the group) that assembled five days a week. On weekends and holidays families enjoyed spending the afternoon or the early evening in these establishments, as there was no other activity so satisfying. It was also an economical choice. In any of these gloriously decorated cafés, a cup of coffee was only 25 cents (of a *peseta*). Customers could order the *copa de l'estudiant* (the student drink), a service available only in Barcelona cafés (and perhaps copied in a handful of other cafés around Catalonia): one was served, in addition to the cup of coffee, a glass of water, sugar (cubes), and a bottle of spirit of the customer's choice (rum, *aiguardent*, or other liquors). When the coffee was served, the bottle of the chosen alcoholic beverage would be left on the table so that patron could serve himself and prolong his stay.[96] Some owners attempted to discontinue this service in 1882, as city regulations forced them to keep the price of the coffee at 25 cents, but the opposition by their customers was so fierce that the owners had to return to their customary service and price after nine months.[97] The customer could linger with his coffee as long as he wanted, reading the newspapers and illustrated weeklies made available to him. He could also request the café letterhead stationery, ink, and pen to attend to his correspondence while enjoying his coffee. Holidays like *Tots Sants* (All Saints), *Nadal* (Christmas), and *Carnestoltes* (the King of No Shame, the central character for the Catalan carnival celebration) were celebrated, and raffles were held for chickens, turkeys, sweets, and liquors.[98]

Cafés were also quick to introduce and adapt innovations, such as the *teatròfon* (the theater phone, which allowed subscribers to listen to opera and music performances over the telephone lines) in 1893 at the Café Alhambra. The Alhambra was known mainly for its billiard tables, housing at one point a total of twenty-four. Women also played billiards, and their poses and plays were followed by an interested male audience.[99] But the establishment renowned for its tables was Café Novedades, which opened in 1896 and was considered one of the most important sites for billiards in Spain and Europe.[100]

The construction of the Eixample meant that the cafés were also being opened in the newly urbanized area, especially during the abovementioned economic boom, the *febre d'or*, which lasted from the late 1870s until the end of 1881. The Catalan stock market was trading all sorts of shares from a wide number of new industries, capital societies, and companies of every kind, giving rise to a new class of rich Barcelonians who were eagerly and actively demanding and consuming high-end products. The establishments that they frequented certainly had to reflect this new taste and economic prowess. The new bourgeoisie wanted a modern and cosmopolitan Barcelona, and their preferred model was Paris, as well as London and New York, which was evident in the many English and French words that appeared in the language of the time. The architecture of the cafés changed during this period as well. Main floors, previously divided into smaller rooms as was typical of the cafés from the Romantic era, were made into a single one, with wrought iron columns replacing the thick pillars and low vaulted ceilings in favor of more open, wider spaces.[101] Electric lighting was also a transforming force during this time, and the cafés were at the forefront of adapting new technology. However, gas lighting was still widely used; curiously, café owners eventually received permission to set up tables on the sidewalk like in Paris by repeatedly complaining to the authorities about the heat produced by the gas lamps.[102]

Another important developing trend of the time was eating out in restaurants, especially on Sundays and holidays. Many cafés responded to this new custom by creating separate dining rooms. There are numerous printed menus of this time written in French, as was the culinary fashion of the time, which continued well into the twentieth century.[103] Eating out, however, should be understood in two ways. The upper class dined out for business meals, parties, and celebratory banquets in large and luxurious restaurants. The working class also started eating out, but typically because factories were often far away from the workers' home or they lived in shared lodging arrangements that made taking care of meals while out easier. Going for a meal to a *fonda* (inn) or a tavern became a quotidian activity, in which workers would be served a simple dish with little variation. In addition to the tourist guidebooks where visitors and locals could find longs lists of dining choices (inns, restaurants, cafés, beer bars, etc.), there was a general guide for Barcelona in the mid-1800s written for the association of factories of Catalonia, a group created to protect the interests of their owners and workers, which listed about 300 taverns serving food and 226 taverns that also sold wine separately.[104] The prevalence of the food-serving inns started in the eighteenth century. The most popular inns were known as the *fondes dels sisos*, which Colman Andrews translates as "inns of the sixes," referring to the price of the menu, 6 *quartos* (a *quarto* was one of the lowest-valued copper coins of the period).[105] These establishments served economical and hearty home-cooked meals like *cap i pota* (stewed calf's head and foot) or *escudella i carn d'olla* (Catalan soup with boiled meats and vegetables) with wine and bread to tradesmen, people of modest means, and factory workers.[106] These *fondes* had a style of their own, in which waiters with rolled-up sleeves and long aprons carried many plates on their arms, serving clients quickly and "singing" comical, made-up names for the dishes, such as *metralla* (shrapnel) for garbanzo beans, *una bicicleta* (a bicycle) for two fried eggs, *un peu de minister* (a minister's foot) for pig trotters, and so on.[107] Néstor Luján provides a list of the most popular *fondes* of the late nineteenth century that served memorable dishes, including the Escudo de Francia (the French shield), Los Caballeros (The Gentlemen), Antonet, Fonda Rincón (Corner Inn), and Fonda Simó (Simon Inn), among others. The specialties they were known for were roasted chicken, lobster with green sauce, grilled meat, peasant stew, and monk fish soup, respectively.[108]

For the upper class, the proliferation of dining rooms that could be reserved was the cause of much social gossip. A cartoon of the time titled "Evening Restaurants" shows a gentleman and a lady asking the waiter for two place settings and the key to the door.[109] Restaurants were becoming so popular among the rich that in March 1881, a newspaper reported that the trendy Restaurant Martin served more than six hundred customers and had to close at 8:30 pm because it ran out of food.[110] Another type of popular establishment during this time was the *ceveseries* (beer bars), which also served food and were located in the lower part of Las Ramblas. The Gran Cervecería Ambos Mundos, located in Rambla number 30, was run by the Amills brothers, well known in the city's hospitality industry, who offered all sorts of dishes for lunch and other meals. They sold the business in 1881 to another famed cook, José Pompidor, who revived the old custom of publishing in the newspapers the day's menu and prices. The dishes mentioned in his May 30, 1881, menu reflect the French and Italian influence in the cooking of the time. For 10 *reales* (2.5 *pesetas*), diners could choose from *Risotto milanaise, Poulets Sautés chasseur, Langouste sauce Tartare,* and *Bifftecs aux pommes,* or, for 12 *reales* (3 *pesetas*), *Potage Julienne, Cromesquis Polonais, Fricandeau Viennoise, Merlan à la Colbert, Asperges en branches, Poulets röstis,* and *Glacier au marasquin.*[111] Another celebrated *cerveseria* was the one located on the corner of Las Ramblas and the Passatge de la Banca, Gran Cervecesería Restaurante Gambrinus, which also had a French cook. The establishment had a large room on the first floor, a back room with two pool tables, and, upstairs, a dining room that could seat up to twenty guests, who could order à la carte or from a set menu. Gambrinus specialized in beers and customers could try different kinds, including the popular medicinal one prepared by Doctor Gelabert, which was recommended for people with weak stomachs or digestive issues. It was also the exclusive distributor of a special beverage, the famed strong beer from Munich, Salvator, made from a recipe from the Order of the Paulaner monks dating back to the fifteenth century. This beer was released once a year, during February and March, and was considered a unique treat by beer connoisseurs. In 1885, the locale reopened as a *petit* hotel with a large dining hall and views of Las Ramblas, which could seat more than two hundred guests.[112]

EATING TRENDS FOR A MODERN CITY

Large banquet halls were popular in the late 1800s, and many establishments, especially hotels, provided ample installations for banquet celebrations, balls, and other social events. These venues also were suited for music performances or shows. A famed establishment was the Maison Dorée, a café and restaurant located on the enviable corner of the Plaça Catalunya and flanked by Las Ramblas, which linked the old part of the city and the new expansion. In 1897, at number 22 of the Plaça, the Pompidor brothers opened the Maison Dorée to bring some Parisian flair to the city. It was located in the house owned by Teresa Maspons de Llopart and designed by architect Jeroni Granell in 1873 and enlarged to create an open first floor and decorated in the Art Nouveau style by August Font Carreras, with Louis XV–style furniture imported from France. The banquet hall had a capacity of three hundred diners, as well as a terrace popular during the warm months of the year. It quickly became a celebrated establishment not only for its location but also because of the excellent cuisine.[113] Its *tertúlia* was attended by famous politicians and artists of the time. It is said to be where the *modernista* artist Ramon Casas fell in love with his muse, Júlia, a young lady who sold lottery tickets. Llúis Permanyer writes that it was the first building in the city with a revolving door, and because the café's coffee grinder was underground, the Barcelonians began circulating the rumor that turning the door helped grind the coffee beans.[114] He also notes that the Maison Dorée introduced afternoon tea to Barcelona, its window displaying the following ad: "Five o'clock tea served at 7 pm." He recounts an anecdote about the 1905 ball organized by the Marquis of Alella that created a moral dilemma: until then, no lady had gone out at night to a public venue to dance. The problem was quickly resolved when it was decided that because the banquet hall had been rented by the Marquises, it counted as an extension of their home, and it was therefore a perfectly respectable place for ladies to dance the night away.[115] The building where the café restaurant was located near what was then the U.S. consulate. It later became the site of a bank and was then rebuilt again to house shops. The building is currently occupied by the Spanish department store El Corte Inglés, which has, as its next-door neighbor, the Hard Rock Café Barcelona.

The star of Barcelona's gastronomy scene in the late 1800s was the Restaurant Martin, known among the locals as Can Marten, surpassing the previously favored Can Justin.[116] The chef was Martin Pagès, a French cook who arrived to the city in 1870 with only 40 francs in his pocket and a contract to work at the Restaurant Parisien. Later, while working at the Restaurant Montserrat, he had the opportunity to prepare a banquet in honor of King Amadeus of Savoy, in which his brother Humbert, the future king of Italy, was also in attendance. Pagès, on his way to become a celebrated chef, went on to cook at the Café Nuevo and, in 1875, became the chef of the restaurant of the opera house, the Gran Teatre del Liceu, where his cooking started to gain prestige among the city residents. In 1879, he opened his own restaurant, the Gran Restaurante Martin, on the boulevard of the Rambla, number 70, across from the Liceu.[117] The restaurant's success was in part thanks to its luxurious decor and comfortable setup, but it was the chef's cooking and the quality products used in his kitchen that quickly built his reputation. Pagès was able to expand his restaurant quickly, adding more rooms, again decorated with fine paintings and sculptures. The specialties of the house were large banquets, some with more than two hundred guests, and the dishes served during these occasions were abundant, displaying a mix of foreign and Catalan culinary traditions. The banquet in celebration of the 1883 literary competition *Jocs Florals* presided by the poet Víctor Balaguer had the following menu:

Puré a la provenzale, Arroz a la milanesa—Fritos: Fritura a la princesa—Principios: Salmón a la medionale [sic]*, Filete a la Godard—Legumbres: Espárragos a la francesa—Asados: Pavo asado—Dulces: bizcochos helados—Postres variados—Vinos: Jerez, vino de Languedoc, Sauterne y Champagne.*[118]

(Provençal-style purée, Milanese-style rice—Fried items: Princess-style fried food—Appetizers: *Meriodionale*-style salmon, Godard-style fillet—Legumes: French-style asparagus—Roasted meats: Roasted turkey—Sweets: ice cream cakes—Other desserts—Wines: sherry, wine from the Languedoc, Sauterne, and Champagne.)

Another of the restaurant's well-known practices was its daily order of oysters from various places (Caucalle, Ostend, Marennes, etc.), which the restaurant made available not only to its dining guests but also to those who wanted to serve them in their own homes.[119]

The cooking career of Martin Pàges reached its apex when he won the contract to service the restaurant built for the 1888 World's Fair. Even though the Castell dels Tres Dragons, designed by the architect Lluís Domènech i Montaner, was not finished in time, the chef was able to successfully deliver his well-known service. A remarkable structure that was greatly admired during the exhibition, the restaurant's entrance led to a salon furnished with marble tables and Thonet chairs, where coffee was served. The kitchen was on the same floor and featured seven large ovens, an enormous stove that could be accessed from all sides, a central reservoir for warm water, and a plate warmer. The pantry, the coal room, and the refrigerated room were installed in the towers next to the restaurant. Three dumbwaiters were used to send the dishes up to the dining room on the second floor, accessible from the main room through a staircase with steps made of marble and wooden banisters carved into vegetal shapes. The restaurant, open from August to December 1888, served all sorts of dishes throughout the day and was the site of many organized banquets.[120] The closing banquet on December 8 was specially prepared by the head chef, who presented the following menu:

Potages: Bisque d'ecrevisses à la Française—Consommé de volaille à la Royale—Hors d'ouvres—Relevé: Saumon du Rhin [sic]*, sauce hollandaise—Entrées: Filets de*

boeuf à la Richelieu—Petites caisses de grives à la Saint-Hubert—Sorbets au Kirsch—
Légumes: Fonds d'artichauts à la Macédonie. Rôti: Chapons du Mans au cresson—
Entremets: Pièces de glaces décorées—Gâteaux suédois. Vinos: Jerez (Medalla de
Oro en la Exposición)—Rhin Johannisberg—Rioja clarete (Medalla de Oro en la
Exposición)—Château Léoville—Moët et Chandon.[121]

The preparations for the World's Fair marked the beginning of a high-end hotel industry as well. For instance, the Hotel Internacional (located on Passeig Colom) was designed and built specifically for the event by the abovementioned modernist architect Domènech i Montaner. Although this hotel was demolished after the World's Fair, it nevertheless signaled a moment at which the city was able to offer elegant accommodations to its visitors in addition to the Hotel Colón and the Hotel Continental. The restaurant built for the Hotel Internacional was famous for its long stove and grill that reportedly could cook four hundred steaks at the same time. What is more, for the first time in the city's restaurant history, it had a separate space to prepare desserts.[122] The hotel was built in record time—fifty-three days—and hosted a historical banquet at the end of its construction. On January 8, 1888, the eight hundred workers who had labored on the building, as well as the architect and the contractors, were invited to a banquet presided by the mayor, Mr. Francesc de Paula Rius i Taulet. The menu for the occasion consisted of rice, stewed veal, hake, *rostit,*[123] desserts, and coffee.[124] Interestingly, the menu for the workers, in contrast to the other banquet menus quoted, reflects the divide between what upper- and lower-class Barcelonians were accustomed to or could actually afford. As Fàbrega points out, it is in the taste and eating habits of the working class that we can see the roots of Catalan regional cooking that prevails today.[125]

Another trend that started at the end of the 1800s was the American-style bar, in which drinks were served along the counter. The shift represents a big change for patrons used to idle time in cafés spent reading and conversing. Villa argues that the bar can be seen as the product of the Industrial Revolution and points to its early success—as gin palaces—in cities like Manchester and London.[126] In Barcelona bars did not become popular until the early twentieth century, along with cocktail bars. The first establishments that opened in Barcelona combined elements of taverns, cafés, and beer bars, even if their names seemed to indicate that they were a different type of business. The Cantina Americana (American Canteen) that opened in 1879 reflected this mix of style. Another business, the Botillería Americana (American Bottler), opened in 1880. It reminded customers of a different type of store, the popular eighteenth-century *botillerías*, which served beverages and ice cream. The Botillería Americana had, in addition to the bar, a room with a few tables where cold dishes were served. It advertised a great variety of wines and liquors, beer from Bavaria, Manzanilla, cognac, absinthe, champagne sold by the glass, and an American drink still unknown in Barcelona: the cocktail.[127] During the World's Fair of 1888 an establishment opened in the style of an American soda fountain serving carbonated beverages. Although it was popular during the fair, it closed after the event. The first automatic bar was opened in 1894 but quickly closed its doors.[128] The surge of American-style bars serving whiskey and cocktails would not begin until the early twentieth century.

The social life in the Barcelona cafés was intense, and each establishment offered a special appeal that attracted different groups. The Café Pelayo, for instance, was where the intellectual and literary group of the *Renaixença* would gather. It was known as the *penya dels savis* (the circle of the wise) or *la colla de la Renaixença* (the gang of the *Renaixença*).[129] The most notable characters of the city gathered here; even famous writers from other parts of Spain like José Zorrilla, José María de Pereda, and the great nineteenth-century writer Benito Pérez Galdós attended the *tertúlia* in the café. One late addition to the group was the future Nobel Prize winner for medicine, Santiago Ramón y Cajal, who arrived in 1887.[130] The Café Suizo, first attended by literary figures and revolutionaries, in the 1880s became the preferred establishment for brokers and important merchants.[131] Even the anarchists had their own café, the Gran Café del Circo Español, where they gathered around Salvador Seguí. The anarchists who assembled in the café did not drink alcohol or smoke. They did not play cards or dominoes or talk about women, but rather lived a revolutionary, bohemian life, using the café tables as a platform to lecture and the furniture as a place to read.[132] However, the most famous (and lasting) café is Els Quatre Gats, a place that not only gathered the most famous artists of the nineteenth and twentieth centuries but also still survives today—albeit as a restoration and not the original café—thanks to the mythical place it occupies in the history of modern art and the tourists who continue to flock to it on their tour of the city following the route of the *Modernisme*.[133]

THE STORY OF ELS QUATRE GATS

Founded by Pere Romeu in 1897 after a trip to Paris, where he met with his artist friend Ramon Casas and became friendly with Santiago Rusiñol and Miquel Utrillo, Els Quatre Gats became a well-known café, tavern, and restaurant where the most prominent artists of the *Modernisme* movement gathered. While in the French capital, Romeu had the chance to learn shadow puppetry with Utrillo at Le Chat Noir, the famed cabaret owned by Rodolphe Salis. In a way, the opening of the café tavern in Barcelona was an effort to replicate the cabaret and its ambiance. Els Quatre Gats eventually offered shadow puppet performances (in Catalan called *ombres xineses* or "Chinese shadows") and later actual puppet shows as well as art exhibits where friends displayed their work. It also published a literary magazine that ran for only fifteen issues, which was important, albeit short lived, in voicing the ideas of the aesthetic movement of the time. This literary review paved the way for other influential literary magazines such as *Pel & Ploma*, *Forma*, and *Joventut*.[134] Villar documents that it was not possible to replicate the Parisian cabaret, because the owner of the building threatened Romeu with eviction if he allowed a certain "type" of woman in the establishment.[135] According to Ricard Opisson, one of the cartoonists and illustrators who frequented its *tertúlia*, the café was quite chaste and, more than anything else, boring, especially for those who did not belong to the social group. The only female companions allowed were the wives, daughters, and sisters of the artists who frequented the café. It worked more or less like a club for the male artists and members of the Catalan bourgeoisie who made their way to the establishment to discreetly stare at the artists.[136] Its significance for art historians, however, is substantial, as it signals the arrival of *Modernisme* in the city of Barcelona, which until then was limited to Cau Ferrat, Santiago Rusiñol's workshop in the beach town of Sitges. What distinguished this café even more was its connection with perhaps the most famous artist of the twentieth century, Pablo Picasso, who frequented the café between 1899 and 1900.[137]

The café was located on the first floor of a neo-Gothic building designed by a young Josep Puig i Cadafalch, who would later become a renowned figure in moderniste architecture. The café had two rooms, the first with the bar and the tables where the artists gathered together for meetings presided over by Casas, Rusiñol, and Utrillo. The second, larger room was used for literary and musical evenings and shadow puppet and stringed puppet performances that were popular in the city. The interior decoration mixed traditional elements of Catalan architecture—ceramics and tile—with wrought iron, and its walls were full of drawings and paintings.[138] Romeu himself studied painting but soon abandoned it after realizing his lack of talent and turned his interest to what he enjoyed most: sports. He practiced fencing, mountain climbing, cycling, hunting, sailing, rowing, and swimming, an activity he enjoyed in the open sea even during the winter months. His disheveled and eccentric look suggested a colorful character: tall, lean, and dark with long, greasy hair and an abundant beard, always sporting a large-brimmed black hat and a frock coat the color of *cafè amb llet* (coffee with milk).[139] His fondness for sports can be seen in the well-known painting *Ramon Casas and Pere Romeu on a Tandem* by Ramon Casas, which hangs in the café (a copy; the original is in the National Art

Interior of the café Els Quatre Gats. *Photograph by H. Rosi Song.*

Museum of Catalonia), where he rides a tandem bicycle with the painter. Romeu is in the back looking directly at the viewer. An outline of a factory chimney is in the background, a common sight in the urban landscape of Barcelona at the time.[140]

Before opening the café, Romeu first opened a gymnasium called Gimnasio Catalán, where he held an art exhibit in its fencing room. He soon shut it down to join a puppetry troupe with Utrillo and even traveled to Chicago to perform at the World's Fair of 1893. In 1897, Romeu opened Els Quatre Gats in collaboration with his three artist friends—Casas, Utrillo, and Rusiñol—with the intention of creating a meeting place for progressive artists and intellectuals of the time.[141] The name of the café referred both to the number of people involved in its inception and to the idiom "to be four cats," which denotes a number so small as to be insignificant.[142] Art historians point to the important role it played in generously supporting young artists, among them Picasso, who staged his first exhibit there at the age of eighteen.[143] He spent many hours at the café drawing, and according to the writer Rafael Moragas, Picasso auctioned off one of his works to his friends at the end of the day in the hopes of earning enough for a late-night snack, when a cup of chocolate with an *ensaimada* (a yeast-based cake baked in round, coiled shapes from Majorca) cost 30 cents.[144] Picasso also created the café's menu, rendering a prosaic item into a work of art.[145]

The food at the café was an afterthought. Anecdotes describe how Romeu suddenly felt the urge to go hunting when creditors were due to show up. He returned to the café only after they had all stopped by, smugly producing half or three-quarters of a rabbit. The writer Josep Pla, who told this anecdote, was sure that Romeu purchased the rabbit.[146] When customers in the café wanted to dine, Romeu became exasperated, his attitude scornful. Els Quatre Gats initially had an excellent reputation for its coffee, but it soon was criticized for having lost all "strength" and "perfume"; it was said that it became a rather insipid liquid with hardly any alkaloid that could liven up a conversation.[147] When Romeu went to the market to purchase supplies for the restaurant, he spent only the money that was available to him without any regard to the actual needs of the kitchen. His cook's solution was simply to reduce the serving size of the dishes. The plates served at the café were mocked, referred to as miniature dishes, painted dishes, or dishes for kindergarten kids. Picasso recounted a dinner he once had at the café that consisted of a salad composed of a couple of slices of tomato and a few lettuce leaves that were already in bad shape.[148] The café closed its doors in July 1903, when most of its patrons—including the founding members Casas, Rusiñol, and Utrillo—started frequenting the Café Continental by the Plaça Catalunya.[149] Els Quatre Gats reopened in 1985 and was restored in 1989 to its original layout and design.

FOOD, ART, AND ADVERTISEMENT
FOR THE NEW INDUSTRIAL ERA

Modernisme as an aesthetic movement was important for the gastronomic experience of the time, since the architects who designed the buildings also supervised the finishing of both its exterior and its interior. The descriptions of the popular cafés, restaurants, bars, and hotels reflect this aesthetic, which contributed to their reputation among their customers. The architect Domènech i Montaner, for instance, established his workshop in the café restaurant he designed for the World's Fair of 1888, where he worked to revive old artistic crafts.[150] He oversaw the construction and the finishing details of his work to give it a unified look, so he worked with designers, craftsmen, and artists to provide the elements necessary for the interior, ranging from floor tiles, stained glass, doors, shutters, ceilings, lamps, rugs, and even accessories for elevators and bathrooms.[151] He even worked with furniture makers and porcelain artists and ceramicists. Inspired by Art Nouveau, Catalan artists like Alexandre de Riquer, Lambert Escaler, and Gaspar Homar achieved great aesthetic innovation at this time with the use of mixed materials, new techniques, and merging artisanal work with new available technology. This style also impacted graphic art and poster designers, which intersected conveniently with the business interests of the time. The imported designs using organic imagery and flowing lines—either in the Art Nouveau or in the Viennese variant, *Jugendstil*, style—publicized the industrial products of the time.[152] Catalan businesses were hungry to promote and sell their goods, and many food and wine products of the time were advertised in this style, including chocolates, oils, sweets, wines, anise, and so on. Some continue to be advertised in this manner, like Amatller chocolates.

Other popular establishments in the nineteenth century were places that served *xocolata* (*xocolateries*) and *orxata*, a beverage made with tiger nuts (*orxateries*).[153] The custom of drinking chocolate was firmly established in the eighteenth century in Spain. The Baron of Maldà wrote in his diary that he drank chocolate every morning and when he had visits. Along with coffee and tea, chocolate was a foreign product in Spain, but one that was quickly adopted (if one could afford it, of course). It was even more popular than coffee. All three beverages were considered exotic and were consumed first in the royal court and by the upper class as a sign of social prestige.[154] They all inspired heated debate regarding their medicinal and moral benefits, but they were considered generally beneficial for one's health. And although all three beverages were consumed privately, they came to be identified as social drinks since people enjoyed them at social gatherings in public spaces, such as the famous cafés described in this chapter. In a way, all three drinks

Advertisement poster created by Rafael de Penagos, submitted for the 1914 advertisement competition organized by Chocolate Amatller, receiving an award for fourth place. *Image provided by Chocolates Simón Coll.*

marked the way Spanish and Catalan bourgeoisie socialized among themselves in urban spaces. In contrast, the popular class mostly enjoyed wine in their social gatherings. Chocolate was the favorite of the three beverages. It was (and still is) made thick, sweetened with sugar, and, back then, infused with pepper, cinnamon, ginger, or vanilla. The drink is made so thick that it inspired a Spanish saying that goes, "things ought to be as clear as the chocolate is thick."[155] Chocolate usually was served with some sort of bread or pastry to dip in it as well as a glass of water to cleanse the palate afterward. Although commonly made with water, during the nineteenth century, it was also made with milk in accordance with how the French made hot chocolate.[156] *Orxata* was also widely consumed and could be made with tiger nuts or even almonds. Drinks made with milk, which were considered more modern, became popular later in the century.[157] Drinking *xocolata* became popular, and many *xocolateries* opened in the 1800s, perhaps because *xocolateries* were one of the few places women could go unaccompanied by men. One of the oldest restaurants in Barcelona, Can Culleretes, started as a *xocolateria*, until 1890 when it started serving food.[158]

Looking at the printed menus from the 1800s in Barcelona and beyond, as well as the accounts of the time, it is undeniable that French gastronomy shaped Catalan cuisine. Yet, according to Jaume Fàbrega, the region unquestionably established its own traditions and culinary characteristics during this century. Part of the explanation for this is that the upper class enjoyed dishes with foreign influences when eating out or at banquet celebrations, whereas for most of the working class, cooking was a more straightforward, pragmatic affair that took advantage of the products seasonally available in the region. This cooking style frequently adapted foreign dishes to local tastes, as is the case of the traditional *canelons* (from the Italian cannelloni), which remains one of the most typical Catalan dishes today, or the *fricandó* (braised veal with wild mushrooms, from the French *fricandeau*).[159] But there is evidence that traditional dishes like *escudella i carn d'olla* or *esqueixada* (shredded salt cod salad with tomatoes, onions, and olives with oil and vinegar) were born from specific rural, urban, or coastal cooking traditions during the period. Dishes from other cuisines (French, Italian, Occitan, American) were also incorporated in the cookbooks of the time with Catalanized or Castilianized spellings, such as *sopa juliana* (similar to Italian minestrone with julienned vegetables), *bullabessa* (bouillabaisse), *bou a l'adoba* (bouef en daube), *puré de patates* (potato purée), *brandada de bacallà* (emulsion of salt cod and olive oil), *ensalada russa* (Russian salad), or *rosbif* (roast beef).[160] Fàbrega argues that dishes that make up a national cuisine are not necessarily unique. For instance, the Catalan dish of salt cod with raisins and pine nuts is made in Greece and also serves as filling in the Galician

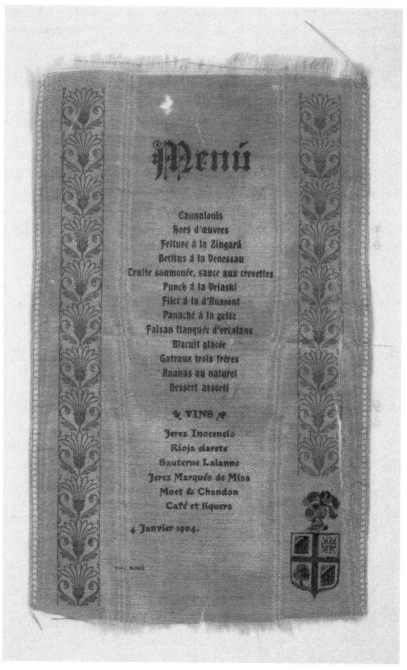

Menú

Cannalonis
Hors d'œuvres
Friture à la Zingará
Betilus à la Venessau
Cruite saumonée, sauce aux crevettes
Punch à la Velaski
Filet à la d'Aumont
Panaché à la gelée
Faisan flanquée d'ortolans
Biscuit glacée
Gateaux trois frères
Ananas au naturel
Dessert assorti

VINS

Jerez Inocencio
Rioja clarete
Sauterne Lalanne
Jerez Marqués de Misa
Moet & Chandon
Café et liquers

4 Janvier 1904.

Wedding Menu for Josep Torres Sampol and Maria del Remei de Prat i Roure at Hotel Peninsular, Girona, January 4, 1904 (in French). Print on cloth, 18x11cm printed Tipografia Masó, Girona. Copyright © Jordi Puig; image provided by Fundació Rafael Masó, Girona.

empanada (a type of meat turnover). Yet, at the same time, they demonstrate a specific local culinary language in the unique ways in which they are prepared. Common ways to start or to finish a dish reflect a certain structure of cooking, as a gastronomic grammar or syntax that imbues each dish with determined character- istics. Fàbrega highlights as an example one of the basic starters of a Catalan dish, *sofregit* (cooking onions down slowly as the base for a sauce), from which many dishes are built.[161] Other examples include *picada* (a paste made of garlic, toasted bread, nuts, herbs, and spices), *allioli* (a sauce made of garlic, salt, and olive oil), *samfaina* (a ratatouille-like dish that can be made into a sauce by pureeing it), or *romesco* (a sauce made of almonds or hazelnuts, dried sweet peppers, and toma- toes). All of these basic preparations can be recognized as part of a distinctive type of cuisine that extends beyond Barcelona and Catalonia into the *Països Catalans*.[162] These cooking practices are indeed present in the cookbooks of the period and in more contemporary recipe books.

COOKBOOKS TO TEACH

Almost three centuries after the publication of the *Llibre del coch*, Rupert de Nola's medieval cookbook, *La cuynera catalana* (The Catalan Cook), was published in 1835. An anonymous text, it is clearly a practical and didactic publication for a wide audience, which is no longer exclusively male. Its appearance should be linked to the emerging cultural movement of the *Renaixença*, as it articulates that the reason it was written and published in Catalan was to make the text accessible for general use. Published in four installments and, later, in multiple editions, it enjoyed great popularity. It was meant to be a practical recipe book, as its original, complete title indicated: *La cuynera catalana, ó sia reglas útils, fàcils, seguras y económicas per cuynar bé escullidas dels autors que millor han escrit sobre aquesta materia* (The Catalan Cook, that is, useful, easy, sure, and economical instructions to cook well, chosen from authors who have best written on the subject).[163] Curiously, in the prologue, the author addresses the book to the heads of households, acknowl- edging their frustration at how costly it is to maintain a home with cooks who do not know how to handle the staples of the kitchen and waste cooking ingredients through poor preparation. The cookbook is therefore a teaching tool about cooking, being healthy, saving money, and maintaining a good kitchen. The book starts with a breakdown of spices, explaining their use in creating dishes and making them more appetizing. The author explains where the spices come from, describes the difference between black and white pepper, suggests uses for cloves and nutmeg, explains that the best cinnamon comes from Ceylon, and mentions herbs like bay leaves, thyme, marjoram, savory, coriander, anise, and fennel and aromatics such as mint, oregano, parsley, chervil, celery, onion, and garlic.[164] In the introduction to a recent edition of the cookbook, Carme Queralt points out its modern notes, clearly directed at a more privileged class, reflecting new insights about nutrition and health. The writer of the book is also mindful of hygiene: he writes about sweeping the kitchen and washing one's hands and gives instructions about what should be washed with bleach, soap, or ashes. These comments reflect a desire to improve quotidian life for readers. The author pays special attention to the preservation of food (food pantries become a staple in the kitchen during this time), how to use natural and manufactured food items, and cooking techniques and formulas that make dishes more economical and healthier.[165] The recipes contained in the book are impressive for their variety and the different ingredients they use. The collection also mentions a large number of dishes with foreign influences marked by their style (*a la castellana, a l'espanyola, a la francesa, a la provençal,* etc.) and specifically lists dishes that have Arabic roots. Some of the recipes call for fish that are no longer available in the area (sturgeon, lamprey, shad) and offal (blood or tripe of lamb or goat) that is no longer sold in the markets. But many of the recipes follow techniques and ingredients that are still used in Catalan cooking today, such as the grilling and stuffing of meats and fish, the slow cooking of meat and vegetables, the use of dried fruit in savory dishes, and the mixing of seafood and meat.

Many other cookbooks were published in Barcelona in the nineteenth century, which indicates a large, well-established bourgeoisie compared to other cities in the Iberian Peninsula. Their interest in food and cooking reflects new ways of understanding nutrition and gastronomy that went hand in hand with the arrival of industrialization and technology. During this period, cookbooks became their own publishing genre with a clear identity, and many times they were geared at educating the professionals of an emerging hospitality industry with the necessary foundational culinary knowledge.[166] But these instructions were also necessary for house kitchens and the women who managed them day after day. One book that was very popular and addressed these needs was *Carmencita o la buena cocinera* (Carmencita, or the Good Cook), published in 1895. Although the book was written in Spanish, its author, Doña Elaida M, widow of Carpinell, was clearly Catalan, as her writing was riddled with Catalanisms. The cookbook became a huge hit and enjoyed multiple editions, becoming a common item in brides' trousseaus. Many women today keep copies from their own mothers or grandmothers. The book was the work of a housewife without any professional training. Her recipes deal with everyday cooking and the struggle to find, prepare, and "recycle" dishes and ingredients to avoid wasting food. Some of her instructions are basic ideas for reusing leftovers: for a piece of fried cod, she suggests flaking it, frying an onion and a tomato, adding it to the fish along with roasted red pepper, and making turnovers. Leftovers from a salt cod and potato dinner could be pounded in a mortar and fried in the Andalusian style (breaded fried fish); half could be sprinkled with sugar and be served as dessert and the other as a main course.[167] Her recipes and those in *La cuynera catalana* clearly mark the path of a modern recipe book in the early twentieth century focused on domestic and daily cooking while establishing a body of popular Catalan dishes and its cooking traditions. Such is the case of the well-known and widely used *La teca* (1924) by Ignasi Domènech i Puigcercós, the *Llibre de la cuina catalana* (1928) by Ferran Agulló, and the *Art de ben menjar* (1923), first published anonymously and later under the name Marta Salvià.[168]

The discussion of Catalan identity and its unique traditions, cooking and otherwise, is an interesting aspect of the diversity that exists in the Iberian Peninsula. As other European nations were building a singular concept of nation by streamlining language and other traditions including cooking, Spain did not give in to culinary or identity homogenization. Lara Anderson follows this effort in her book *Cooking Up the Nation* (2013), in which she argues that the strength of Spanish cooking lies in the variety found in its many regions.[169] The idea of diversity as the only characteristic that applies to the entire geographic area is repeated again in Rebecca Ingram's reading of a culinary map of the nineteenth century.[170] Talking and writing about food of the period undoubtedly intersect with notions of identity, nation building, and modernization. As writer Ramón Gómez de la Serna's early twentieth-century culinary map reveals, although the cooking in the peninsula is indeed rich and varied, these different cuisines reveal the failure of a singular Spanish identity. Considering the map, it is not surprising that Spain's food-writing pioneer Dionisio Pérez (known as Post-Thebussem) wrote a book praising the nation's cooking and cataloging its regional cuisines—and always highlighting it was the variety that made Spanish gastronomy superior to others on the continent.[171] This book, published by the Patronato Nacional del Turismo (the National Office of Tourism) in the early 1900s, indicates that when it comes to food, the Iberian Peninsula should be identified by its multiplicity—a trait that has been used to promote tourism among its own citizens as well as foreign visitors—rather than its singularity. The writing about Catalan gastronomy reflects, at times, a palpable attempt to assert its particularities over the other culinary practices of Spain; yet it is precisely this effort that helps us distinguish and better understand what Fàbrega aptly calls the grammar of Catalan cooking.

4

❖ ❖

The Greatest Fresh Markets
in the World

Among the attractions that bring millions of tourists to Barcelona are its world-famous fresh food markets like La Boqueria. Located on one of its central boulevards, the market has become an obligatory stop for visitors strolling up and down Las Ramblas while visiting the old part of the city. The market is well known around the world, and some of its food stalls, like the Pinotxo bar near the entrance, have been reviewed or mentioned in food and cooking magazines worldwide. The crowds and the long lines at the eateries hide the fact that the market still functions as a shopping place for residents of the area. Local chefs make trips to the market to talk with purveyors, check out produce, visit seafood stalls, and shop for their businesses. The tension that exists between these uses of the market represents one of the challenges that the city faces when trying to balance the quality of living of its inhabitants and the profit it receives from the tourism industry. The benefit from tourism goes beyond employment and revenue for Barcelona, as the global recognition it receives through these visits plays a significant role in promoting Catalan culture inside and outside Spain. Catalan culture places vital meaning on the use of its language, and teaching Catalan has become a sensitive political issue on the Iberian Peninsula. The "normalization" of Catalan started in the 1980s through its teaching in schools and use in local government, media outlets, and workplaces. Even today, this policy periodically comes under scrutiny and attack when political tension erupts between Madrid and Barcelona. The debate around the Catalan language is important to consider when discussing any aspect of its culture today. Part of maintaining a strong regional identity comes from engaging in quotidian life practices that define a way of living. The use of markets for daily or weekly shopping falls into this category, and, for the residents of Barcelona, the presence of these markets, whether the iconic La Boqueria or a more modest neighborhood market, represents a quality of life that is distinctively local.

The current perception among the residents of the city is that tourism negatively affects the way the markets of Barcelona function in the city. Tourists visit markets, mostly to peruse them, take photographs, dine at food stalls, and purchase ready-to-eat products like cut fruit, freshly made juices, coffee, baked goods, and sandwiches (*entrepà*, "between bread"). They do not provide the business needed for vendors to maintain butcher stands or fish stalls, poultry or salt cod counters. Yet the real threat to the continued existence of these vendors comes from other modern trends that push shopping in market halls into the past. The advent of retail food trade, with its chain supermarkets, convenience stores, trendy organic and health food shops, and home delivery services, combined with the busy schedules of the majority of shoppers, make food shopping a task dictated by pragmatism and time-saving measures. A considerable population continues to shop almost daily in the markets. Contrary to public belief, senior citizens do not solely constitute the clientele. However, it is true that the access to these shopping places are affected by traffic, economic considerations, and limited hours. Although many markets were closed by midday, more than 70 percent of the renovated markets in the city currently open in the afternoon or evening from Wednesdays to Fridays. In the end, the survival of the traditional market halls and the social role they play depends on balancing popularity, accessibility, affordability, and convenience while maintaining their traditional role in neighborhood socialization.

Throughout the long history of the fresh food markets, it is clear that their significance always aligned with the political and cultural context of Barcelona. From the beginning, in addition to their traditional role of organizing provisions for residents, the vendors who gathered near the religious convents of Las Ramblas or the entrance of the city's walls to sell their products were an important part of the urban social fabric. Everyday activities offer another perspective into the history of Barcelona: working, shopping, cooking, and eating ground the existence of its people and intersect with their experience of the events that take place during their lifetimes. These regular actions are intimately connected to food production, provision, distribution, and consumption. Public market halls provide good landscapes from which to understand these experiences and the "Catalan" way of living.

Entrance to La Boqueria market. *Printed with permission from Bryn Mawr College; photograph by Kate McCann.*

THE HISTORY OF FOOD MARKETS IN BARCELONA

There are currently thirty-nine public food markets distributed throughout the various neighborhoods in Barcelona.[1] The list includes four non-food-related markets near the market halls, such as the large Sunday market next to Sant Antoni, which deals exclusively in books, magazines, postcards, and video games, and the flower market along Las Ramblas. Some of these markets are more popular among the visitors to the city than others. La Boqueria is clearly the most visited, but since its renovation in 2005, the Mercat de Santa Caterina, with its distinctive and colorful tile roofing, rivals La Boqueria in popularity.[2] Another important market is the recently renovated Mercat de Sant Antoni, which opened in the summer of 2018. Tourists visit markets because of their history or gastronomic prestige (as well as their proximity to historic sites that are typically part of the tourist itinerary), but the residents' relationships to the markets depend on their location and proximity to neighborhoods. Despite emerging later than in other European cities, Barcelona's market halls have remained very much relevant until the present. They continue to draw attention from the local government, which remains committed to their renovation and to finding ways to revive the social role they play in the neighbor-hoods where they are located. In stark contrast to other historic market halls in the rest of Europe—and even in other cities in Spain—markets in Catalonia have become a strong part of its regional identity. From the first wrought-iron construc-tions built in 1876, they have developed into a polycentric system that today serves as a wide network of public covered markets.[3]

The building of market halls in Europe during the second half of the nineteenth century represented a new form of architecture and town planning. The technology that allowed the use of wrought-iron and glass in large quantities in the construc-tion of buildings was perceived as a sign of modernity. The massive structures were seen as an expression of municipal pride, innovation, renovation, and the new edi-fices of commerce for capitalist cities.[4] Although the construction of wrought-iron market halls in Barcelona would start later, the city began to work on providing space for their food markets during the first half of the 1800s. The municipal regu-lation of 1834 ensured the creation and the administration of public facilities that would function to provide food and drink for its inhabitants marked an important political moment for the city. It was the first time that the local government inter-vened to regulate a matter of its economy; from then on, the experience changed the role that the Catalan capital would play in its own affairs.[5] When two convents burned down in 1835 along Las Ramblas during a popular rebellion, the city de-cided to use the lots to build its first two covered markets. Although the widespread anger that led to these acts of violence was connected to the ongoing Carlist Wars of the time, the underlying frustration was the poor living and labor conditions of the working class.[6] The population of the city had grown rapidly in the late 1700s thanks to its booming industries—especially textiles—fueled by the wealth that Catalans made in the American continent when the Bourbons allowed their par-ticipation in the trading routes along the Atlantic coast.[7] Barcelona's population, for instance, grew from 35,000 inhabitants to 117,000 from 1717 to 1787.[8] The increase steadily continued until the next century, which created a critical need for housing and also a huge demand for provisions. Suddenly the quantity of foodstuffs sold in the city multiplied, and the area around Las Ramblas, the Plaça del Born, and La Ribera was overflowing with vendors and shoppers. There had been local initiatives to regulate the chaos by grouping the vendors according to the products they sold, but the complexity of the situation quickly surpassed their efforts. When the convent and churches around these areas were burned down, the city suddenly found the space to start planning the construction of markets.[9] The locations of the first markets proved to be appropriate, since vendors already had been selling their products along the walls of the convents as a type of open-air market. Interestingly, the municipal authorities trying to regulate these markets ultimately created a hierarchy between the farm workers from the countryside and the urban dwellers. The farmers, limited in their contact with individual buyers, were forced to sell their goods wholesale at a cheaper rate. Meanwhile, vendors who lived in the city continued selling directly to the public. Because city-dwelling vendors and other food-selling intermediaries had better access to local politicians, the market trade functioned to their benefit for a long time, pitting rural vendors against city ones.[10] It is interesting to note that farmers continue to bring their produce for sale into the city near La Boqueria today. They are situated at the Plaça de Sant Galdric, located to the right of the main entrance to the market and are referred to informally as the plaza of the woman farmers (Plaça de les pageses).

The effort to regulate vendors and the way markets function was not a nineteenth-century phenomenon. In Catalonia, markets (or other places where vendors gathered to sell their goods) existed even before the medieval period. They were usually located in a spacious place close to villages or towns, near major arteries, and in proximity to sites where animals were slaughtered. The butchering of animals required more permanent installations, so other vendors would gravitate toward them. In locations where tables were provided for these tasks, the vendors who worked them were under the careful control of the local feudal authority eager to collect the appropriate taxes. Other, more permanent locations secured by vendors included the communal ovens where local residents baked their breads. The first documented market in Barcelona was located close to a public oven in the tenth century.[11] Even though there were regular markets, spontaneous markets, especially in rural areas, were born from immediate needs, such as a particular harvest or some artisanal production that surpassed basic exchange or consumption. The availability of surplus farm products like vegetables, combined with increasing mobility, developed into a type of commerce. Carme Batlle i Gallart traces the evolution of Catalan merchants from farm laborers and later from the rise of artisans.[12] But in order to engage in the trading of goods, these early vendors in medieval Catalonia needed the protection of their feudal lords or the church authorities. Therefore it is not surprising that markets often were located near convents and monasteries, since they provided protected space. There was serious competition among the feudal lords to provide locations for markets because they represented a good income. They collected taxes and leased the scales and weights that vendors needed in order to sell their goods. Sometimes feudal lords and their men engaged in violent confrontations to protect their market sites or tried to attract vendors by offering them lodging the day before or after the market.[13] There were set days for markets and documentation indicating that Jewish and Muslim residents could engage in commerce on days permitted by their religions. Jaume I, for instance, in 1268, gave Jews the right to negotiate with Christians so they could buy grains, wheat or barley, oil, and other goods. A regulation from 1235 indicated that Jews needed to carry a stick or a cane to point to the goods they wanted to purchase so as to avoid physical contact with food items, because they were rumored to have contaminated the water wells, spreading the plague.[14] A popular day for markets was Wednesdays, *dimecres*, a practice from antiquity, as Mercury was the god of commerce. Despite pagan roots, Wednesday markets remained in practice, and most of the Catalan markets took place that day.[15]

Well before the convents and churches burned down, the vendors around Las Ramblas and El Born had long occupied the areas next to the church properties, near the access points of the city. As mentioned, their numbers multiplied in the 1800s, creating the need for better organized open-air commerce. As the century advanced, it also became clear that the stalls in the center of Barcelona displeased the new Catalan bourgeoise. Public socialization started taking place on urban streets, and ladies and gentlemen with their families enjoyed promenades around the city. They were increasingly displeased about the noise, smell, and fights that characterized the markets.[16] But even before these complaints, municipal regulations were put in place in the two largest open-air markets near Las Ramblas and El Born. A director controlled the scales used in the market and maintained order in the area. City officials regulated the cost of food to prevent excessive prices and tried to prevent the sale of contaminated meat, which could contribute to the frequent epidemics that plagued Barcelona. These regulations eventually led to the creation of uniform rules for the stalls, which in turn created a new business: providing equipment for the vendors. In addition to building identical stands for fish vendors, a new system gave merchants the opportunity to lease equipment such as chairs, scales, and awnings.[17] Yet these new rules did little to address the nuisances the markets caused for the city and its residents. Even though the conduct of the vendors and other workers around the market area was increasingly regulated, the stalls along Las Ramblas were an eyesore.[18] The obvious solution was to provide enclosed spaces for the markets. Enclosed buildings would shield inhabitants from noises, smells, and the constant fights that broke out among the vendors. Enclosed markets also shielded the children who had to walk across the market area to get to their school from foul language. Remember that an important part of the modernizations of the nineteenth century involved improving manners. Each citizen was expected to learn a code of conduct that would be more compatible with a modern and cosmopolitan Barcelona; this expectation only increased as the city prepared for the 1888 World's Fair.[19]

The revolt of 1835 that burned down the church properties created the space for new construction. In 1836, disentailment laws passed by Juan Álvarez Mendizábal, the prime minister of Queen Isabella II, allowed the city to confiscate the necessary lands for the construction of its first two covered markets. Although similar buildings existed in other parts of Europe since the thirteenth century, Barcelona had only the Llotja building, which was used to sell wheat. The idea of gathering a diverse group of vendors in one place for retail sale was a new development linked to the industrial era.[20] The first market would house the vendors from the old open-air market on Las Ramblas known as La Boqueria into a new building to be called the Sant Josep market. The second market, to be named after Queen Isabella II but later known as Santa Caterina, was to be located where the church of the same name once had stood. The plans for Sant Josep, with porticoes and Ionic columns, reflected the wealth of the neighborhood, which was home to the increasingly wealthy Catalan bourgeoisie. The second market, situated near working-class neighborhoods, was a more modest design based on Saint-Germain in Paris.[21] The construction for La Boqueria began in 1840 and Santa Caterina in 1844. However, they took so long to build that by the time they were finally completed in the late 1800s, they already looked outdated, especially when compared to contemporary projects like Les Halles Centrales in Paris.[22] Part of the difficulty was the growing population, which necessitated altering the plans for La Boqueria during construction. In 1869, adjacent lots were incorporated into the project, and in 1888 the convent Sant Joan de Jerusalem was demolished to create room for the Plaça de Gardunya, where the current market stands today.[23] Meanwhile, the opening of Santa Caterina was intended to coincide with the birthday of Queen Isabella II on October 10, 1848, but it was only partially finished. Because the construction was plagued with problems from the beginning and required constant adjustments, and even a renovation, the building was not considered complete until the late nineteenth century. One of the initial complaints was the lack of glass in the windows of the building, as air and bright light inside the market spoiled meat and other products. Around the 1860s, the city finally dropped the original, intended name for the market and began calling it what the neighbors did, remembering the old church.[24] Today both markets continue to be called by their popular names: La Boqueria and Santa Caterina.

Meanwhile, after the medieval walls of the city were torn down in the 1850s, plans for urban expansion included more markets around the city. According to the 1856 survey prepared by Ildefons Cerdà, whose urbanization plans for the Eixample district were approved by Madrid in 1860, there were five working markets: La Boqueria, El Born, Santa Caterina, Barceloneta, and El Pedró, which would later become the site for the construction of the Sant Antoni market. These markets sold vegetables and fruit, meat, dried fruit, fresh and salt pork, offal, game, eggs, fresh fish and seafood, hens, bread, and lingerie fabrics and ranged in size from more than eight hundred vendors (La Boqueria) to only forty-five (El Pedró).[25] Part of Cerdà's vision was pragmatic urbanism, the desire to redesign urban spaces according to their specific social functions, and his plan tried to address the needs of the residents, their access to provisions, education, and outdoor space.[26] Markets were part of this vision, as were schools, green spaces, and even the optimal volume of air per person. As discussed in the previous chapter, what later happened in Barcelona shows the disparity between the aspired modernization of the city and its reality, bogged down by the greed of developers and land speculation. Cerdà's original design for the city included the opening of three large avenues, one of which, avenue B, would have directly affected the area where La Boqueria was located. The 1878 plan by architect Àngel Baixeras temporarily stopped this development because he considered the market a great attraction for Las Ramblas.[27] Originally built on the periphery of the city, over the years La Boqueria acquired absolute centrality, holding the largest share of market sales in the city.[28] With its construction, Las Ramblas was suddenly free of three hundred stalls, which dramatically changed the landscape of the boulevard. It is not surprising that the city marked the beginning of the project in 1840 with great fanfare. In addition to the local authorities and plenty of residents, the national army and artillery and spearman units were invited to celebrate the occasion. With the ceremonial first stone placed on the site of the construction, a lead capsule containing some coins, a copy of the Constitution, and a scroll with the statement from the mayor, Josep Maria de Gisper, was buried. The document addressed the decision to build a market capable of selling food items and other merchandise befitting the good taste of the people of Barcelona.[29]

While construction of Barcelona's first two markets continued, the city already was considering building more covered markets. The designs would follow the European trend of using wrought-iron and glass. Modeled after the popular arcades and exhibition pavilions of the nineteenth century, these new market halls created the ideal space for display. They also reflected the creation of a consumer culture aided by movement, enabled by railway travel.[30] People traveled to places to see and to peruse merchandise and other objects, and buildings were designed to provide the space to engage in this activity. Barcelona, as a modern city, was interested in having these "modern" buildings, and their construction was also planned in preparation for its 1888 World's Fair. The first two "modern" covered market halls following this design were El Born and Sant Antoni. As with the previously built markets, their locations were chosen based on the area's existing open-air markets, El Born and El Pedró. The construction of these markets also related to the city's ongoing urban planning and expansion in the 1800s. The dimensions of these two markets were very large because the city was trying to ease the congestion of La Boqueria and Santa Caterina by better distributing vendors and customers across the city. But this plan was not successful, and both modern markets ended up being underutilized. After this failure, markets were built with more modest dimensions, and the city began seeing the markets as a network to be regulated in conjunction with each other as a system.[31] By 1888, Barcelona had completed the construction of three more iron and glass markets (La Barceloneta, Hostafrancs, and La Concepció).[32] In the guidebooks for the World's Fair and other publications for visitors to the city written in the late 1800s, food market halls were suggested as places to visit.

The building of the market system in Barcelona continued until the 1930s. As the city tore down its medieval walls, it absorbed the markets of adjacent towns, including those from Gràcia and the municipality of Les Corts, such as La Llibertat, Abacería Central and El Ninot (which recently underwent a renovation and reopened in 2015). The building of the market system also resulted in the relocation of slaughterhouses in the city, moving them away from the its more central locations.[33] After completing the first wave of wrought-iron markets, Barcelona started using cheaper building materials, such as concrete pillars.[34] The markets embodied the profound transformation that was taking place in the way the city received its food. The railway system allowed for the fast arrival of far more diverse products than ever before. Newspapers regularly published the prices for food items. An 1850 edition of the *Diari de Barcelona* mentions rice from Valencia; wheat from seven different places; corn, oats, barley, flour, and semolina; chickpeas, fava beans, and white beans; salt cod from Norway, Iceland, and Newfoundland; fresh cod; cheeses from Holland; almonds from Majorca; saffron from the Mancha and Aragon; cloves; black pepper; cinnamon from Holland and China; oil from Tortosa, the Empordà, Malaga, and Seville; six types of sugar; cocoa; and coffee.[35]

News about food and commerce in the city of Barcelona was varied and abundant in printed form in the late nineteenth century despite the food and financial scarcity experienced by the working class. Shipping companies often announced the arrival of shipments through newspapers. Ads in the 1890 edition of the *Diari de Barcelona* communicated the arrival of 200 bushels of wheat bran and semolina on the Cabo Creus; 50 barrels of oil, 500 bushels of flour, and 30 barrels of beer on the Andrés; and 8,419 bags of corn from Buenos Aires.[36] As bulk commercial items, the goods mentioned in the newspaper might not have made it into the markets for retail sale, but they provide important information about ongoing food trade of the time. There is also plenty of information during this period about the types of vegetables cultivated, animals raised for meat, and fish being caught in Barceloneta, the port neighborhood. Among the publications where this information can be found are agricultural magazines and archives of the daily menus of the inns and restaurants that have survived until today. The agricultural magazine *L'art del pagès* (The Art of the Farmer) contained news about agricultural conferences, open-air markets, food fairs, lists of orange and almond varietals, the latest machinery, instructions on how to grow particular vegetables or mushrooms, forecasts of the harvest season, and the prices of grains.[37] During this time, the Institut Agrícola Català was founded to improve farming in the area. The institute organized regular exhibitions in the Camps Elisis open gardens in the Eixample district on farming and machinery as well as competitions for growing vegetables like pumpkins, radishes, and carrots.[38]

If the construction of markets can be explained as a way of organizing and regulating the existing open-air markets while containing their visibility and controlling the conduct of its workers, the markets were also educational and opened more and newer opportunities for commerce. The World's Fair of 1888 served that purpose for many countries and especially for Barcelona, which used the venue to showcase Catalan food products. The guidebooks published for the exposition mentioned the new, wrought-iron market halls of El Born and Sant Antoni as among the city's most important attractions.[39] At the World's Fair, the local products from the city and the region included different types of flours, soup bouillons, noodles, chickpeas, oils, vinegars, almonds, hazelnuts, olives, preserved meat, lunch meat, the famed dry sausage from Vic, preserved vegetables, nougat, cookies, chocolate, candies, wines, liquors, and anise. Spain, for its part, displayed its products—sugar, sweets, coffee liquor, cheese, chocolates, preserves, dried fruit, and legumes—according to the provinces and cities from which they came.[40] A novelty in the exhibit was the display of about one hundred mineral waters from all over Iberian Peninsula, which until then had been sold exclusively in drugstores. Even more groundbreaking, however, were the new machines made for the food industry that prepared and packaged meats, fish, tea, milk, butter, bread, and pastries; manufactured cold cuts, chocolate, and broth concentrates; brewed beer; and made carbonated beverages.[41] According to Jaume Fàbrega, it was after the World's Fair of 1888 that the Industrial Revolution started entering the kitchen. During the first half of the twentieth century, products that were designed to make cooking quicker and easier (mostly for the working class) entered the market: bouillon cubes, meat extracts, dehydrated soups, packaged yogurt, powdered and condensed milk.[42]

More important, the first electric and gas stoves, which eventually were available to the working classes, changed the way that meals were prepared at home, marking the slow end to wood and coal stoves.

SELLING FOOD THROUGHOUT THE CITY

While there was an increase in fresh food markets in the nineteenth century in Barcelona, there were also other kinds of food retail. Bakeries were regulated by the government to control the price of bread. When the wheat that entered the city was milled, the flour was delivered directly to the municipal bakeries (*fleques*; singular *fleca*). Bakers took control in the late eighteenth century, and in 1854 there were 130 bakeries and two flour mills.[43] A bakery from 1889, Fleca Sarret, still operates on Girona Street (Carrer Girona, 73) as Forn Sarret. Many bakeries now identify as *forn* (oven) instead of the old *fleca*. Another popular *botiga* (shop) was one that sold pasta and rice, as it was common to eat soup with *fideus* (short pasta noodles) every day and rice and *macarrons* (macaroni cooked with tomato sauce) once a week. These shops also sold butter, cheese, and dried fruit. In a city guide from 1888, sixty-four shops specialized in pasta for soups.[44]

Meats first were sold in separate shops according to the type of meat: lamb, pork, veal, or mutton. The municipality supplied the meat and also collected taxes on top of its base price. Some farms were located just outside the walls of the city, and the animals grazed in pastures nearby. This proximity allowed the local municipality to guarantee the safety of the meat butchered and sold for consumption. During times of upheaval like wars, revolts, or epidemics, fresh meat was replaced by salt pork or beef. In the mid-1800s, there were more than two hundred butcher shops in the city. A shop that sold cured meats was the *cansaladeria* (*cansalada* means "salted meat" and refers to a form of salted pork fatback used in many Catalan dishes). *Cansaladeries* sold ham and charcuterie from Majorca and Aragon and meat products from Italy, northern Germany, Ireland, and Romania. Sometimes the shops were run by French and Italian immigrants who sold local products and specialties imported from their own countries. An interesting practice was that the *cansaladeries* gave away every day the *brou bufat*, the leftover broth from cooking *botifarres* (fresh sausages). The broth was valued because it was useful to cook with, but it also served as a meal for the poor. It could be served with *fideus* or bread.[45] Unlike the salt cod shops that were popular and existed in higher numbers in the city, offal and fresh fish were mostly sold in the stalls in the markets, although there were a few independent fish shops.

Queviures Múrria on Roger de Llúria Street, number 85, Barcelona. *Image provided by Queviures Múrria.*

A special kind of shop that was popular in Barcelona were the *colmados*, also called *queviures* in Catalan.[46] The shops sold many food products that were not available in the fresh food markets. If they specialized in imported foods, such as coffee and chocolate from the Americas or spices from other countries, they were referred to as *ultramarinos* (overseas).[47] The list of products on sale, however, was not limited to foodstuffs; they sometimes offered other "exotic" items from abroad that usually would be available only in drugstores, such as tonics made of special herbs or fragrances. The *colmados* or *queviures*, with their abundant and copious goods, located in the most central commercial areas, served as a prominent display of the wealth of Barcelona in the nineteenth century.

Lluís Permanyer, who traces stories around the city of Barcelona, relates the story of its first *colmado*: Juan Nepomuceno Conde Núñez, born in 1795 and originally from Asturias, married a woman in Andalusia whose father ran a tavern called El Colmado. When she died, Conde moved to Barcelona with his daughter and took over a food store belonging to a relative, which he renamed El Colmado and moved to Escudellers Street, an area that enjoyed great social and commercial prestige. Conde profoundly disliked the French after having been kicked by a French soldier during the Spanish War of Independence. His daughter Dolores fell in love with a French cook, Emil Martignole, who had been hired by the rich *indiano* Josep Xifré (mentioned in the previous chapter). The distressed father sent Dolores to Tarragona and then to a convent in Mataró, but Martignole did not give up easily and followed her to the convent, where he befriended its gardener, who eventually helped him to reunite with his lover. Dolores and Emil married, and although Conde was invited to the wedding, he never accepted the match and died soon afterward. The daughter inherited El Colmado and, with Martignole's help, expanded the business to include a selection of wine and built their home on the floor above the shop.[48] An advertisement for the store from 1849 lists its products, highlighting its generous selection of wine (from fruity to dry and from different parts of the Spanish kingdom and abroad), cured meats, cheese from different parts of Europe, pork, fish in *escabetxe* like hake, langoustines, tuna, seabream, squid, oysters, clams, and other products. El Colmado also advertised *gordal* olives, large caperberries, cornichons, preserved truffles, peppers, and tomato sauce. Buffalo Bill supposedly bought whiskey there in 1889 while touring with his show. Because he was as tall as Martignole was short, he had to reach for his bottles and also help the owner with other items on high shelves that he was selling to his customers. The shop was highly appreciated for the quality and variety of the products it sold, especially its canned meats, and in particular the canned partridge. Martignole even developed a gelatin that sick people could consume, which became extremely popular during the 1918 flu epidemic, making him a wealthy man. In 1922, a second shop opened on the ground floor of the famed *modernista* building Casa Batlló, and the shop on Escudellers closed in the 1930s. Later fights among Martignole's descendants surrounding the patent rights for the gelatin marked the end of the family retail business.[49] This story reflects the social significance and popularity of these types of shops.

Other *colmados* or *queviures* were also popular, and the handful that survive today are considered Catalan institutions. The Queviures Múrria on the Eixample opened in 1898 and at first specialized in roasting coffee beans and making *neules* (rolled wafers traditionally consumed at Christmastime and sometimes dipped in *cava*).[50] It later became a prestigious shop as it began to offer a rich selection of food products. One of the most emblematic shops of Barcelona, it is easily recognizable for its Anís del Mono poster display, the original liquor advertisement created by the artist Ramon Casas.[51] Although the shop remains in operation, it represents a type of business in danger of extinction. A few *colmados* have closed recently because business becomes unsustainable when their clients are mostly tourists who come to peruse the store, take a picture, and walk out. Like the fresh food markets such as La Boqueria, the *queviures* also have become more tourist attraction than useful (or affordable) shops. A newspaper article lamenting the closing of Can Ravell at the end of 2016 expresses the remaining shop owners' desire that local customers help the stores by buying their products; otherwise, the survival of these stores is doubtful.[52] Residents are sentimental about the remaining *queviures*, but nostalgia alone will not keep them in business. The shops face competition from supermarkets and convenience stores around the neighborhoods in addition to the decline of cooking at home (except for holiday meals). Because Barcelona is enjoying a tourist boom and real estate is becoming increasingly expensive, these shops cannot afford to keep their doors open despite creating foot traffic with their colorful window displays filled with attractive culinary delights.

A NEW CONSUMER CULTURE

The construction of the market halls in the late 1800s and early 1900s, according to historian Montserrat Miller, coincided with the maturation of consumer capitalism. The popularity of food retail shops during the period is a testament to the flourishing trade around food taking place in the city. These activities also indicate changing food tastes and, curiously, give rise to discourse about women's responsibilities as consumers. As mentioned in the previous chapter, the domestic economy addressed in the 1800s cookbook *La cuynera catalana* reflects precisely the gender shift in purchasing practices around food. Market vendors and neighborhood shopkeepers benefited from the attention people paid to food trends. Miller points out the important role that women vendors played in this economy, transmitting carefully crafted oral discourses to help guide consumers in their food shopping and culinary practices.[53] Part of the reason that food became fashionable in Barcelona was because it still did not have the large department stores or shopping arcades that existed in other European cities. In the Catalan capital, social activity revolved around its elegant cafés and fashionable restaurants, to which the nearby market halls served as sources of food. These eating establishments depended on a neighborhood-based clientele, which contributed to the development of a commercial subculture consisting of everyday food shopping. Shops thrived on the personal connections between vendors and shoppers. Business relationships thrived when shops were located near restaurants, which were in constant need of food products.[54] This reality encouraged the clustering of shops around the restaurants, both of which were sustained by the daily foot traffic of shoppers looking for food provisions for their meals and of diners who frequented these venues. Boosted by a symbiotic connection, fresh food markets coexisted with small-scale commercial shops and specialty stores, in addition to the inns, taverns and other eateries, which acquired a large part of their stock from these businesses. The daily commerce maintained by these organizations not only allowed vendors to earn their living but also helped popularize public eating and drinking.[55]

The move of open-air markets into enclosed structures is charged with symbolism. For anthropologist Danielle Provansal, open market spaces tend to become venues for collective festivities where social transgressions happen and therefore need to be contained. But even if markets become covered spaces, they still function as places where people socialize, albeit possibly in more private, modest, or individualized ways.[56] We should remember that the legislation seeking to enclose the open-air markets was connected to politically liberal policies of the nineteenth century to regulate urban hygiene and moral conduct. But the transition to these enclosed places also tells us something about how social and cultural spaces worked in the city. Miller, in her fascinating and exhaustive study of fresh food markets in Barcelona from their origins to the late 1970s, traces a history in which the open-air markets, in addition to providing food to the city, played an important social role that formed part of the fabric and rhythm of its quotidian life.[57] El Born, for instance, attracted all types of people of all ages, and spontaneous comedic moments could arise among those present, which created a fair-like atmosphere. Also in these markets, all social strata of the city intersected, especially when they were located in public areas where people gathered during religious and civil celebrations. Areas around El Born as well as La Boqueria served multiple social, political, and cultural functions.[58] Starting in the eighteenth century, the elite of the city withdrew from these public spaces and, interestingly, the social distance created by this change also had linguistic consequences. Even before the Bourbons tried to suppress the use of Catalan, the trend among the upper class was to adopt Castilian as their language of choice. Although the intellectual elite undertook the project of modernizing Catalan so it could be written and taught, the language survived because the popular class never stopped speaking it. As Miller writes, "marketplaces in Barcelona, which were enmeshed in the everyday lives of the popular classes, and especially those of women, remained public spaces in which Catalan persisted."[59] After the Spanish Civil War, when only Castilian was expected to be used for communication in government, law, and education, markets served as important places for the preservation of the local language, as commerce and family life functioned around it.

The construction of market halls contributed to the creation of tight-knit communities, especially among women vendors. Miller has examined the gendered nature of small-scale commerce in food and how, in the history of Barcelona markets, women as independent business owners catered directly to other women in quotidian neighborly life.[60] These women passed stall titles through family lines to create market dynasties that extended generations. Many of them also continued to work after marrying, which offers insight into the division of labor, the family economy, and the culture of work that prevailed in the late 1800s and early 1900s.[61] In the mid-1800s, when most vendors worked in open-air markets, 90 percent of stalls were run by women. By the 1930s, with fifteen markets in the city and more men entering the trade, close to 60 percent of the business permits for the markets still were issued to women.[62] The rate of ownership is remarkable given that, in other areas, women were not allowed to own businesses or even to work outside the home without the permission of their husbands well into the twentieth century, but they could own and transfer market stall titles on their own. Women vendors were especially suited for this line of work, as they were able to develop a closer connection with their female clientele and, in general, they contributed to the everyday life of the community and the forming of social networks around the market halls. These connections encouraged the development of neighborhood retail clusters; women vendors tended to expand their businesses horizontally through kinship and other connections, taking over neighboring stalls or small shops, which functioned in a complementary rather than a competing way.[63]

This organization of retail also created areas with a strong sense of working-class solidarity exemplified in the tolerance of the street vendors. In the early 1900s, during periods of economic hardship and high unemployment, many jobless workers peddled foodstuffs around the market, and because of their low prices, they were popular with working-class consumers. They sold products they either bought from other market vendors or seized from farms or distribution centers. Although they represented a form of competition, their presence around the markets was unavoidable. For instance, during one of the hardest economic crises of the early twentieth century, a *mercadet* (small market) was organized around the working-class neighborhood of El Raval so that sellers and shoppers could have free access to each other, reflecting another form of proletarian economy.[64]

The social dynamic that characterized life around these shopping spaces had its own traditions and festivities. One of the most popular celebrations was the market balls, where they would crown a "queen of the market" from among the eligible women vendors of the different markets of Barcelona.[65] The presence of women in the market is abundantly documented through photographs of the time, which show their visibility as vendors and shoppers.[66] Yet men still ran the most profitable businesses. Records show that the most expensive stalls, such as the ones for fish and cafés, were purchased by men, whereas the cheaper ones, for fruit and vegetables, were mainly owned by women. Interestingly, when El Born market

Women shopping at Mercat de l'Estrella. *Image provided by mercatsbcn.cat—IMMB.*

was transformed into a wholesale and vegetable market in 1921, the gender composition changed dramatically. Three-quarters of the 150 stalls were run by men; taking into account the male laborers doing the loading, unloading, and transport, the gender difference was even higher.

The transformation of El Born into a wholesale market was an effort to address the lack of guaranteed provisions available to residents of Barcelona, which was especially evident during World War I, even though Spain remained neutral. The wartime shortage eventually led to an insurrection of women in January 1918 after a harsh winter protesting the lack of gas and electric power amid rumors of yet another increase in the price of bread. There were food shortages despite its abundance outside the city, where farmers fed potatoes and corn to their livestock.[67] The women demanded that the city regulate the price of coal, bread, olive oil, meat, and potatoes. The informal networks of women formed around the city markets had enough support for protests to last six weeks.[68] The solution offered by the government to address this situation was the creation of a free central market, where trading would be public and prices would be competitive. The idea was not to intervene in retail prices but rather to promote production and centralize the sale of food products in the city, thus eliminating intermediaries, which would contribute to lower prices.[69] Maintaining an uninterrupted supply of provisions to the city while keeping the costs down also would play a role during the Spanish Civil War, when

El Born was under the control of the CNT (National Confederation of Labor; the Spanish confederation of anarcho-syndicalists labor unions).[70] The problem of supply and distribution of food products in the city (and in Spain in general) continued until the 1970s. In Barcelona, a central fruit and vegetable market, the Mercabarna, finally opened in 1971 and remains in business today.[71]

RENOVATING AND REBUILDING MARKETS FOR TODAY

The continuing renovations of the fresh food market halls in Barcelona are a testament to their significance in the daily lives of their residents. Renovations of the Mercat de Sant Antoni concluded in 2018, and the Mercat del Ninot in 2015. The new installations for Mercat del Ninot reflect an ongoing effort to make the market attractive not only to shoppers but also to visitors. Now more spacious and with better lighting, the market incorporates sleek new eateries that are clearly different from the more traditional local bars that operated in the old market. It has gastronomic boutiques catering to customers who want to purchase food gifts like high-end olive oil, vinegar, cheese, and wine. It also offers more prepared foods for its regular customers and perhaps even for tourists, who can assemble a quick meal to take to their short-term rental apartments. The renovation of the popular Mercat de Santa Caterina pointed the way for how old markets could be revamped. When it opened in 2005, it had a fancy restaurant and a gourmet boutique selling high-end products like specialty olive oil, vinegar, and salt. It also had stalls that offered high-end produce like wild mushrooms or decoratively assembled fruits and vegetables, which, though not sourced locally, nevertheless worked beautifully as food displays. The market has since become part of the iconic image of the city. Its reconstruction was delayed many years because of the discovery of the archaeological remains of the church and convent of Santa Caterina. Another marketplace near the Santa Caterina that was planned to be renovated and reopened was the market of El Born, which had been abandoned after the end of the Spanish Civil War. When excavations started in the 1990s, archaeological remains of the city from the 1700s were uncovered. After much discussion, the local government decided to abandon the initial plans to revive the market. Instead, the site was turned into a cultural center and museum dedicated to the memory and the history of the city, El Born Centre de Cultura i Memòria, which opened in 2013. The decision to preserve the remains of the 1700s and the memory of the siege of Barcelona by the Bourbons, which basically ended Catalonia's political autonomy is significant. The recent commemoration of the 1714 siege was organized around the idea that the Catalan capital was a vibrant city with a distinct culture of its own easily seen through its gastronomy. Food tasting routes organized throughout the region of Catalonia highlighted each town's significance and local flavors. Cookbooks were published to commemorate the siege, and an app was created to help tourists follow the culinary trail of Catalonia.[72] The events organized to mark the historical event highlight a distinct Catalan identity, evident not only in the archaeological remains of the capital city but also through the history of its eating practices.

Considering the existing nostalgic narratives about the history of fresh food markets in Barcelona, the evolution of El Born reflects how markets have become important referents for Barcelona and its own way of life. First the area served as the site of an open-air market; later the first wrought-iron modern market hall was erected in its location. The market then underwent many changes, including its first conversion from a retail to a wholesale market in early 1921, later to a food distribution center during the civil war, a storage space, and finally an events site for meetings, parties, and concerts before closing permanently in the 1970s. The 2017 exhibit celebrating the market organized by the El Born center captured this nostalgic view of the past with testimony from the market's surviving vendors and porters and abundant photographs and footage from the daily activities in and around the market.[73] The accompanying texts emphasized the idea of loss as well as the importance of remembering the significance of the market for Barcelona's residents: not only was it a place of business, but it also represented a style of socialization and coexistence that has now disappeared. The exhibit seemed to be directed toward encouraging locals to preserve and value the city's memory, which is closely connected to its food practices. Given the importance that gastronomy has acquired as part of the Catalan identity at home and abroad, it is not surprising to encounter food exhibits in other parts of the city.[74]

Underlying these narratives about Barcelona's past, there seems to be criticism about the current tourism boom, which affects the city and is somehow responsible for the loss of a certain urban lifestyle. But perhaps the loss is not entirely due to the number of enthusiastic visitors to the region, but also to the rhythm of modern life and the way shopping and cooking practices have changed in the late twentieth and early twenty-first centuries. Despite all the doomsayers, walking today around the fresh food markets and observing the local customers engaged in daily shopping shows that these markets have retained their practical and social roles in their neighborhoods. Although it is true that supermarkets, convenience stores, and vegetable and fruit shops have cut into their business, markets continue to operate. The energy that emanates from these places on busy mornings makes it hard to believe that they will soon disappear. Even if some of the more centrally located markets have become tourist attractions, they are the minority and do not reflect what happens in every neighborhood of the city.

Shopping in the markets today affords customers full immersion in one of the most important foodways of the city and, by extension, Catalonia. The size and distribution of the vendors and stalls vary from one market to the another, including the number of stands, restaurants, coffee or lunch counters, and other retail stores. But they share basic characteristics in terms of the food products available for sale so regular customers know what to expect. The markets tend to be divided into areas by the type of food they sell. Usually the fish and seafood sellers are located in a specific area of the market with access to storage and refrigeration, as are the fruit and vegetable sellers. The meat sellers likewise work near each other, their products sold in different stalls depending on the type: red meat (beef, veal, lamb, and pork) or poultry (chicken, turkey, duck, quail, and eggs, but also rabbit). Meat stands can also sell breaded or marinated meat, especially the poultry counter, which often has *croquetes* and canned *foie* and duck confit. There are also stalls that specialize in offal like tripe, brains, sweetbreads, kidneys, hearts, lungs, liver, and animal heads (particularly lamb and occasionally pig). Stalls also sell dairy products (milk, cheese, butter, cream, and yogurt), cured meats, and dry goods like pasta and rice. They also have dishes ready to be cooked like *croquetes, canelons,* and stuffed and rolled meats for roasting like pheasant or lamb. Separate stands sell salt cod, including presoaked, shredded salt cod, and other canned fish like anchovies and tuna; these vendors also sell different types of olives, large caperberries, and pickled vegetables. Buying presoaked salt cod is a great time-saving measure for home cooks. Spices and other condiments might be sold here or at stands with dried nuts and fruits. Frozen products like vegetables, fruits, and meats of all kinds are sold in bulk in one or two specialized stands in every market. There are bakeries, of course, where one can buy both freshly baked bread and pastries (and breadcrumbs) and sometimes stands that sell chocolate and other candies. Specialized fruit and vegetable stands may carry expensive goods like wild mushrooms, exotic fruits, or edible flowers. Most of these types of stands can be found in other market halls in Spain, but one that is found only in Catalonia offers presoaked and cooked legumes: chickpeas, lentils, and *mongetes* (Catalan white beans). Particularly helpful for the home cook who might not have time to soak and cook beans, they are ready to be incorporated in dishes and salads.

Going to the market continues to be an important aspect of neighborhood socialization. In Catalan, *anar a plaça* (going to the square) also means going to shop at the market, which derives from the old open-air markets in the plazas or adjacent to convents or monasteries. Shoppers have itineraries of their favorite or usual *parades* (stalls or stands, literally "stops"), where they are waited on by vendors who are familiar with their shopping habits or tastes. Stall owners suggest items that are good or have recently arrived or let clients try certain items before they make their decisions. Customers who see other clients waiting usually ask, "*l'últim(a)?*" (the last one?), to identify the buyer who arrived before them. An efficient way to identify one's turn, it allows the shopper to avoid cutting in line. It is always a good idea first to ask whether any of the items on display can be touched or to get permission to select one's fruit and vegetables, since the vendor usually picks the produce for the customer. In vegetable stands, it is typical for the vendor to cut off parts of the vegetable that the customer requests, like the green tops of carrots or onions. Customers can ask for free parsley in vegetable and fish stalls. The fishmongers in the market are friendly when asked preparation and cooking advice about the products they sell. They are always happy to share tips and to suggest ways of preparing the fish or seafood available that day.

Regular shoppers might struggle with the decision to go to a stall that might have a better product than their regular *parada*, so as not to offend their usual vendors (with whom they might have varying degrees of familiarity or friendship). The casual conversations between shoppers and vendors can extend across the life span of both sides of the counter: birth, education, job and life changes, including happy and sad events that create a personal bond. Even if this relationship cannot be properly defined as friendship, it creates a sense of camaraderie and familiarity that is part of the social bonds of each *barri* (neighborhood). The importance of these establishments in maintaining the social fabric of the city is being recognized and emphasized, perhaps more so today by the local government. City officials recognize the importance of maintaining the attractiveness and social relevance of these markets in their neighborhoods. Many markets have started hosting market nights with live music and inexpensive tapas served in different stalls to attract local residents. For instance, in 2017, according to the Institut Municipal de Mercats de Barcelona, more than seven hundred events were organized by local markets, including tasting events, activities for kids, cooking demonstrations, art exhibits, and other cultural activities. These events add a social dimension to the space that goes beyond the use of its installations for everyday shopping or, for some, as a tourist stop during the day. Markets halls also have bars and eateries serving breakfast, coffee, lunch, and the *menú del día* (the conspicuous Spanish daily set menu that provides an appetizer, entrée, beverage, and dessert for a fixed low price), which gather not only the market workers but also those who work nearby.[75] Another tradition is the *esmorzar de forquilla*, literally "breakfast of fork," referring to a breakfast eaten with a fork, unlike the more typical breakfast pastry eaten with

Fish stall from the Mercat de l'Abaceria, before its renovation. *Image provided by mercatsbcn.cat—IMMB; photograph by Jordi Casañas.*

coffee in the morning. These breakfasts are informal but quite substantial and are served in the market eateries. Many Catalan chefs partake of these breakfasts when they go to the market to do their daily shopping for their restaurants. The food offered in these market stalls is part of many people's daily food experiences, and the quality of the locales inside or near the market speak to the high-quality dishes they offer to their customers and neighbors.

It is undeniable that fresh food markets are part of Barcelona's attraction for tourists. However, a balance between the needs of the local shoppers and the visitors must be achieved. An issue at hand is the density that groups of tourists bring to the market during shopping hours for regular clients. The key to remedying this situation is managing tourists' expectations while addressing the local needs.[76] A recent measure, for example, regulates the times when organized tour groups can visit busy markets frequented by tourists, such as the Santa Caterina and La Boqueria, in order to avoid congestion during the peak local shopping hours.[77] However, the markets always have made efforts to attract all visitors. An example of this effort was the inclusion, for the first time, of a high-end restaurant with a bar in the renovated Santa Caterina market. Cuines Santa Caterina, a restaurant run by the popular restaurant group Tragaluz, advertises its *cuina de mercat* (market cooking) and has been widely successful in signaling the close connection with the market and its cuisine based on seasonal and local products.[78] When it first opened, it used a ticker like Wall Street, advertising the fresh products from the market used in the daily menus and demonstrating the direct link between the kitchen and products from the market. A close relationship between market and restaurant has become an identifier for eating establishments, and guidebooks now offer a separate category for them. Even the physical organization of some of the recently renovated markets denote their dual existence, with fancier stalls and those with more prepared food like cut fruits or juices at the front of the market and the stalls selling meat and fish toward the back of the building. Another famous market eatery, in addition to the Bar Pinotxo of La Boqueria, is El Quim de la Boqueria, whose chef, Quim Márquez, has become a regular in the market. His cooking is now synonymous with tapas made from the seasonally varied and exceptional products of the market. Other chefs associated with the market are Iker Erauzkin, for example, who for many years served as head of La Boqueria culinary school. He now runs the restaurant Uma in the Eixample. Markets today regularly feature collaborations with famous chefs around the city, which are attractive to both residents and visitors. There is a clear effort to connect what the diners taste in eating establishments with their source of origin. The events that chefs organize in conjunction with the markets are a way to link their customers with local produce and Catalan cooking traditions.

Part of the challenge faced by these markets today is to avoid becoming too gentrified or touristy.[79] The markets often cannot compete with cheap products sold in supermarkets or in neighborhood shops that specialize in fruit and vegetables, but they cannot focus solely on high-end products catered to tourists and a small sector of the clientele either. As Manuel Guàrdia and José Luis Oyón suggest, they need to focus on offering access to local and seasonal fresh produce at affordable prices and organizing with other food market retailers to compete with large-scale food distribution. They also need to promote medium- to low-scale food demand, which is met by the many stalls run by immigrants in the city. Most important, markets need to continue to function as social hubs for the city.[80] The markets must be preserved as privileged spaces where interactions between different social classes take place and where the needs of many—no matter how different—intersect.[81] The recent market renovations undertaken by the city in the past two decades reflect how Barcelona markets have addressed these needs, making them models for other similar establishments around the world.[82] More recently, there have been initiatives to explore a way to combine e-commerce with the traditional market business. Today, many stalls offer home delivery services and even allow purchases made through the messenger program WhatsApp. As stated in the publication by the Ajuntament de Barcelona, its markets "are the heart and soul of the city and its neighborhoods, as well as local commerce leaders, driving forces, and health-care and sustainability benchmarks."[83]

Finally, we close this chapter by offering perhaps another reason why fresh food markets survive in Barcelona. Their endurance is owed not only to the rich and wonderful array of food products that they consistently offer to its residents but also to the many anecdotes that have become part of the social fabric of the city. These are stories that give the Catalan capital a sense of its own history and cultural identity. Genís Arnàs and Matilde Asina, in their informative book about the Barcelona markets, tell a noteworthy one about a man named Ramon Cabau who was intimately connected to La Boqueria. He is considered to have revolutionized Catalan gastronomy in the 1970s and 1980s, well before the appearance of chefs like Adrià. He was an agronomist, a pharmacist, and a lawyer. He was what could be called an authentic *Senyor* of Barcelona, always donning a tie and straw hat in his hand. With his daily effort and passion for work, Cabau became a local legend, running one of the most emblematic restaurants of the city, the Agut d'Avinyó, which he opened in 1962. In his restaurant, he offered an early version of the *cuina de mercat*, from La Boqueria in this case. His dishes had a clear influence from French cuisine, as well as touches from traditional Catalan gastronomy. He popularized items like *foie*, which he would buy in France and bring back hidden in his car. He also started using tiny zucchinis that he grew on his farm. He enjoyed teaching about food products from around the world and trying them himself. He was known to sleep very little. Every morning, before 8:00 am, he made a triumphant entrance into the market, ready to buy the best products for his restaurant. Before entering the stalls, he walked down Las Ramblas, greeting and buying from the flower vendors. He entered the market with a wooden cart full of flowers that he distributed among the salespeople of the different *parades*, bringing color to a place that was still gray and sad after a long dictatorship. When he had to give up his restaurant for financial reasons, he became deeply depressed and was unable to overcome his grief. On May 31, 1987, he bumped into the wife of Isidre Gironès, the owner of the famed restaurant Ca l'Isidre (still open today) at La Boqueria, greeting her with enigmatic words. He asked her to thank everyone who loved him. He had decided to end his life that morning after walking around the market. He took cyanide and died in the arms of his friend and chauffeur Petràs, with whom he made trips to the French border, returning with the car loaded with cheeses that filled the vehicle with many distinct smells. The shock caused by his death was incredible. The day of his burial, April 2, 1987, thousands of clients and vendors filled Las Ramblas and the front of the market in a last but deeply felt homage to the inimitable Ramon Cabau. Today, one of the columns by the market's entrance carries a plaque with his name.[84]

5

❖ ❖

Detecting Catalan Cuisine

Following the Trail of Pepe Carvalho

One of the most celebrated and popular "foodies" of Barcelona is a fictional character created by the writer Manuel Vázquez Montalbán (1939–2003). Created in the noir style of the hard-boiled American detective, Pepe Carvalho is a disenchanted middle-aged gourmand who combines crime solving, eating, and cooking with bouts of reminiscing about the past and the changes that the city he loves has undergone. He is also an accomplished cook, as was his creator, and after a couple of decades of crime-solving adventures, he and his sidekick-cum-cook Biscuter leave a sizeable number of recipes. They were published as a cookbook and now form part of the Carvalho detective series. The influence of Vázquez Montalbán on crime and gastronomic literature of the twentieth and twenty-first centuries is remarkable. He left a trail of modern gumshoes dreaming about food and savoring it as part of their adventures. He also wrote extensively on Catalan culinary history and was deeply committed to the slow food movement.[1] The writer deployed the popular detective to trace the culinary history of Barcelona and to document its most emblematic eating establishments.[2] Today, city guides and other cultural associations offer itineraries of Barcelona based on Carvalho's eating preferences and recommendations.[3]

At first, Pepe Carvalho's cynical view might appear unsuited to explain the gastronomic landscape of the Catalan capital, but it is precisely his distrust of the nonstop urban transformations around him that offers insight into the relationship between the city and its eating establishments. Néstor Luján pointed out in his *Vint segles de cuina a Barcelona* (Twenty Centuries of Cooking in Barcelona) that the city lacks restaurants with long histories compared to other European cities. He speculated that perhaps it had to do with Barcelona's political history, one that has continually pushed it to seek new things, always trying to differentiate itself from other cities (mainly those in Spain).[4] Given the Catalan capital's subordination within the Spanish state, especially since its defeat by the Bourbons, Barcelona is a city trying to prove that its second-class political status does not reflect its cultural excellence, especially in culinary terms. Many exceptional restaurants have existed in the city's past—such as the ones mentioned in chapter 3 about the dazzling late nineteenth century—but few, if any, have survived until today. We cannot forget, of course, that part of the reason for the changes in the restaurant scene was due to the political instabilities of the early 1900s that shook the city and the civil war that almost bombed it into oblivion. The long years of the Franco dictatorship should be remembered as an extended period of gloominess that forced into submission a large part of the city's population. In terms of food and nutrition, these years were characterized by hunger and rationing, which propelled the thriving black markets where vendors peddled whatever foodstuffs they could get their hands on through smuggling or other illegal means.[5] The frenzied culinary scene that emerged from this political and cultural context was perceived with suspicion by Pepe Carvalho, who relentlessly questioned the urban transformation that seemed to erase the memory of a city shaped by repression. At the same time, his memories of a childhood marked by lack of food manifested through a deep longing that made him continually engage in gastronomic excesses throughout his adventures. But even when indulging in food, Carvalho was worried about his city, as it appeared to be seduced by novelty alone, forgetting the values of its own tradition. Instead of working to repair the damage caused by a regime that had almost succeeded in erasing its cultural identity and progressive politics, Barcelona seemed to embark on a development craze that left many lost in their own city.

The city's transformation started in the 1960s, when Spain became a destination for vacationing northern Europeans in search of sunny coasts. The Catalan coast, the Costa Brava, received part of this wave of tourism, and many of its eating establishments started catering to this crowd. In addition to the contact with the outside world, Catalans of a certain social standing, taking advantage of their proximity to France, started crossing the border with more frequency to gain access to cultural events and works that were censured in their own country. The city was clearly changing as the flow of new ideas began to spread among its residents despite the repression that was still part of their everyday experience. Publishers started printing books in Catalan, and students more openly protested the government. Indeed, political opposition to the Franco dictatorship played an important role in shaping a generation of intellectual writers like Manuel Vázquez Montalbán, who was jailed for his ideas. It was also a time when a younger generation, socially and politically active and fond of meeting in bars, restaurants, and clubs, helped to transform the city's restaurant scene.[6] The group known as the Gauche Divine, for instance, enjoyed meeting in public spaces and gathering in bars like the Boccaccio, which quickly became part of the city's modern legend.[7] In a way, oppositional politics drove the city's cultural and social life until Franco's death in 1975. The arrival of democracy in Spain in the early 1980s, however, ended in disappointment for many of these young intellectuals. The political transformation did not dismantle the power structure put in place by the dictatorship, but rather allowed it to endure a political compromise, which since then has been labeled a "pact of silence." Most of the ministers remained in public life or embarked on other political careers, and the dictatorship was never condemned for its violence. Even if many of the complaints about the regime today seem symbolic, it is undeniable that Spanish (and Catalan) society remains divided about its recent past.

Barcelona's urban transformation began in the 1980s with an ambitious plan to reorganize the city following a model that linked urban and political citizenship with social welfare. The initial plan included revising the urban plans of existing neighborhoods, identifying their collective needs, and creating spaces where social participation could take place.[8] But many of these urban initiatives were abandoned when the city won the bid to host the 1992 Olympics, and Barcelona's priorities shifted dramatically. Vázquez Montalbán saw with great skepticism this urban transformation; he considered it a twentieth-century variation of enlightened despotism, one that forged ahead with an elitist view of the city without regard for the needs of actual residents.[9] He harshly criticized urban interventions in old neighborhoods like Barceloneta and Poblenou to open the beach area to make room for the Olympic Villa, expelling residents who had lived in the area for decades. Ultimately, however, the 1992 Olympics in Barcelona enabled the city to showcase its culture. It also started to be regarded as a good example of how international events can bring positive urban change to a city. Such praise overlooks the fierce protest and criticism that the plans for Barcelona's urban transformation drew during the 1980s. In regard to the city's culinary history, it could be argued that this global visibility contributed to the meteoric ascendance of Catalan cooking in the gastronomic world. Yet, for Vázquez Montalbán, the urban projects undertaken for the international occasion felt eclectic and contradictory, and many Catalans felt trapped in a dilemma between what to do about the continuity of its heritage and how to preserve or reject the legacies of the past.[10] The rambling of his detective through the city revealed this quandary, and as Carvalho ate his way through Barcelona, he helped to reveal a maddening race toward modernity fueled by real estate speculation and the dangers of losing the defining flavors of a place and the memory of its residents.

It is perhaps the tension between innovation and tradition that defines the restaurant scene in Barcelona. In a city obsessed with change, it is not surprising that few eating establishments survive for long periods of time. At the same time, many restaurants are turning to traditional Catalan cooking now that its gastronomic prestige is being recognized around the world. From this perspective, discussing the most representative or emblematic eating institutions becomes a complicated affair. At times, they embody tradition and history, which is important to recognize. Sometimes, however, the tradition identified with a restaurant is little more than nostalgia packaged for the consumption of tourists who flock to the city in search of "authentic" experiences. Despite its culinary prestige and its recognition for being on the cutting edge of the gastronomic world, the city did not have its first three-star Michelin restaurant until 2017 (Lasarte). The high-quality and technology-oriented cuisine that brings fame to local chefs is made outside of the city (and in other parts of Spain like the Basque Country). It is only when apprentices and collaborators of chefs like Ferran Adrià, Joan Roca, Carme Ruscalleda, or Juan Mari Arzak started migrating to Barcelona to start their culinary ventures that the Catalan capital became a restaurant hotspot. Comerç 24 by Carles Abellán, for instance, was one such early gastronomically prestigious restaurant. Today the city has many establishments with chefs whose culinary training has taken them to the most acclaimed kitchens in Catalonia and beyond. Unfortunately, even though these restaurants create much excitement and admiration, the road ahead of them is all but guaranteed in a city that craves new experiences.

In Barcelona, a restaurant sometimes typifies a style of eating and the social enjoyment that comes from that experience, such as sharing dishes or partaking of traditional dishes, rather than simply highlighting the qualities of a particular establishment. Curiously, our somewhat cautionary statement is similar to what Carmen Casas wrote in one of the earliest restaurant guides for Barcelona in the 1980s. Even though the context in which she wrote is very different from ours, it is telling that her selection of restaurants was based on types of food and styles of eating rather than particular establishments.[11] Specific restaurant names appeared in the middle of stories describing trends of the time or the way that they related to the history of the city. Her views on Barcelona's restaurants resonated with Luján's beliefs about them: they were to be considered temporary experiences rather than lasting ones. Given that Casas learned from the legendary food critic, it is not surprising that they shared that perspective.[12] In our case, we argue that it is important to remember and preserve the historical specificities of certain restaurants. But we also believe that there is something fun and pleasurable about focusing on the way food is enjoyed by the city's residents rather than concentrating on the specialties of a few selected places. From that perspective, we emphasize that in addition to the restaurants we mention in this chapter, attention should be paid to the type of eating and drinking that happens in small tapas bars near markets; in the *xiringuitos* (in Spanish, *chiringuitos*), or eating posts, along the beach; the *terrasses* (in Spanish, *terrazas*) across the city; or the numerous hotel rooftop bars sprinkled around the city. Paying close attention to new restaurants is part of the gastronomic tradition of Barcelona, including the latest ventures of the city's long list of famous chefs. When Luján wrote about eating out many decades ago, he was always mindful of how strongly restaurants had been influenced by immigrants and other newcomers to the city. Barcelona today is amid such transformation, though our list does not reflect this trend. If, a century and half ago, those who shaped the restaurant scene were from France, Italy, and Switzerland, today they come from much more diverse places, and the mix of flavors and ingredients they offer encompasses greater geographic and cultural distances.

The eating venues we include in this chapter continue to operate and represent different stories that reflect the diverse culinary landscape of the city. Sometimes a visit is recommended for the exceptional quality of the food; at other times their history provides incentive for a gastronomic visit. In no way is our list exhaustive or objective in its selection, but we do believe that it offers an interesting collection of eating and drinking venues that are part of Barcelona's gastronomic landscape. Having carved their places in a city that seeks to continually reinvent itself, perhaps some of these venues stand a chance of prolonging their existence into the future.

CASA LEOPOLDO

Situated in the neighborhood of El Raval, Casa Leopoldo is one of the restaurants that Pepe Carvalho frequents with great nostalgia. Historically, it is the area where the red-light district was, closer to the port and known for its seediness. It was also a working-class neighborhood that housed many of the immigrants that came from Andalusia. Today it is a more gentrified area of the city with large immigrant communities from other parts of the world. Casa Leopoldo is special for Carvalho because it is where he first shares a restaurant meal with his father, a character not always present in his recollections, but one who reminds him of the pain and suffering caused by the Spanish Civil War. Eating the traditional dishes of the restaurant as an adult returns him to his earliest memories. Recognizing the familiar flavors of his childhood helps the detective feel grounded in a city where he often feels lost amid its incessant reconstruction. Luján describes the restaurant as a *petit* restaurant in the center of the old dodgy part of town, which offers Barcelona's most perfect popular cuisine. He explained that its cooking was favored by many loyal gastronomes and praised the restaurant's fish dishes, the Mediterranean lobster dish, the tripe, and the *cap i pota* (stewed calf's head and foot), as well as its opulent steaks. Above all, the critic emphasized the generosity of the cook and its manager and declared himself a loyal, disciplined, and happy customer of the restaurant.[13]

When the restaurant closed in 2015 for financial reasons, it was considered a significant loss for the city and its culinary history. Given the popular interest, it was not surprising that the locale was acquired by two famous chefs and restauranteurs, Romain Fornell (Caelis) and Óscar Manresa (Torre de Alta Mar), who renovated and reopened it in 2017. They have discussed the challenges of reopening such an emblematic establishment. Their intention was to honor its legacy while maintaining a high culinary standard that reflects current gastronomic practices.[14] Many memorable literary *tertúlies* took place there, as it was a favorite restaurant of many writers and other famous chefs. The new chefs addressed the importance of preserving the essence of the restaurant and considered their project almost a civic duty to the city. The newly opened restaurant has preserved most of the original décor, and dark walls highlight the many photos of the original restaurant. They were left by Rosa Gil, the previous owner of the restaurant and the granddaughter of its founder, who first opened it as a *tasca* (bar) by the port. Her father opened the restaurant Casa Leopoldo in 1936. The remodeled restaurant has a photograph of Manuel Vázquez Montalbán, one of its most famous and loyal customers, more prominently displayed than before. His favorite dish, oxtail stewed in Priorat wine (*cua de bou*), holds a special place on the newly designed menu.

CAN LLUÍS

Another traditional Catalan restaurant favored by Pepe Carvalho, Can Lluís continues to be recognized as an emblematic restaurant of El Raval. It was founded in 1929 by Lluís Rodriguez and Elisa Vilaplana. Before that, it was an inn known as Can Mosques (the house of flies), because barrels of fresh cod were kept by its doors, which attracted flies in the summer. Can Lluís began serving homestyle cooking and popular dishes became its culinary signature. Three generations have maintained its friendly and familiar atmosphere, and today it continues to be a popular eatery for local residents. The restaurant never closed during the civil war despite food scarcity and difficulties in buying provisions to prepare the dishes. During the war, clients were warned, "If you want to dine, we don't have bread." Acts of solidarity were common during the war, and neighbors lined up by the restaurant with pots to receive the leftover soup or stew that the restaurant distributed at the end of the business day. The restaurant was also the site of a tragic event during the repressive years of the Franco dictatorship. In the afternoon of January 26, 1946, the dining room was full of lunch customers. The police entered searching for some people. Because of the electricity restrictions, the establishment was not sufficiently lit, so the owner accompanied the officers with a fuel lamp as they stopped at each table. When the police arrived at the table where a couple was eating with their four-year-old daughter, they yelled, "Hands up!" The woman left the table to get their coats, and when she returned, she threw a hand grenade into the dining room. The explosion killed the owner Lluís and his son Fernando. You can still see the impact of the explosion on the floor of the restaurant. Manuel Vázquez Montalbán wrote a short account of the event, which is preserved in a ceramic tile above table number four and is signed by the writer.

After the death of the owner, his son Lluís and daughter Elisa took charge of the family business. Under their management, the restaurant embarked upon a period in which it played an important social function in the neighborhood. Both siblings were young, outgoing, and social. Lluís's friendship with the patriarch of the gypsy community brought many musical and culinary events to the restaurant. His love for soccer also meant that Barça players gathered at the restaurant. In 1965, Ferran Rodríguez started working at Can Lluís as a sixteen-year-old. When he shopped at the Sant Antoni market for the restaurant, the women vendors often made playful and salacious comments offering "langoustines like yours." The 1960s were a period of change and protest against the regime, and the culture of the city was becoming overtly Catalan after many years of repression. Can Lluís was one of the first restaurants in Barcelona to offer its menu in Catalan. Actors, writers, and artists started frequenting the locale, like the theater group Els Joglars, the entertainers of La Trinca, the writer Terenci Moix, the singer Ovidi Montllor, and other intellectuals associated with the already mentioned Gauche Divine. The restaurant was used as a site for radio programs, press conferences, literary award ceremonies, and other cultural presentations. Its active cultural agenda continues today, and the menu of the restaurant reflects its traditional Catalan cooking, hearty dishes like

The owner of the restaurant Can Lluís Ferran Rodríguez Abella talking with the head waiter Dídac Rodríguez (seen inside). *Image provided by Can Lluís; photograph by Esteve Vilarrúbies; Fons d'imatges del Cormeç de Catalunya.*

tripe with chickpeas, pig trotters with snails, and other seasonal ingredients that change throughout the year. The restaurant also has a good wine list. Guests can try a set menu named after Manuel Vázquez Montalbán with his favorite dishes. When the restaurant became very popular and the lines too long, it was decided that Can Lluís needed a bigger space. Ferran Rodriguez, his brother Xavier, and Ferran Agüir worked together to open a second restaurant, Els ocellets (Little Birds), in the 1980s. It became a popular venue on Ronda Sant Pau near the original restaurant. Later, Ferran Agüir opened his own restaurant, Racó de l'Agüir (Agüir's corner), which is another exceptional restaurant offering traditional and innovative Catalan dishes near the Sant Antoni fresh food market.

CA L'ISIDRE

One of Pepe Carvalho's favorite restaurants, Ca l'Isidre was reserved for special occasions: when he needed to drown his sorrows and stop worrying about his financial future by eating well. Also located in El Raval, this classy and traditional restaurant continues to be regarded as one of the most outstanding eating venues of the city. It opened in 1970 and, from its earliest days, its founder, Isidre Gironés, shopped for the restaurant daily at the famous fresh food market La Boqueria. He ran the restaurant with his wife Montserrat, and together they made it into a culinary institution in Barcelona. Its cuisine is known for using the best locally sourced and seasonal products and offering a "Catalan-Mediterranean market cuisine." The kitchen and the management of the restaurant has been under their daughter Núria since 2017. A professional chef trained in France and Switzerland, she developed her love for the kitchen learning from her grandmother Angela and her father Isidre. She brings to Ca l'Isidre innovation and creativity that respects the traditional identity of the restaurant. She works with a team of chefs and professionals from the service industry, with José Millán as the head maître d' of the house. The restaurant boasts an extensive wine cellar with more than four hundred classic wines from around the world. The walls of the restaurant are decorated with numerous photographs of the many political and cultural figures who played important roles in the transformation of the city in the late 1900s. Through this photographic documentation, it is easy to imagine how gathering for meals and special dining events also played an important part during that period of political change for Barcelona after the end of the dictatorship.

SET PORTES

One of the oldest and most emblematic restaurants of the city, Set Portes continues to be a popular eating venue for locals and visitors alike. It is located in the famous building constructed in the mid-1800s by the wealthy Catalan *indiano* Josep Xifré (mentioned in chapter 3). He wanted the building to have arcades (*porxos*) like the buildings in Paris, and it became known as the Porxos d'en Xifré. Its reliefs illustrating allegories about the conquest of America and colonial trade can still be appreciated today. In 1836, the famous restaurateur Josep Cuyàs opened the Café de les 7 portes, one of the luxury cafés of the nineteenth century. The name alluded to the seven doors of the establishment (an eighth door is used by the staff and for deliveries). Néstor Luján wrote about the restaurant and its complicated story: its conversion from a café to a variety show venue, then back to a café, and finally to a restaurant. In 1949, Paco Parellada, who had been the legendary owner of the Fonda Europa in Granollers, took over the restaurant with his daughter Carme and his son-in-law Joan Solé.

It has since become a successful restaurant known for its rice dishes and traditional Catalan stews and seafood casseroles. According to Luján, it was the favorite eating establishment of the writers Josep Pla and Manuel Brunet. When they came into the city for meetings for the weekly *Destino*, they ate at the restaurant, which was also conveniently located next to the França train station. Pla told of an encounter with the owner of the restaurant in Paris during the Spanish Civil War. Without much to do during his exile in France, Senyor Paco visited the Les Halles market every morning. He examined the products for sale and discussed them with the vendors while making an imaginary shopping list for his fictional restaurant. One day it would be fish that looked magnificent that day and was offered at a good price, while another day the shopping list consisted of vegetables and legumes, and every day he made a list of the meat and game available in the market. His morning walk around the market lasted about two hours, after which he happily walked home, fantasizing about his shopping and the dishes he could serve to his clients. For Luján, the story was an emotional and poetic anecdote about a man born to work in a profession in which happiness was feeding others and helping them feel content. In the 1940s, the restaurant employed a famous waiter who delivered the check for each table as a poem, listing the items consumed by the guests in perfectly rhymed verses.[15] In 1980, Francesc Solé Parellada took over the restaurant, continuing the Parellada family's tradition of more than three hundred years in the restaurant business, combining good and generous traditional cooking with excellent customer service, values that his grandfather cherished as a professional restauranteur. In 2016, the locale celebrated its 180th anniversary.

CAN CULLERETES

Founded in 1786 as a *xocolateria*, Can Culleretes is today the oldest restaurant in Catalonia and the second oldest in Spain. Located just off Las Ramblas between the small streets of Ferran and Boqueria, its entrance is on Quintana Street. It was opened by Joaquim Pujol as a place that specialized in serving hot chocolate, a very popular one among the many *xocolateries* of the time. It also served desserts. Lluís Permanyer tells the long history of the establishment that is available on the restaurant's website.[16] Pujol's grandmother was the caretaker of a convent located outside the medieval walls of the city. She had the idea of putting a few tables out by her lodging on public holidays and offering drinks and snacks as an afternoon treat. She offered *orxata* or other sweet drinks, her almond dessert or Catalan cream, always served with a spoon. She made her dessert by first making almond milk and then adding sugar, lemon peel, and cinnamon to it, which was brought to a boil and gradually mixed with starch. She poured the liquid in molds that produced stiff, shiny, cheese-like disks. When her post became too popular, the monks were not amused by the crowds gathering near the religious residence. She first moved to the corner of Plaça Sant Jaume and Jaume I Street and then to the current locale on Quintana Street. She continued to serve sweet drinks and her desserts with spoons. It is said that it was the first establishment that used metal spoons instead of wooden ones. As the venue became more popular and busier, waiters continually could be heard yelling, *"noies, culleretes!"* (girls, teaspoons!), as the container for clean spoons emptied quickly. Customers started referring to the place as Can Culleretes (House of Teaspoons).

The Regàs family bought the establishment around 1890 and turned it into a restaurant. From then on, it served typical Catalan dishes like *escudella*, pork sausage with white beans, and game dishes. It was popular for its affordable meals. At the end of the Spanish Civil War, the Regàs family was forced to hand over the business to the guild of hoteliers and chefs. The reputation of the restaurant suffered during the dictatorship, as the food it served was not good. In 1958, the restaurant was bought by Sisco Agut and Sussi Manubens; since then, they have restored its reputation for solid homestyle cooking and reasonable prices. It is, like other older establishments, full of memories and connections to important people of the city. Their list of distinguished guests is long, but their favorite was Mario Cabré, a Catalan actor, poet, and bullfighter, also known for his affair with Ava Gardner. He visited Can Culleretes almost every day and was like a brother to Sisco. The Agut-Manubens are a reputable family in the restaurant business in Barcelona.

The food served today is far from the innovative and cutting-edge dishes that many new restaurants serve in Barcelona. Theirs is a traditional cuisine, connected to their neighborhood fresh food market and characterized by hearty dishes. A typical dish is a fish or seafood appetizer, a plate of *canelons*, cod brandade, Catalan-style roasted suckling pig, wild boar, or pheasants. While the chefs prepare the entrées, Sisco and Sussi's daughters, Montse and Alicia, prepare the desserts that will be included on the menu of the day, including their signature dessert, "El Sisquet," in honor of their father. The locale is unassuming and offers an ample room decorated with frescoes that illustrate social scenes of the past. Pulling the door open and stepping into the restaurant is to travel in time to another period amid the busy and touristy old city of Barcelona.

Interior of the restaurant Can Culleretes. *Image provided by Can Culleretes; photograph by Oliver Martínez.*

AGUT

Located in the Gothic Quarter of Barcelona, Agut, founded in 1924 by Agustí Agut and his wife Paquita, is known today for its affordable menu and excellent traditional Catalan cooking. The restaurant preserves the atmosphere of an old inn: a traditional, local, and "authentic" Barcelona eating establishment of bygone times. Its history is complicated, and the restaurant is often confused with another establishment owned by the family, which was situated near the current restaurant. The other restaurant, Agut d'Avinyó, was opened by Paquita Agut, the daughter of the owner of the original Agut restaurant, and her husband Ramon Cabau. He was a lawyer, a pharmacist, and a specialist in agronomy who grew produce on his own farmland. Cabau's restaurant played an important gastronomic role in bringing innovation and creativity to Catalan cuisine in the 1960s and 1970s. With his marriage to Paquita, Cabau became part of one of Barcelona's most important families in the restaurant business. He opened his own restaurant close to his father-in-law's, on Avinyó Street, already a famous area thanks to Pablo Picasso's painting *Les Demoiselles d'Avignon* and its reference to the brothel on the same street. Agut d'Avinyó quickly gained culinary prestige and by the late 1970s was considered a gastronomic temple. The dishes imagined and served by Ramon and Paquita began to reflect the culinary sensibilities of a city slowly awakening to a new era of cultural and political change. Combining French cuisine and traditional Catalan cooking, the dishes served were lighter and well executed, using good-quality ingredients. Suddenly traditional dishes seemed new, such as duck with figs or hare stew. Cabau believed in Paul Bocuse's philosophy and strived to use only fresh, quality ingredients in his dishes. He shopped every day in La Boqueria fresh food market. He frequently traveled to France, bringing his car back full of cheeses and *foie* for his restaurant. He became a local personality, easily recognized by his impossible mustache, bow tie, and straw hat, which he carried everywhere. The establishment was popular with politicians, writers, and artists of the city (like the already mentioned Gauche Divine), people who, according to Néstor Luján, liked to eat well.[17] At the height of its popularity, the restaurant was invited to participate in the gastronomic conventions that were being organized in the city and in Spain. But above all, Cabau loved La Boqueria. He not only bought products there but also offered suggestions, shared improvement ideas, and encouraged vendors to offer certain products. He convinced Llorenç Petràs, who ran a chicken farm near Montserrat, to open a wild mushroom stall in the market. Bolets Petràs is today one of the most important stands of the market.[18] But the story of this family restaurant does not end well. Due to financial reasons, Cabau gave up the restaurant in 1984 and continued to work his farm. He sold his produce to the fresh food market, but he had become depressed after leaving the restaurant. One morning, after finishing his regular morning walk around the market, he asked for a glass of water and swallowed a cyanide pill. He died on the spot, but not before saying good-bye to his friends, giving them flowers and enjoying the market at its busiest hour. Today, one of the entrances of the famous fresh food market has a plaque with his name. He had been a beloved customer, and his funeral was attended by people who stood on Las Ramblas to pay their final respects. The restaurant Agut is part of this culinary history of Barcelona and continues to be owned by the Agut-Manubens family. It is a popular restaurant for both locals and visitors for its friendly, attentive service and quality traditional dishes.

LOS CARACOLES

In the middle of the Barri Gòtic, the Gothic quarter of Barcelona, the Bofarull family opened a restaurant in 1835 by the name of Can Bofarull. It was first a tavern selling bulk wine, oils, liquors, and soap. Later, the son, Felicià, decided to start selling small dishes, what we would call tapas today. The snails he served with sauce and black bread became so popular that clients renamed the joint Los Caracoles in 1915. The neutrality years and the happy 1920s brought much prosperity to the restaurant, which enjoyed long lines of clients waiting to dine on lamb heads or *cap i pota*. The small tavern moved to a larger locale during these years, to number 14 on Escudellers Street. It had an oven in which they started roasting chicken, and the restaurant subsequently became one of the most popular roast chicken venues in the city. After the war, Felicià's sons, Ramón and Antoni, took charge of the restaurant, the former running the kitchen and the latter taking care of the public relations side of the business. Described as a Fellini-esque character, Antoni transformed the restaurant into one of the most popular establishments of the city. He was an actor who appeared in more than twenty films and also a film producer. He embraced tourism and served as a host for American actors who came to town. His connections explain the many photographs of famous people on the walls of the restaurant today. Perhaps the restaurant owes its longevity to indulging the city's famous personalities and visitors.[19] The list of guests to the second oldest restaurant in Barcelona is impressive: Burt Lancaster, Vittorio de Sica, Ava Gardner, Bing Crosby, John Wayne, Julio Iglesias, Pablo Picasso, Salvador Dalí, and, more recently, Robert DeNiro and Lenny Kravitz. But do not be fooled by the restaurant's popularity with personalities and tourists; its traditional cooking is excellent and worthy of a culinary visit. Los Caracoles is the only kitchen in the city that continues to use a charcoal stove, and the dishes prepared in its fiery heat are something to cherish.

VIA VENETO

Considered one of the finest eating establishments of Barcelona, Via Veneto still inspires a nod of approval from residents when they hear it mentioned. An upscale restaurant, it recently celebrated its fiftieth anniversary with a tasting menu that featured its most popular dishes, including a tartar of langoustines, sea urchin gratin, black truffle with *foie*, and beef Wellington. Clearly not a traditional Catalan restaurant or an establishment that all diners can afford, its presence in the city still should be noted, as it represents a shift toward high-end dining establishments. It was one of Néstor Luján's favorite restaurants. Curiously, it was Salvador Dalí's, too. (We will get to Dalí's story later.) Luján praised the restaurant for offering luxury combined with great cooking, perhaps reminiscent of the great *modernista* restaurants of the late nineteenth century. The restaurant was not initially successful until it was acquired by the maître d', Josep Monje, who transformed it into one of the top eating establishments of the city. According to Luján, Monje had a clear idea of what a luxury restaurant in a city with many centuries of culinary tradition should look like. He harmonized his superb gastronomic knowledge with the flavors of popular cookery.[20] Once again, it is the story of excellent Catalan cooking presented as a combination of old and new and perfected with impeccable technique. The food critic praised its Catalan fish soup, its stuffed pig trotters, its mysterious wild mushroom dishes, and its browned lamb ribs. But above all, it was Monje's impeccable service that made Via Veneto distinctive. Luján believed that what made a restaurant really special was not only the chef but also someone who knew how to run it and wait on its guests. Eating at Via Veneto was described as a complete experience in which food and service combined to provide an unforgettable gastronomic experience. Perhaps it was Monje's absolute discretion that made the restaurant Dalí's favorite as well. He was known to arrive with a large entourage and organize varied performances. Each dinner with Dalí has been described as something new and unique. One time, the artist asked Monje for fresh sausages, which Dalí hung on his female guests as necklaces. The owner likely acted as nothing out of the ordinary was happening in his classy establishment. On the restaurant's website, guests can reserve Dalí's favorite table.

RESTAURANT GAIG (GAIG A CASA)

Carles Gaig's development as a chef and restaurateur is interesting because it represents a culinary trend that explains the ever-changing Barcelona food scene during the last twenty years or so. He just announced the move of his well-known Restaurant Gaig to the hotel Torre del Remei in the town of Bolvir in Cerdanya in July 2019. In addition to his Barcelona restaurant once located in the Eixample, he has one in Singapore (run by his daughter Nùria). The international prestige Catalan (and Spanish) cuisine achieved in the late twentieth century has allowed a select group of chefs to embark on culinary adventures around the world, such as Carme Ruscalleda, the late Santi Santamaria, Ramón Freixa, and Paco Pérez, among others. But Gaig's trajectory and the cooking that the chef and his restaurant represent tell us something important about the recent developments in Catalan gastronomy.

Born into a family with ties to the culinary world, Gaig grew up in the Horta neighborhood of Barcelona. His parents owned the Taberna d'en Gaig, which had been in the family since 1869. Although he helped in the kitchen, it was his mother's blindness that brought him into the kitchen full time. He learned to cook classic Catalan dishes from his mother, and his great-grandmother's *canelon* recipe always has been present on his menus. As the restaurant website explains, Gaig's passion for innovation and tradition led him to renovate his traditional restaurant in 1989 and rename it Restaurant Gaig, which went on to win a Michelin star in 1993.[21] He soon was recognized with more awards, such as the Royal Spanish Academy of Gastronomy's national award for best chef in 1999. In 2004, he closed the doors of his restaurant in Horta and, along with his wife Fina Navarro and his team, moved to the Eixample and into the Hotel Cram, where they opened their restaurant, Gaig. In the restaurant hotel he explored avant-garde cuisine (or the so-called "molecular" cuisine) and practiced "market cuisine," a term popularized in the early 2000s. More than a style, it is a term that links cooking with local produce obtained from the fresh food markets in the city. The label became popular around the time when markets started gaining recognition as valuable assets to the city's gastronomic scene. In the hotel restaurant, they served elaborate tasting menus for local and international customers. In 2004, the restaurant won the best restaurant of the year award from the Catalan Academy of Gastronomy. More accolades followed, including the San Sebastian Gastronomic Conference's 2005 award for Best Dressed Table for Fina Navarro, who served as the maître d' of the restaurant. In 2008, Carles and Fina opened a new restaurant, Fonda Gaig, where their last restaurant stood, returning to more traditional Catalan cooking. Their customers clamoring for the old Gaig, they decided to open a venue where they could revive many of their classic dishes. The year they opened the restaurant, they won an award for the preservation of Catalan cultural heritage. Eventually they left the hotel and settled on Còrsega Street as Restaurant Gaig. The restaurant was beautifully and elegantly decorated and attracted a privileged local clientele. Now, with the restaurant's announcement of its move outside of Barcelona, Carles Gaig leaves in its place Gaig a Casa on the street Nau Santa Maria, number 5. A bistrot with ready-made meals that can be taken home, the chef plans to travel to the city to cook a few days a week in front of his clients in his last venue in the Catalan capital, perhaps offering a final chance for visitors and residents of Barcelona to try his grandmother's famous *canelons* prepared by the chef himself.

Carles Gaig continues to embark on culinary ventures, but, as his restaurant website states, he and his wife Fina are staying faithful to the roots of his family restaurant in Horta and to traditional Catalan cooking. The evolution of their culinary adventure, which returned them to their gastronomic origins, speaks to the culinary development of Barcelona during the late twentieth and early twenty-first centuries. Chefs have brought innovation and creativity to traditional Catalan cuisine. As explained by many star chefs, including the world-famous Roca brothers, contemporary Catalan gastronomy is a cutting-edge and imaginative cuisine based on the region's culinary tradition.

BAR XAMPANYET

Located down the narrow, cobbled alley in the Gothic quarter near the Picasso Museum, the Xampanyet is a little tapas bar with few tables and always full of clients. Its name comes from the fizzy wine it serves, along with freshly made tapas with products procured from the nearby Santa Caterina fresh food market. It also serves quality canned seafood, and it is known for its cured meats and anchovies. You can order ham, grilled vegetables, or whatever the waiter or bartenders recommend. The tapas are not cheap, but they are fresh and well prepared. The place is small and old school, and one needs courage to step in to try to make space at the bar or one of the barrels that serve as standing tables. Getting sit-down tables is difficult, but they can be reserved. It is a place for a quick bite or a *vermut* (an appetizer before a meal). The staff is friendly and increasingly more patient with tourists and more proficient in English. There are many places like this bar around Barcelona, especially around the food markets. If one does not have much luck creating a space by the bar, try similar places like La Cova Fumada by the Barceloneta fresh food market or Bar Pinotxo at La Boqueria market.

QUIMET I QUIMET

A special tapas bar in Poble Sec, Quimet i Quimet easily can be confused with a wine shop or one of the traditional *queviures* or *ultramarinos*, the nineteenth-century stores discussed in chapter 4 that were known for carrying imported food products. The bar is standing room only, and its specialty is *conserves*—that is, food preserved through curing, canning, or jarring. They are displayed in their containers on shelves for sale. The store first opened in 1914 as a wine shop, which sold the wine that the grandfather of the current owner produced outside of Barcelona. To help sales, he offered some traditionally preserved food like anchovies or olives to accompany the wine. Over the years the store underwent some changes, especially in the selection of its food products. It added a carefully curated selection of wines and vermouth and more variety to their tapas menu—such as smoked sardines, sun-dried tomatoes, and cured salmon—in addition to the traditional anchovies. Now it offers *montaditos*, small Basque-style open-faced sandwiches made with imaginative combinations of products sold in the store and a wide selection of wine by the glass. It offers almost eighty different combinations with ingredients like cockles, sardines, hard and soft cheeses, cured meat, *foie gras*, baby squid, asparagus, and swordfish. In the nineteenth century, doors of bars were painted maroon or red to indicate to illiterate customers that they sold alcohol. The doors of the restaurant still maintain their reddish color.

The owner explains that high-quality canned foods in Barcelona represent a culinary tradition that has nothing to do with the industrialized food sold in supermarkets. Although the preservation technique might have originated during industrialization when technology entered the kitchen, these products are not for mass consumption, but rather for selective tasting of vegetables, meats, and fish. Quimet i Quimet represents a different eating experience from the more popular tapas or sit-down restaurants. These tapas are not cheap because they come out of a can or a jar. The food items served are culinary treats that should be savored as such.

BAR BOADAS

The oldest cocktail bar in Barcelona, Bar Boadas has become a required stop for anyone who loves a good mixed drink. The place is cherished not only by cocktail connoisseurs but also by the locals who have frequented the establishment since its opening. It is possible to get a look at this loyal clientele by visiting at noon, when the bar opens. It is quiet, the expert bartender works alone, and regulars stop by, one

Exterior of Quimet i Quimet. The doors of the establishment still maintain the reddish color to indicate the sale of alcohol as it was done in the nineteenth century. *Image provided by Quimet i Quimet.*

or two, never too many, sitting quietly at the bar, reading a newspaper, or chatting with whomever is working behind the counter. If you do not know what to order, tell the bartender your preferences and something special will be prepared for you. Meanwhile, you can peruse the walls of the bar, examine the many photographs that document its long history, and find familiar faces who have journeyed to this mythical place. Its story begins in Cuba, in another famous bar called El Floridita. Known as the birthplace of the daiquiri and one of Hemingway's favorite hangouts, it had been owned by a Catalan immigrant. His cousin's son, Miquel Boadas, was born in Cuba but returned to his parents' hometown, Lloret del Mar, where he lived with his mother until the age of thirteen, when he returned to Cuba and started working for his cousin in El Floridita. He quickly became a popular member of the bar and discovered his passion for making and serving cocktails. He spent his formative years in the cocktail business during Havana's intense nightlife scene of the 1920s. Due to personal circumstances, Miquel Boadas decided to return to Catalonia. By then, the city had been slowly awakening to the craze for American-style bars and mixed drinks, which were seen as a sign of modernity. When Boadas arrived in Barcelona in 1922, it already had a few popular bars, like Au Pingouin and the American Bar at the Hotel Colón. He worked as a barman in a few places, but he became known for his work at the Canaletas, a kiosk bar in the middle of Las Ramblas that was open twenty-four hours a day.

The Canaletas Kiosk Bar on Las Ramblas (now disappeared). *Printed with permission from Arxiu Fotogràfic de Barcelona.*

In 1927, he met a woman from Lloret and with her found the locale where he would make his dream come true. He opened Boadas in 1933, decorating it in the style of La Floridita. Despite public opinion that it would not last long due to its proximity to the Canaletas kiosk, the bar enjoyed much success. It remained open during the Spanish Civil War—it is said that George Orwell and Joan Miró had been clients—and the sad and dark postwar years of the 1940s. Boadas and his wife worked and lived in the building, and after welcoming their daughter, María Dolores, the three became fixtures of the locale. María Dolores, who passed away in 2017, continued her father's labor of love, making the bar a cultural institution of the city. Quite the character, she surrounded herself with friends and clients she liked (among them, of course, Manuel Vázquez Montalbán) and maintained the bar's ambiance according to her own taste. Stepping into the bar with its wooden furniture and dark lighting, it feels like traveling to some distant time and place, especially in contrast with the bustling streets around Las Ramblas. Unfortunately, some of her comments about how Barcelona changed in the last years drew criticism and reflected her disconnect with its rapidly transforming urban landscape. Her death marked the end of an important part of the history of the establishment. Despite her absence, the bar continues on, maintaining its rightful role as part of the culinary and cultural legacy of the city.

6

Traditional Catalan Dishes Today

To read about Catalan cuisine is to learn to recognize its distinguishing particularities, especially as a cuisine that exists within Spain and the Mediterranean region, both areas with which Barcelona is often closely identified from abroad. Writing about food and recipes has acquired much cultural value in Catalonia, especially now, when the area's most innovative and avant-garde restaurants firmly express their connection to the traditional cooking of the region. To learn about this cookery is to understand the backbone that fuels the famous Catalan chefs' gastronomic imagination. More than the internationally acclaimed restaurants of Barcelona and its surroundings, what makes Catalan cooking special is its own sense of culinary identity. In it, there are traits that come from its medieval tradition but also from other cultural influences, still detectible through the favoring of certain ingredients. Cooking with lard in combination with olive oil, for instance, has been pointed to as one of its more unique characteristics (even though the use of lard is no longer common today), as well as its penchant for aromatic herbs. The use of a mix of nuts, bread, and herbs as a thickener for sauces and to finish dishes is an old practice that still endures, as well as the slow cooking of chopped onions and herbs that starts many of their dishes. The combination of sweet and savory flavors also is noted as a distinct Catalan practice, as is the harmonious pairing of sea and land products in the same recipe. Rice features frequently in its traditional dishes, more so than in other regions of Spain. Vegetables also appear more prominently in the Catalan diet compared to others in the country. Although salt cod is used as frequently as in other parts of the peninsula, Catalans boast a couple of unique ways of preparing it. Closely connected to its mountains and the sea, Catalonia enjoys the mild Mediterranean climate that provides bountiful foodstuffs throughout the year. Eating seasonally and locally is a habit that Catalans practiced long before it became trendy. Finally, the culinary specialty that each village or town offers around the coast and mountains of Catalonia has become part of its strong gastronomic identity and has propelled its culinary prestige around the world.

In this chapter we have collected a sample of traditional dishes, paying close attention to their significance in everyday cooking and regular menus. We have also asked some Catalan chefs to share some of the traditional recipes they use in their restaurants. The ones included here have been adapted for the home cook and ingredients available in the United States; however, even when simplified, they might appear more intimidating than the regular recipes. In our selection of recipes, we have focused on the importance of sauces in Catalan cooking, from which many dishes build their distinct and deep flavors. We also chose dishes to showcase traditional ingredients—albeit ones that can be procured without too much difficulty—and suggest variations and possible adaptations. The recipes gathered here illustrate some of the particularities of the region's cuisine that we have mentioned throughout the book. The order of the recipes follows the idea of building a final dish, usually an entrée, which starts from a basic sauce. Each sauce recipe is then followed by a couple of dishes that highlights the use of the sauce. We also draw attention to some cooking techniques and combinations of unusual ingredients in a plate. In a way, each recipe embodies a distinct character that can be linked to a Catalan gastronomic tradition. Among these recipes, you will not find any that could fit into the "tapas" category, so common and internationally popular when talking about eating in Spain. The reason is that although Catalans enjoy the *pica-pica* (to eat a bit of this and that), they prefer to sit down and eat a complete meal, be that for lunch or dinner. Informal eating is done before a meal in the late afternoon or before lunch (in that case, called a *vermut*) during the weekend. Honoring this practice, we offer recipes for entrées rather than small dishes. Mealtimes in Barcelona follow those of other Spanish cities, although dinnertime tends to be earlier than, for instance, in Madrid, where dinner reservations can be offered as late as 11:00 pm onward. Catalans enjoy dinner around nine at night and usually have an early evening compared to other cities. Large and long lunches are common during the weekend, as in other parts of the country, and Catalans enjoy them as well, after which they are likely to have a frugal dinner. Dishes prepared at home tend to be simpler, even modest, and richer in vegetables (in fresher forms as in salads) than when eating out.

Although the number of recipes here is small, there are fortunately other great cookbooks on Catalan cooking published in English. They offer a wide variety of recipes along with useful information about the region's culinary tradition. The classic and still unbeatable source is by Colman Andrews, *Catalan Cuisine*, first published in 1988 and now available in a newer edition. A recent cookbook on Barcelona (and its ties to New York) is *Boqueria* written by Marc Vidal and Yann de Rocherford published in 2018. Two more were published in the same year: *The Catalan Kitchen* by Emma Warren from Australia and *Catalan Food* by Daniel Olivella with Carolina Wright. Another recent book, also from Australia, was *Catalonia: Recipes from Barcelona and Beyond* by José Pizarro, published in 2017. The important cookbook on essential Catalan cooking by Joan Roca of the famed *El Celler de Can Roca* was translated into English in 2012. Its original title in Catalan, interestingly, is *La cuina de la meva mare* (The Cooking/Kitchen of My Mother). The book offers an eye-opening breakdown of ingredients and paints a clear picture of the roots of Joan Roca's cooking, becoming, alongside his two brothers, the most creative chef, sommelier, and pastry chef in the world, respectively. In 2004, Paul Richardson published a cookbook called *Barcelona* for the Williams-Sonoma Foods of the World series. There is a curious book on Catalan cooking by Irving Davis, an antiquarian book dealer and bibliophile with great love for the Mediterranean. His *Catalan Cookery Book* was published privately after his death in the late 1960s and reprinted in 1999. Two other books that focus on the culinary cultures around the Mediterranean Sea are both by Patience Gray, *Honey from a Weed* (1986), which has enjoyed multiple editions, and *Centaur's Kitchen* (2005), published after her death. She features Catalan cooking in both of her books while drawing interesting connections with other culinary traditions from the area. There is a recipe book on Catalan country cooking by Marimar Torres called *The Catalan Country Kitchen* (1992) and one that focuses on Majorcan culture, *Bread and Oil* (2000) by Tomás Graves. Cookbooks that focus on Spain, yet offer a good selection of Catalan recipes, are Claudia Roden's *The Food of Spain* (2011) and Penélope Casas's *¡Delicioso!* (1996). More recently, two cookbooks in English on Catalan food have been published in Spain. *Barcelona Served* (2005) is part of the gastronomic tourism initiative supported by the Ajuntament de Catalunya, published in three languages (Catalan, Spanish, and English), and edited by Montse Palacín. It is a combination of recipes and biographies of chefs with descriptions of their restaurants. Another one, *Catalan Cuisine* (2014) by Juliet Pomés Leiz, was designed as a sketchbook that visually traces Catalonia's cooking tradition while offering its most basic recipes and other culinary-related comments about the region's culture.

For the recipes we offer here, we have consulted the abovementioned cookbooks and other classic ones in Catalan and Spanish that have not been translated into English, such as *La cuynera catalana* (1851), Ignasi Domènech's *La teca* (1924), Ferran Agulló's *Llibre de la cuina catalana* (1928), Marta Salvia's *Art de ben Menjar* (1925), Néstor Luján's *La cuina moderna a Catalunya* (1991), Manuel Vázquez Montalbán's *La cocina de los mediterráneos* (2002), Santi Santamaría's *Una reivindicación del buen comer* (2012), and Jaume Fàbrega's *L'essència de la cuina catalana* (2013), among others. We also relied on our own personal experiences in the kitchen and the recipe collections of our family and friends.

THE CATALAN MADELEINE?

Having documented how bread (and wine) constituted most of the daily intake of food for people living in Barcelona during a great part of its history, it seems appropriate to start our recipe collection with one of the most emblematic Catalan dishes, the *pa amb tomàquet*. We know that bread was baked from the very beginning of the history of the area using different grains until wheat became the favored one. The bread and the tomato, despite the latter's late addition after its discovery of the American continent, hold a special place in the Catalan imagination. Anecdotes abound about the confusion of visitors when they enter an eating establishment and find themselves at a table with a basket of tomatoes, a container of oil, salt, and maybe a few cloves of garlic without any instruction about what to do with them. A close friend tells of having a hard time finding fresh vegetables on restaurant menus during her trip through Catalonia in the late 1990s. When she and her traveling companions saw the tomatoes in one of the restaurants they stopped at during their journey north, they thought of them as the table decoration and ate their meal while gazing at them longingly. After finishing their lunch, they realized that other people were using the tomatoes to moisten the bread and pouring oil on it before eating it, and they badly wished they could start their meal all over again. Colman Andrews also tells of his own puzzlement when faced with bread and tomatoes in the Empordà region until his traveling companion explained the mechanics of the *pa amb tomàquet*.

Frankly, calling it a dish is an exaggeration because of its simplicity, but its genius is undeniable, a combination of a few essential ingredients that produces a most delectable experience. Perhaps the dish's origin can be explained by the practicality of the Catalans: what better way to eat day-old bread than softening it with tomato pulp and juice and pouring some oil over it? Although it is certainly a dish that is simple to assemble and common to eat, it is also one that arouses many nostalgic memories and could be considered the comfort food of many Catalans.[1] The bread used for the dish varies, as well as the taste depending on the quality of the bread and the oil. Sometimes the breads used for the dish are *coques* (*coca* being a type of Catalan flat pastry made of simple dough usually topped with sweet and savory toppings) but usually a country-style white bread. The tomatoes used for the dish are smaller, and you can see them hanging in the stalls of the fresh food markets and vegetable shops. They are called *tomàquet de penjar* (tomatoes to hang) and also *tomàquet d'untar* (tomatoes to spread). You can buy just a few or the entire cluster and leave it hanging in your kitchen. You can eat *pa amb tomàquet* alone, or you can top it with an anchovy fillet, cured ham, a piece of Spanish omelet, or cheese. In Catalonia most sandwiches (*entrepans*) are made with bread with tomato. In restaurants a side of *pa amb tomàquet* usually is ordered to accompany the appetizers or when sharing tapas. Outside Barcelona, it is still common in restaurants to find the ingredients on the table, except for the bread, which is served once the diners sit down and order their drinks and food.

Pa amb tomàquet

Adjust the ingredients depending on amount of bread and tomato desired.

INGREDIENTS

Thick slices of white country-style or artisanal bread, plain or toasted
Very ripe small to medium tomatoes (look for ones with lots of juice and pulp)

Salt
Garlic cloves (optional)

PREPARATION

If using garlic, cut in half and rub it on the bread (toasted if desired). Cut the tomato in half and rub it on the bread, squeezing the tomato to get its juice (and even some pulp) on the slice of bread. Pour oil and sprinkle some salt on the bread before eating it. Alternatively, you can salt the bread first and then pour the oil. Chef Carme Ruscalleda's tip is to start squeezing the tomato on the bread's crust to begin breaking up its pulp. Once the process of making the bread is completed, you can eat it topped with an anchovy filet or some *pernil ibéric* (the Spanish cured ham, the *jamón ibérico*).

Chapter 6

BUILDING BLOCKS OF CATALAN COOKING

Allioli

One of the most emblematic sauces of Catalan cuisine, *allioli* consists of garlic, olive oil, and salt. Garlic, one of the most basic and frequent ingredients in many Catalan dishes, was once considered a plebeian food by Spaniards because of its pungent smell. Néstor Luján follows the story how the bulb gained prestige when identified as a health food and now occupies an important place in Catalan (and Spanish) cuisine.[2] Although an egg is often used as a binding ingredient in the sauce, purists will tell you adamantly that you would have garlic mayonnaise but not an *allioli* (which means garlic and oil). Luján, for instance, recommends against using an egg since it makes the sauce heavy. He explains that even though the taste of the classic *allioli* can be considered strong, it is easier to digest when it is used as an accompaniment to grilled meats (or snails). The sauce also is used as a finishing touch for casseroles or served with *fideuà*, a type of paella made with short pasta and seafood, typical of Valencia.

The binding happens in the mortar, where the garlic is crushed with salt and oil added slowly while making a circular motion with the pestle. For the author of *La cuynera catalana*, it is important that the mortar is completely dry and warm, which aids the binding. If the sauce breaks, a couple of drops of lemon or sour orange juice will help bind it. Joan Roca recommends using room-temperature (or warmer) ingredients, since warmth aids binding. He also splits the garlic to take out any sprouting because it inhibits binding. Ferran Adrià similarly recommends removing the garlic sprouts, noting that they impart a bitter taste to dishes. Roca suggests using a mild olive oil for the sauce. His instructions involve chopping the garlic first, adding salt, and mashing it to a pulp with the pestle before proceeding with the sauce. Start the sauce with a splash of oil while slowly making circular motions with the pestle (or a whisk), always in the same direction, and then gradually add more oil. His solution for mending a broken sauce is adding some vinegar-soaked breadcrumbs or even a boiled potato. *Allioli* is a sauce that should be served and eaten right away. Because the garlic oxidizes, the sauce's flavor becomes unpleasant with time.[3]

Classic *Allioli*

Adapted from Jaume Fàbrega's *L'essencia de la cuina catalana*

INGREDIENTS

2 peeled garlic cloves (or more depending on how much sauce you want)

Salt

5 ounces mild olive oil at room temperature or warmer (this is an approximate measure, so use more as needed)

Mortar and pestle (and whisk, if desired)

PREPARATION

Chop the garlic and transfer it to a mortar (make sure it is completely dry and not too cold), add some salt, and mash it with the pestle until it becomes a smooth paste. Once you have reached this consistency, start adding oil very slowly, almost drop by drop while whisking the sauce in circular motion, always in the same direction. Once you have started incorporating the oil, finish with a steady small stream while whisking it faster. The sauce is ready when it is thick and peels off the mortar bowl. If the sauce is broken, add a few drops of lemon, vinegar-soaked bread, or boiled potato. This recipe makes about half a cup.

This sauce is made to accompany grilled meats (chicken, pork, lamb, rabbit, and snail dishes) and even fish. It also is used to finish other stewed dishes, frequently in a "broken" form (*allioli negat*). It can be made with fruit as well. We offer these variations and a few recipes that use them later in this chapter.

Allioli by Albert Raurich

We asked the chef from Dos Pebrots (and Dos Palillos) to share his recipe for *allioli* used in his restaurant dedicated to classic Catalan cuisine. He told us he learned this recipe from a fisherman from Cadaqués, his hometown. We are keeping the measurements in grams, as it reflects the precision measurement used in the restaurant's kitchen. This recipe yields ten servings.

INGREDIENTS

64 grams garlic
600 grams extra-virgin olive oil

12 grams table salt
20 grams sherry vinegar

PREPARATION

Peel the garlic and cut it into small pieces. Crush the garlic with the salt in a mortar until it becomes a smooth paste. Add the vinegar and keep pounding the paste until it becomes creamy. Add the oil, drop by drop, stirring the creamy paste without stopping until a thick emulsion forms. It is very important not to stop stirring at any time. When it is ready, the emulsion should be thick enough that it can fold on itself without breaking, producing a log that can be sliced like butter. Cover with plastic film in the mortar until serving.

Allioli sauce. Image provided by Dos Pebrots Restaurant; photograph by Daniel Jiménez.

Allioli Negat ("Broken" *allioli*)

This is the "broken" form of the garlic sauce—that is, "denied" from the form it should have: smooth and creamy. Clearly it is much easier to prepare and it is often used to finish soups and stews. Joan Roca's version does not use eggs, which means it is the classic *allioli* but without a smooth texture. Colman Andrews calls it "drowned" *allioli*, and his version uses eggs but also lists them as optional. The final result should look like a curdled sauce. The recipe below is adapted from Andrew's *Catalan Cuisine* and makes about a cup.

INGREDIENTS

5 cloves of garlic, peeled
Salt to taste
2 egg yolks (optional)

1 cup (or more as needed) mild olive oil

PREPARATION

Make sure all ingredients are at room temperature. Start by following the instructions for the classic *allioli* and adding the egg yolks (if using). Keep adding oil after an emulsion forms, but only until it breaks and the sauce begins to thin. Watch carefully when preparing it so you do not use more oil than what you need to "break" the sauce. When ready, it looks curdled. This sauce is used to finish other dishes.

Sweet *Allioli*

In some parts of Catalonia, such as in Lleida, people add roasted quince to the *allioli* sauce. In Majorca honey can be added, and in other parts of the Catalonian Pyrenees, apples or pears may be used. Andrews observes that these sauces make unusual but superb accompaniments for grilled or roasted meats. In this version there is no need for eggs, as the fruit will form a nice emulsion with the oil. The recipe that follows is adapted from Andrew's *Catalan Cuisine* and makes about a cup.

INGREDIENTS

1 large ripe quince or 2 small ripe apples or pears
3–4 cloves of garlic, peeled (or more if desired)

Salt to taste
3–4 ounces (or more as needed) mild olive oil

PREPARATION

Peel and core the fruit, cube it, and cook it in water in an uncovered pot until soft but not mushy. Drain and cool. Roasting the fruit is another option that would bring more sweetness to the sauce. Once the fruit is cool to handle, prepare the classic *allioli* and then stir in the fruit and add the olive oil slowly until an emulsion forms. Adjust salt and use immediately or refrigerate until ready to serve.

Potatoes with *allioli*

This is a brilliant side dish that Colman Andrews offers in *Catalan Cuisine*. He suggests serving it with grilled or roast meat, especially lamb. Andrews prefers to use eggs in the *allioli*, as it puffs up nicely when broiled. This adapted recipe serves four.

INGREDIENTS

4 large potatoes
Olive oil

1 cup of the classic *allioli* (or made with eggs)
Salt

PREPARATION

Preheat oven to 350° Fahrenheit. Parboil the potatoes in salted water, drain, and cool. Peel and cut into half-inch to three-quarter-inch slices. Place a layer of potatoes in an oiled baking dish, slightly overlapping. Spread a thin layer of the *allioli* and repeat the process until you end with a top layer of potatoes. You can salt the layers of potatoes depending on the saltiness desired. You should have some *allioli* left, less than half a cup. Bake the potatoes 30–40 minutes until done; then spread with the remaining sauce, broiling it until slightly brown. Serve with meat.

Espatlla de xai amb alioli negat (Lamb shoulder stew with "broken" *allioli*)

This recipe, adapted from Joan Roca's *Roots*, calls for the use of the "broken" form of the garlic sauce. It is cooked in a cassola (in Spanish, *cazuela*), a shallow, round, glazed terra-cotta casserole often used in traditional Catalan cooking. A heavy cast-aluminum or cast-iron pot can be used instead. You can also add sliced onions or tomatoes to the dish, some bacon, and a bay leaf. The dish also can be made with a kid shoulder, which is harder to find in the United States.

INGREDIENTS

1 lamb shoulder (about 3 pounds, bone-in or boneless)
3 Yukon Gold potatoes
1 head of garlic

Extra-virgin olive oil
Salt and black pepper to taste
Water or beef broth (about a cup)

PREPARATION

Preheat the oven to 320° Fahrenheit. Peel and cut the potatoes in 1-inch slices and arrange them in the dish you are using to make the stew. Wash and pat dry the meat, make a few incisions, and salt and pepper it, and lay it on top of the potatoes. Pour olive oil generously on top and place it in the oven for about an hour and a half. In the meantime, prepare the "broken" *allioli* by crushing the garlic, pounding it into a paste in a mortar, and adding olive oil while stirring. Remember that the finished sauce should look curdled.

Halfway through cooking, take the meat out of the oven, turn it, and add some liquid (water or beef broth) before returning it to the oven. Baste the meat with the juice from time to time to prevent the meat from drying out. Once it is done, add a few spoonfuls of the "broken" garlic sauce and serve the meat with the potatoes.

Suquet de verat (Mackerel fish stew)

Néstor Luján considered the fish dishes cooked along the Costa Brava one of the highlights of Catalan cuisine, especially when prepared with olive oil. The *suquet* is primarily a dish made by the fishermen of the Mediterranean Sea. Along the coast and across the border, it can vary, but around the Catalan coast, the traditional way to prepare it is to cook oil, fish, parsley, tomato, and onion all together, at a strong boil, over a wood fire. It also could be made in different ways, building the soup from a *sofregit* (as we will see later) with generous amounts of onion and little tomato. Potatoes became an ingredient of the dish much later, after they were brought over from the American continent and became part of country's general diet in the nineteenth century.[4] In Joan Roca's version of the traditional *suquet*, the finishing touch is the "broken" *allioli*. The dish is surprising for its choice of an oily fish, although he explains that using an oily fish in *suquet* (with mackerel, anchovies, or sardines) is common along the coast. Potatoes can also be added to this dish. We have selected this dish from Roca's *Roots* as an example of a *suquet* that is more distinct than other traditional fish soups or stews and because mackerel is increasingly available in supermarkets in the United States. The recipe serves four.

INGREDIENTS

1 cleaned mackerel (about 2 pounds), cut in large pieces
Half a garlic head
2 tomatoes (grated without their skins)
1 tablespoon Spanish sweet *pimentón* (can substitute with paprika)

Salt to taste
White pepper
Olive oil
Water or fish stock
"Broken" *allioli*

PREPARATION

Finely slice the garlic cloves and grate the tomato. The best trick for producing the grated tomato that is often called for in Catalan recipes is to use a square cheese grater. Cut the tomato in half, place the grater on top of a plate, and carefully grate the tomato over its largest holes, ensuring that the skin is not grated, only the pulp. If you put pressure on the tomato and move it from side to side, or even in a circular motion as you start grating it, you will soon be able to grate the tomato down the side of the grater. You will be left with just the skin of the tomato, which you can discard. You should try to do this slowly at first to avoid hurting yourself, but once you have mastered the technique, you will use it often, especially when making the *sofregit*.

Fry the sliced garlic in olive oil in a heavy-bottomed enamel cast-iron pan and add the grated tomato and paprika. Season the fish pieces and add them to the pan with enough hot water or stock to cover. Boil for about 5 minutes until the fish is cooked and remove from heat. Add a tablespoon of the "broken" *allioli* and serve. You can add potatoes to this dish. If so, boil the potatoes first until nearly cooked and then add the fish.

Picada

Ferran Agulló identifies *picada* as one of the four basic sauces of Catalan cooking. The other three are *allioli*, *sofregit*, and *samfaina*.[5] *Picada*, indeed, is one of the oldest and most characteristic sauces of Catalan cooking, which was in use in its oldest known cookbook, the *Sent Soví*. A paste prepared in a mortar with a pestle consisting of garlic, parsley, toasted nuts, and breadcrumbs, *picada* is used to finish or thicken sauces or soups. Recent interest in Catalan gastronomy has revealed its long history and use; Jaume Fàbrega points to Colman Andrews as among the first to recognize *picada* as unique among the cuisines around the Mediterranean Sea.[6] For Luján, *picada* is what makes Catalan dishes special, giving it another layer of complexity. He declares with conviction, "it invigorates it, making any Catalan dish more delectable while giving it a touch of class."[7] He recommends the use of most nuts—roasted almonds, pine nuts, hazelnuts—but never walnuts (though other recipes use them), because walnuts give the dish a bitter taste.[8] The nut paste can be adjusted as needed, but it is used mostly to give the sauce a luscious body. Depending on the region, different ingredients may be used. Some use a bit of oil, water, leftover wine, bitter chocolate, saffron, pepper, tomato, red pepper, dried peppers, boiled egg, or parsley. It is common to prepare a simple *picada* with parsley and garlic to add to a rice dish, grilled fish, sardines, squid, and so forth. Below we offer a basic *picada* recipe and two dishes in which it is used.

Picada

Adapted from Jaume Fàbrega's *L'essencia de la cuina catalana*

INGREDIENTS

1 clove garlic	½ ounce bread (breadcrumbs can also
1½ ounces roasted almonds (or nuts	be used)
such as hazelnuts or pine nuts)	Salt to taste

PREPARATION

Fry the bread in oil or simply toast it. In a mortar, mash the garlic with salt. Add the roasted almonds and bread and make a paste. It is necessary to loosen the *picada* with some liquid—either the broth of the dish to which it will be added or some other broth, water, or even some wine—before using it in a dish. Once the *picada* is added to the dish, simmer for 10–15 minutes to allow the flavors to meld and the dish to reach the desired consistency.

Conill amb xocolata (Rabbit with chocolate sauce)

This stew is a traditional dish from the Maresme, a county located along the Catalan coast, north of Barcelona. Its largest city is Mataró. Manuel Vázquez Montalbán collected this recipe in his *L'art de menjar a Catalunya* and explained that it was served during the area's *festa major* (a yearly festivity in honor of one or more patron saints of a locality).[9] The recipe is quite informal and does not provide measurements, but it is forgiving, so there is no need to be exacting with the amounts. Here we offer approximate quantities. The chocolate gives the dish a deep, extraordinary flavor.

INGREDIENTS

1 quartered rabbit
1 onion, chopped
1 medium-sized tomato, grated

Extra-virgin olive oil
1 tablespoon pork lard (optional)
Salt and pepper to taste

For the picada:

2 cloves garlic (if there are any green sprouts, slice them in half and re-move them)
1–2 tablespoons chopped parsley (and more for serving, optional)
1 tablespoon roasted almonds

½ tablespoon pine nuts (or more to taste)
½ tablespoon walnuts (or more to taste)
1.3 ounces of dark bitter chocolate (or more to taste)
Salt and pepper to taste

PREPARATION

Season the quartered rabbit with salt and pepper. In an enamel cast-iron pot, brown the rabbit pieces in oil (and lard, if using) until each piece is nicely golden. Lower the heat and add the chopped onion. When the onions are lightly browned, add the grated tomato. Cook on low heat and stir it from time to time. If the dish becomes dry, add some water (or broth or wine). Meanwhile, prepare the *picada*. In a mortar, pound the garlic, parsley, nuts, and chocolate with the pestle until it becomes a paste. Coat the meat with a couple of spoonfuls of the *picada*. Start tasting at this point to determine how much chocolate you want to use. Mix some warm water into the remaining paste in the mortar and pour it over the rabbit. At this point, the meat should be almost covered with liquid. Simmer over low heat, stirring from time to time, for about 45 minutes. Most of the liquid should have evaporated by this point, leaving a glossy, thick, dark sauce. Serve it with chopped parsley on top (optional).

Rap a l'all cremat (Monkfish with burnt garlic)

The dish is very popular and there are many different versions of it, all using garlic, though not quite burnt as the name indicates, or it would make the dish bitter. The garlic is fried until very dark and used in a *picada*. Be careful not to burn the garlic. The resulting garlic sauce can accompany different kinds of fish, usually ones with firm, white flesh. The culinary encyclopedia of Catalan recipes, the *Corpus del patrimony culinary català* (Corpus of the Catalan Culinary Patrimony), curiously focuses on the burnt garlic sauce rather than the fish. Both Vásquez Montalbán and Andrews offer a version of the dish with monkfish. Since the Catalan writer's version is more complicated, we offer an adapted version from Andrews's *Catalan Cuisine*, which serves as a main dish for six. He amusingly notes that the residents of Costa Brava serve this dish with plenty of *allioli*, as if the dish did not provide for the day's proper ration of garlic.[10]

INGREDIENTS

8–10 cloves of garlic, peeled and finely sliced
Extra-virgin olive oil
1 or 2 slices French or Italian country-style white bread

2 pounds monkfish (or other white firm-fleshed fish such as halibut or cod), cut in large pieces
Flour for dredging
3 cups fish stock
1½ teaspoons minced parsley
Salt and pepper to taste

PREPARATION

Sauté the garlic in olive oil over medium-low heat until dark brown (be careful not to burn it); remove from the pan with a slotted spoon and set aside. In the same oil, fry the bread on both sides; then remove and set aside. Dredge the fish in flour and, again, in the same oil (adding more if necessary), fry until golden brown on all sides; then remove and set aside. Deglaze the pan with the fish stock and simmer to reduce the liquid by about a third. Meanwhile, make the *picada*. In a mortar, mash the garlic, the fried bread, and parsley with a little fish stock to make a thick paste. After the stock in the pan has reduced, stir in the *picada* and simmer for a few minutes until the flavors of the paste meld into the stock. Return the fried fish to the pan and simmer, partially covered, until the flesh is cooked and the sauce is thick. If the liquid evaporates too quickly, add more water or fish stock. Salt and pepper to taste before serving.

Sofregit

Sofregit is one of the most basic starters for many dishes. Many Catalans see it as one of the foundations of their culinary identity. *Sofregit* is not to be confused with the Spanish *sofrito*, which Fàbrega reminds us is a tomato sauce more than anything else. Nor is it similar to the Italian version, which includes carrots, celery, and butter.[11] The Catalan *sofregit* is mostly diced onion, slowly cooked until caramelized, along with other ingredients, some fresh herbs, or garlic. The inclusion of tomatoes, which is rather recent considering the sauce's long history, continues to be debated, and most agree the tomatoes should not dominate the onion. Yet Agulló's version of the sauce uses a one-to-three ratio of onion to tomatoes, which reveals that the dispute is still not settled.[12] He also suggests, probably to the dismay of many, that canned tomatoes or tomato paste can be substituted for fresh tomatoes. Fàbrega help us distinguish two versions of the *sofregit* and their traditional uses.[13] He explains that the variation with only garlic and tomatoes serves as the base for *suquets* (fish soups and stews) and some other types of *guisats* (stews), whereas the one that uses only onion is used in rice dishes (usually with squid ink), dishes with white fish, and *niu*, an old Lenten dish from the town of Palafrugell, which is made with cod entrails, dried cod (not salted), boiled eggs, and potatoes.[14] Comparing different cookbooks, one thing is clear: the *sofregit* admits many different versions. The medieval text discussed earlier, the *Sent Soví*, offers perhaps the earliest form of the sauce, using only onions and herbs. Since then, it developed multiple versions. The preparation of the sauce varies from cook to cook, depending on how one has learned to make it. Anna and I had long discussions about the sauce because our experiences of making and using it had been so different. Albert Adrià, the brother of elBulli's famed chef and a renowned chef in his own right, told Anna that before opening his popular Bodega 1900, he researched the sauce extensively. Puzzled by the existence of the many variations, he tried dozens of them to understand the technique and the flavors it developed according to the ingredients used. His restaurant offers more traditional Catalan-style tapas, whereas Tickets, the world-famous tapas restaurant he runs with his brother Ferran across the street, continues their foray into avant-garde gastronomy, offering playful and more experimental dishes. Below we offer Joan Roca's traditional version of *sofregit*, as it seems to embody the basic structure of the sauce, followed by a few recipes that start with a *sofregit*. We also include one of Albert Adrià's versions of *sofregit* that he shared with us.

Sofregit

Adapted from Joan Roca's *Roots*

INGREDIENTS

1 tablespoon lard (optional)
Dash of olive oil (more if not using lard)
1 finely chopped medium-sized onion (grating is not recommended, as it would lose its juice and burn more easily)
1 finely diced or grated tomato, depending on desired consistency of the sauce
1 garlic clove, finely diced (optional)

PREPARATION

In a frying pan, heat the lard (if using) and olive oil, toss in the chopped onion, and cook slowly over low heat. Once the onion starts browning, add the diced garlic (if using), and then add the grated (or finely diced) tomato. Continue to cook slowly until the flavors meld and it acquires a jam-like consistency. If it becomes too dry, add a bit of water or (vegetable or chicken) broth, depending on the dish in which the *sofregit* will be used. The color will darken as the sauce becomes more concentrated.

Sofregit by Albert Adrià

INGREDIENTS

40 grams extra-virgin olive oil
15 grams garlic
150 grams finely chopped onion
5 grams sugar
1 bay leaf
$1/8$ teaspoon dried thyme
$1/8$ teaspoon dried rosemary
60 grams tomato (fresh or canned)

PREPARATION

Using a hand blender, crush the garlic with the oil, pour the mixture in a pot, and put it on the stove. Start with the oil and garlic cold to better adjust and control the heat. When the garlic starts turning golden, add the finely chopped onion and the dried herbs, turning up the heat so the onion becomes golden, always stirring. Once golden, turn down the heat to the lowest setting, cooking until completely soft. The cooking time can vary depending on the heat, the type of onion, and the quantity of the *sofregit* being made, but it could be anywhere from 1 to 2 hours.

Add the tomatoes, but not until after tasting the onion to ensure it is completely soft. Once the tomato is added, the onion's texture can no longer be changed. Cook until the tomato liquid is evaporated. Use *sofregit* as a base for other dishes.

Arròs amb carxofes (Rice with artichokes)

As already noted, *sofregit* is generally used for rice dishes, and we chose this recipe since it also incorporates one of the most popular vegetables enjoyed in Catalonia, *carxofes*. You can find artichokes in stews, grilled, breaded and fried, roasted, sometimes served with *allioli* or simply with a sprinkle of salt and a wedge of lemon. The rice used for the dish is one commonly used for paella: *bomba* rice. Although increasingly available in specialty stores in the United States, it is not always easy to find. You can substitute it with Arborio rice, which is used to make risotto, but you will need to adjust the liquid. The ration for Arborio rice is about two cups of liquid to one cup of rice. The following recipe is adapted from the cookbook that is part of the Pepe Carvalho detective series written by Manuel Vázquez Montalbán.[15] The recipe will feed four generously.

INGREDIENTS

About 2 pounds artichokes
Olive oil
1 medium-sized onion, finely chopped
1 medium-sized tomato, grated
1 roasted red bell pepper (from a jar or roasted, peeled, and seeded at home)

About 4 cups vegetable broth
14 ounces *bomba* rice (or Arborio)
A pinch of saffron
1 clove of garlic
A sprig of parsley or basil
Salt and white pepper to taste

PREPARATION

Start by cleaning the artichokes. Remove the tough outer leaves and the choke, keeping the hearts and the softest parts of the leaves. Soak in water with lemon juice or pour some lemon juice directly on the artichoke to prevent browning. Dice and fry them for a few minutes in a casserole with a couple of tablespoons of olive oil. Remove from the oil and set aside. Using the same oil, add the diced onion and start the *sofregit*. Add the grated tomato when the onion has passed its translucent phase and it is starting to caramelize. Once it has acquired the consistency of a jam, add the broth. When it is boiling, add the rice, artichokes, and saffron. Season the dish at this point with salt and white pepper. Let the rice simmer for a few minutes; then lower the heat, cover, and cook for about 20–25 minutes depending on the desired texture of the grain. Rice usually is served al dente. While the rice cooks, cut the red pepper in thin strips, chop garlic with the parsley or basil, and add them to the rice about 5 minutes before taking it off the heat. Let it stand a few minutes before serving.

Pollastre amb bolets (Chicken with wild mushrooms)

Cooking with wild mushrooms in Catalonia is very common. Mushrooms also appear in early cookbooks like in the 1800s' *La cuynera catalana*, where it is suggested to serve them with a sauce made with a *picada*.[16] Luján writes that the Catalans' favorite wild mushroom is the *rovelló*, which is not much appreciated outside the region, according to the gastronome.[17] He disagrees vehemently with this perception, praising its flavor. Andrews also likes the *rovelló*, with its oxidized bronze color and aromatic fragrance. He explains that the variety found in Catalonia, *Lactarius sanguifluus*, is more delicious than the better known and more common *Lactarius deliciosus*.[18] Basques and Catalans have great appreciation for wild mushrooms and also enjoy picking them in the forest. There are more than a thousand varieties in the region of Catalonia, but ones that are frequently sold in the markets are the *rossinyols* (chanterelles, *Cantharelus cibarus*), *surenys* (porcini, *Boletus edulis*), and *múrgules* (morels, *Morchella vulgaris*), among others.[19] The recipe below is an adaptation from the *Corpus del patronomi culinari català* and uses, in addition to *sofregit*, *vi ranci*, a Catalan wine generally fortified and oxidized through extended periods of aging in wood and heating in sunlight. Joan Roca explains that it is a wine of tawny brown color with a rich, nutty, and sweet aroma. The recipe serves six.

INGREDIENTS

1 whole chicken (cut in pieces to serve six, reserving the rest, along with the neck, giblets, wing tips, etc., to make the broth)

18 ounces wild mushrooms, chopped roughly (a mix of shiitake, oyster, chanterelles, hen of the woods, puffballs, etc.—whatever is available in your store or market except white button mushrooms)

4 cloves garlic, finely diced, divided

2 medium-sized onions, finely chopped

2 medium-sized ripe tomatoes, grated

1 cup dry sherry (or *vi ranci*)

1 bouquet of herbs (thyme, dried orange peel, bay leaf), tied with twine

1 or 2 tablespoons chopped parsley

Flour for dredging

Olive oil

Salt and pepper to taste

Water

PREPARATION

Prepare the chicken broth by boiling the reserved parts with enough water to yield about 4½ cups of broth. While the broth is being made, season the remaining chicken parts with salt and pepper, dredge in flour, and fry them in a casserole pot with olive oil, a few pieces at a time, until browned; remove and set aside. In the same pot with the oil, start the *sofregit* with the chopped onion on low heat. Once they are cooked, add half the diced garlic, and later the grated tomato. When the sofregit has melded into a jam-like consistency, return the chicken to the pot with the herb bouquet. Pour in the sherry, reducing it while stirring, and then add the chicken broth. Let it simmer for about 30–40 minutes. While the chicken is cooking, clean the mushrooms and sauté them in olive oil with the rest of the diced garlic and the chopped parsley. Add the sautéed mushrooms to the chicken about halfway through cooking. Alternatively, this recipe can be made with turkey pieces and water rather than chicken broth. You can also add your *picada* of choice to finish the dish.

If fresh mushrooms are not available, you can use dried ones, too, after soaking them in warm water. Save the soaking water to use in the dish to enhance its flavor.

Samfaina

As already noted, for Ferran Agulló, *samfaina* is one of four basic sauces of Catalan cooking, and he describes it as a type of a *sofregit* that is not reduced as much.[20] There are other vegetables in the sauce, such as zucchini, eggplant, bell peppers, and so forth. Roca calls it a Catalan ratatouille-like dish and the ingredients can vary depending on how it will be used later. The name of the dish creates a bit of a confusion because there is a Castilian dish called *chanfaina*, a stew made with chopped offal, that is made in various ways along the Iberian Peninsula. For instance, in Andalusia, *chanfaina* is made with meat and sausage in a thick sauce of oil, vinegar, bread, almonds, garlic, red bell pepper, oregano, and thyme.[21] The version from La Mancha is called *pisto* and does not use eggplants. The Catalan version is entirely vegetarian, at least at the start of the dish, though it could incorporate some sort of protein in its finished form. You could use it to cook with eggs, chicken, rabbit, lamb, salt cod, and so on. Below is the classic recipe for *samfaina* from the already mentioned *Corpus del patrimoni culinari català* followed by its combination with one of the most popular ingredients in Catalan cooking, *bacallà* (salt cod).

INGREDIENTS

4 medium-sized tomatoes
2 medium-sized onions
2 garlic cloves
2 red bell peppers

2 eggplant
Olive oil
Salt

PREPARATION

Dice all the vegetables into small cubes and chop the garlic. In a deep, heavy-bottomed pot, sauté the diced onion in a couple of tablespoons of olive oil. After it cooks down a bit, add the garlic, peppers, tomatoes, and eggplant. Add the ingredients slowly, letting each vegetable cook before adding another to the pot. Once all the vegetables are in the pot, salt to taste, and then cook over low heat until it becomes a sauce. There are many variations to this dish. You can cook all the vegetables at once or use green bell pepper, zucchini, parsley, or black olives (or some combination), and you can also omit the garlic.

Bacallà amb samfaina a la catalana (Salt cod with Catalan samfaina)

This dish can be made by using the basic *samfaina* recipe above, with the slight variation of adding parsley and pepper to it. It also calls for the "broken" *allioli*. The recipe is adapted from Ignasi Domènech's *La teca* (1924). It serves four to six people as a main course.

INGREDIENTS

1½ pounds thick-cut salt cod, desalted, skinned, boned, and cut into pieces
2 cups *samfaina* (see above)
2 tablespoons "broken" *allioli* (see above)

Flour for dredging
Olive oil
Salt and pepper

PREPARATION

To desalt the cod, soak it in plain water in the refrigerator for at least 48 hours, changing the water one or two times a day. Before soaking, it helps to cut the cod into large pieces (small pieces disintegrate) and be sure to use cold water. Holding the cod under cold running water to wash off the salt before soaking also helps in the desalting process. Once desalted, cut the cod into smaller serving-sized pieces, dredge lightly in flour, and fry them in olive oil in a heavy bottomed pot until golden brown. Remove the pieces and drain them on paper towels. Discard any oil remaining, return the cod pieces to the pot, and cover them with the *samfaina* sauce. Cook the fish over low-medium heat until done, around 10–15 minutes. Add the "broken" *allioli* after removing the dish from the heat and before serving it.

VARIATIONS

The desalting and frying process of the *bacallà* can also be used for one of the most emblematic Catalan dishes, *Bacallà a la llauna*, which was popularized in the nineteenth century and much loved by Néstor Luján. It was often served in taverns and at home because of its simplicity.[22] Preheat the oven to 400° Fahrenheit. Once the cod is fried, transfer it to a shallow baking dish. Use the leftover oil from frying to sauté a couple of finely chopped garlic cloves with parsley until the garlic is golden brown. Remove from heat and stir in a teaspoon of sweet paprika (*pimentón*). Pour over the cod and bake in the oven for 10–15 minutes until done.

MAR I MUNTANYA (SEA AND MOUNTAIN)

Mixing ingredients from the sea and the mountain, which developed in the fishing towns along the northeast coast of the region, is considered one of the most defining characteristics of Catalan cuisine. Andrews points to other cuisines that have experimented with this mix and observes that even back in Roman times people combined poultry with shellfish.[23] Yet he acknowledges that the Catalan way of combining these flavors—in contradiction to the simple side-by-side assembly of, for example, American surf and turf—is special. In the Catalan cooking style, these ingredients are cooked so that they can absorb each other's flavor in a single dish embodying the harmonious landscape of the Empordà region between the mountains and the sea. For his part, Fàbrega powerfully sings the praises of this style of cooking, which, he asserts, does not exist anywhere else in Europe or Asia. Unmeasured enthusiasm aside, he probably is correct in guessing that part of the reason this cuisine has received global recognition is because it clearly influenced the first culinary steps of Ferran Adrià.[24] The recipe we chose to illustrate this culinary practice mixes two unlikely ingredients that are different not only because of their habitat but also because they also belong to opposite poles of what is considered an indulgence: chicken and lobster. Andrews points to the historical contradiction of this perception, as seafood was once considered common and poultry more exclusive, since it was expensive to raise. But now lobster has acquired a more prestigious status. The original recipe calls for spiny lobsters, but because they are not widely available, the recipe that follows uses regular lobster (*llamàntol* in Catalan).

Pollastre amb llagosta (Chicken and lobster)

The writer Josep Pla mentions this dish in his collection of essays *El que hem menjat* (What We Have Eaten) published in 1972 as a recent trend in restaurants in the region of his hometown, Palafrugell. He was not impressed by it because he saw it as a quest for culinary novelty to attract tourists. What he remembers, nostalgically and with much longing, is the homemade version of this dish, in which the careful preparation of the *sofregit* harmonized distinct flavors to produce a delightful experience. Néstor Luján agreed with this observation; he criticized the frozen ingredients used in the restaurants that could not do justice to the dish. If prepared correctly, it is a sumptuous and noble dish enriched by its opulent sauce: golden, perfumed, thick, and at the same time light in taste.[25] We offer Luján's version, which he obtained from the influential Catalan restauranteur Lluís Cruañas (1937–2016). He was the owner of the famous restaurant Eldorado Petit in Sant Feliu de Guíxols. After his success, he opened a second one in Barcelona and even one in New York City, which closed in 1992.[26] His restaurants are now run by the Grup Eldorado. The recipe serves four.

INGREDIENTS

1 whole chicken, approximately 2¾ pounds

1 lobster, approximately 2.2 pounds

5 ounces finely chopped onion

9 ounces grated tomato

2 garlic cloves, finely sliced

16 ounces fish stock

1 bay leaf

200 milliliters (about ¾ cup) dry white wine

200 milliliters (about ¾ cup) brandy (or *aiguardent*)

A pinch of saffron

2 teaspoons grated dark bitter chocolate

3–4 white button mushrooms, thinly sliced

1½ tablespoons almonds or hazelnuts, roasted and chopped

A few sprigs of thyme and parsley

Olive oil

Salt and pepper to taste

Flour for dusting

PREPARATION

Cut the chicken into small pieces, discarding the neck, wing tips (cut at first joint), and backbone. Season with salt and pepper, dust with flour, and fry in oil until golden. Set aside. Clean and cut the lobster in pieces, saving the head and the legs for later. Fry the lobster pieces in the same oil; set aside. Next, prepare the *salsa americana*, a sauce made with fish stock.[27] Fry the sliced garlic until golden in a pan with olive oil, add the onion, and later the tomatoes. Add the fish stock, the reserved lobster parts, and the wine and brandy. Boil until reduced and then add the saffron. Arrange the pieces of fried chicken and lobster pieces in a pot, pour in the sauce, grated chocolate, and sliced mushrooms, and cook over low heat for about thirty minutes. Prepare the *picada* in a mortar with the the roasted nuts, herbs, and olive oil. Add to the dish at the very end, adjust seasonings, and serve.

SAVORY AND SWEET

Like mixing unexpected flavors and ingredients, another characteristic of Catalan cuisine is its practice of mixing savory and sweet flavors, as well as cooking with fruit, dried and fresh. Again, what is emphasized about this cooking is the harmony that results from combinations in which the ingredients complement each other. Both of the recipes below have many variations. The second version of the duck dish is by chef Fina Puigdevall, which she serves in her restaurant Les Cols in Olot, a town in the province of Girona. The final dish in this section displays its medieval and Arabic roots.

Ànec amb peres (Duck with pears)

This recipe has many variations, ranging greatly both in the number of ingredients used and in the extra steps required. We chose to adapt the simpler version offered by Manuel Vázquez Montalbán in his *L'art de menjar a Catalunya* since it reflects the simplicity of a traditional dish.[28] The recipe serves four.

INGREDIENTS

1 whole duck, approximately 4 pounds
1 medium-sized onion, finely chopped
1 tablespoon lard (or olive oil)
2–3 ounces cognac
2 pears (or 2 Granny Smith apples) peeled, cored, and halved

200 milliliters (about ¾ cup) white wine
Water or chicken broth (if needed)
Salt and white pepper to taste

PREPARATION

Cut the duck in pieces to serve four. Save the extra skin and fat to render for later use (always a good addition when roasting vegetables). Fry the duck pieces in a heavy bottom pot with lard or olive oil. Remove, drain, and set aside. In the oil (pour some off if there is too much), fry the onion slowly until golden, and then add the cognac and the fruit. Return the duck pieces to the pot, salt and pepper to taste, and add the white wine. Cook on low heat, covered, for about 30–40 minutes. Check from time to time ensure that there is liquid in the dish, adding water or broth as needed. Serve the duck and fruit with the sauce.

Ànec amb peres i salsifis (Duck with pears and salsify)

This is an adapted recipe from Fina Puigdevall's Les Cols menu. Because salsify, the root of the wildflower (*Tragopogon porrifolius*) native to the Mediterranean region, might be hard to find elsewhere, we have replaced it here with the more easily found parsnip. Serves four.

INGREDIENTS

For the pears and compote
3–4 pears (Anjou or Bosc)
½ cup sugar
Peel of one orange

1 vanilla bean
1 cinnamon stick
1 bay leaf

For the duck and sauce

Legs and the wings from 2 whole ducks (reserve breasts for another dish)

Duck stock made from the leftover carcasses, strained and skimmed

Muscatel (or another sweet wine, like cream sherry), enough for two generous pours

1–2 teaspoons agar-agar powder (or 1–2 tablespoons of agar-agar flakes), prepared as directed (see notes below)

A sprig of fresh thyme

A sprig of fresh rosemary

Salt and pepper to taste

Olive oil

For the vegetable garnish

2–3 parsnips, peeled

PREPARATION

Wash the pears and peel them. Put the whole pears in a pot with enough water to cover them, along with the sugar, vanilla, cinnamon, orange peel, and bay leaf. Bring to a boil and then reduce to a simmer until fruit is soft but firm, about 20 minutes. Check for softness. Reserve half the pears and the water for the compote. Cut the remaining pears into small (about ½ inch) cubes and set aside.

In a food processor, pulse the reserved pears, adding the reserved water only as needed to create the texture of a compote. Set aside.

Next, salt and pepper the duck legs and wings and brown them in a heavy bottomed casserole over medium-high heat with a generous amount of olive oil, thyme, and rosemary. Once browned, add a generous pour of the muscatel (or cream sherry). Lower the heat and cook slowly until the meat comes off the bones easily, for an hour or two. Be sure to cook the meat skin-side down so the meat does not dry out or darken while braising. Remove from heat. Once cool enough to handle, skin and debone the cooked meat, reserving the meat and its juices and the bones to use later in the preparation of the duck sauce. Return the meat to the pot over low heat and cook some more, shredding it as it cooks, until the meat is almost dissolved. Mix the agar-agar (either the dissolved and previously prepared agar-agar or the gelatin powder—see notes below) until all the ingredients are well blended. Cut a rectangular piece of aluminum foil and place a rectangular piece of plastic wrap on top of it. Spread the meat onto the plastic wrap, avoiding contact with the foil, and form it into a log, applying pressure so the meat roll is firm. Cover the roll with foil and keep cool.

For the duck sauce, boil the reserved duck bones, juices, and some of the duck stock previously prepared and add another pour of the muscatel (or the cream sherry). Once the consistency of a sauce is reached, strain, cool, skim off the fat, and set aside.

Meanwhile, preheat the oven to 350° Fahrenheit. Clean and peel the parsnips. Roast them in the oven for about 30–40 minutes with olive oil until cooked. Cool and cut them into small (about ½ inch) cubes. Set aside.

To serve: Warm the sauce on the stove and the unwrapped duck roll in the oven for about 20 minutes. Divide the roll into four servings. You can use circular molds to retain the shape of the roll while plating the duck. Place the duck on the plate, followed by the sauce around it; add three drops of the pear compote on top of the duck roll, and then place the cubed pears and parsnips on top. Divide the compote, the cubed fruit, and vegetables as you plate so you have enough to create four dishes. Serve.

NOTES
You can substitute the agar-agar with cornstarch or gelatin powder, which might give the dish a creamier consistency than the firmness obtained by using the red algae. One teaspoon of agar-agar is equivalent to eight teaspoons of gelatin powder. To prepare the agar-agar, dissolve it in cold water and boil it (or follow the instructions in the package). About two to three serving sizes of prepared agar-agar following the instructions of the package is enough to make the duck roll. If you want a firmer duck roll, you can use more prepared agar agar or less, especially if you just want the duck roll to hold together and are using a mold ring to plate the duck.

Espinacs amb panses i pinyons (Spinach with raisins and pine nuts)

Also called *Espinacs a la catalana* (Catalan-style spinach) or even *a la mallorquina* (Majorcan style) or *a la valenciana* (Valencian style), the variations for this dish include making it with Swiss chard and cauliflower. Fàbrega traces the long history of the dish in his *L'essencia de la cuina catalana* and calls it the best spinach recipe. This recipe is adapted from his book and can be served as an entrée or a side dish.

INGREDIENTS
4½ pounds spinach, washed
¼ cup pine nuts
¼ cup plump raisins (soaked in water
   to make sure they become plump
   and juicy)

Olive oil
Salt to taste

PREPARATION
In a pot with water and salt, blanch the spinach leaves for a minute or two. Shock them in cold water, drain in a colander, and squeeze small handfuls of spinach until it is as dry as possible. Chop it roughly and set aside. In a large frying pan, slowly sauté the pine nuts in olive oil until golden brown. Add the spinach and raisins and continue sautéing for a minute or two. Season with salt, remove from heat, and serve.

COOKING WITH EMBERS

A preferred way of cooking in Catalan is *al caliu*, in the hot embers of a wood fire. The most popular dish using this cooking method is *escalivada*. Néstor Luján explains its etymological origin comes from the word *escarmentat* ("chastised"), and although it once referred to anything cooked in embers, now it refers to vegetables like eggplants, red bell peppers, onions, tomatoes, and even potatoes cooked (or grilled) in this way.[29] Another popular culinary tradition that uses this cooking method comes from the region of Valls, where a varietal of spring onions, *calçots*, harvested during the cold months were grilled as snacks for laborers who were working the land and were served with grilled meats like ribs or sausages.[30] The traditional *calçotada* has spread beyond the region in the last fifty years or so, and now it has become a common outing for family and friends to travel to the countryside or the outskirts of the city to eat the grilled onions accompanied by grilled meats either in restaurants or in their *masias*, their country (or farm) houses. The dish is usually served with a sauce called *salbitxada* but it is common to see it paired with the more known and popular *romesco* sauce, which is originally from Tarragona. As with the other sauces, there are many variations, but the classic recipe for *calçcots* offered by Josep Lladonosa i Giró does not use *nyoras*, a type of red pepper, which is an important ingredient in the *romesco*.[31] The spring onions are usually presented whole and almost charred on a clay roof tile, as it is the perfect vessel to contain them. Learning to eat the spring onions is a bit tricky but can be mastered quickly: Pinch the head of the onion—the bottom of the white part—with one hand and with the other find the unburnt greens and pull the tender spring onion out whole. Holding the onion by its green parts, dip the *calçot* in the sauce and eat it head first. An awkward eating position, it provides enjoyment and comical moments among the families and friends who gather for the occasion. We offer a recipe for a classic *escalivada* that can be served as a vegetable or side dish, followed by an adapted recipe for *romesco* and *calçots*.

Escalivada

Adapted from Joan Roca's *Roots*. The recipe includes potatoes, which is unusual. It also offers different cooking methods, since grilling outdoors is not always possible.

INGREDIENTS

2 red peppers

2 medium-sized onions

4 potatoes, approximately the same size as the onions

2 young eggplants (to avoid seeds, use the longer Asian eggplants if you can find them)

Extra-virgin olive oil (Aberquina olive oil is recommended)

Salt to taste

Good-quality red wine vinegar to taste

PREPARATION

Wash and dry the vegetables well. Roast each of the vegetables on an open flame on the stove or over charcoal embers, being careful not to burn them. Cooking the potatoes this way might be more complicated than the other vegetables and requires more time. You can also coat the vegetables with olive oil and roast them together in a 375° Fahrenheit oven for 30–40 minutes. If grilling, start the potatoes first, since they take longer than the other vegetables, and then cook the eggplants, peppers, and onions. Place the cooked vegetables in a bag for a few minutes to make them easier to peel. Cut the eggplants into long strips, seed and slice the peppers into strips, and slice the onions and potatoes. Serve them together on one large serving plate or on individual plates, drizzling the vegetables with olive oil. Guests can salt and add oil or vinegar according to taste.

Grilled Leeks with *Romesco* Sauce

A good substitute for *calçcots* is young or baby leeks. In late spring into early summer in the northeast, you can find red spring onions, which are sweet and tender and grill well. Suzanne Goin, from the famed Lucques restaurant on the West Coast, writes about her enchantment with the tradition of the *calçotada* and speculates that, given her love for the culture that created an entire festival around grilled spring onions, she should have some Catalan genes, though her family tree does not agree with her.[32] In her version of the recipe, she uses baby leeks and baby artichokes, serving them with the *salbitxada* sauce in which she also incorporates burrata. We offer below a version of a *romesco* sauce to accompany the calçots, along with straightforward instructions for grilling the leeks or red spring onions. The sauce is also very good with other grilled vegetables, grilled chicken, and roasted or grilled white fish. The recipe is from the culinary school of the Universitat de Barcelona, the CETT (Campus de Turisme, Hoteleria i Gastronomia). The sauce makes about 4 cups. The red spring onions or leeks serve four as an appetizer.

INGREDIENTS

8–12 red spring onions or small, young leeks
½ cup roasted almonds
¼ cup roasted hazelnuts
4–5 medium-sized tomatoes *escalivats* (roasted and peeled)
1 garlic head *escalivat* (roasted and peeled)

1 ½ cup olive oil
¼–½ cup red wine vinegar (start with ¼ cup and add more according to desired acidity)
1 roasted red pepper (peeled and seeded; see note below)
A couple of springs of parsley
Salt to taste

PREPARATION

Put the nuts, tomato, and garlic in a mortar or a food processor and slowly add oil and then the vinegar. Adjust salt as needed and set aside. Start the grill (or heat an oven to 375° Fahrenheit) and prepare the onions. Wash them and trim both ends, leaving some of the head. Grill or roast them whole or halved depending on the size of the onions. Coat with olive oil and grill over hot coals or in the oven, turning until golden brown or charred according to your preference. Serve them with the sauce.

NOTE

Usually, the pepper recommended for a classic *romesco* is the *nyora*, a roundish red pepper with some heat that is not available in the United States. A good substitute is a roasted red pepper and a dry ancho chile soaked in hot water and seeded.

HOLIDAY DISHES

It could be argued that the most traditional holiday dish is *escudella i carn d'olla*, which is paradoxical, since it used to be eaten almost daily, when frugality dictated that the meat was boiled first for soup and then served separately as a meat and vegetable dish. In fact, many texts have railed against its pungent smell, due to its use of cabbage, as well as the monotony of this daily dish.[33] The cooking of many ingredients in a pot exists in different varieties along the Iberian Peninsula, and one that is much acclaimed is *cocido madrileño*. Néstor Luján points to an important difference between *escudella i carn d'olla* and *cocido madrileño*, two (almost) national dishes: the latter uses *chorizo* (*xoriço*), as many Castilian stews do, and blood sausage (which tends to be made with rice), whereas the former omits *xoriço* but uses both blood and white sausage and a meatball called *pilota* (ball) made with ground veal and pork, parsley, bread, and egg. For almost a century, until 1936, the daily meal of a Catalan was *escudella* (made with a variety of ingredients) and rice dishes on Sundays. Today the dish is tinged with nostalgia and enjoyed as a family meal during the Christmas holidays. Despite its unassuming name—Colman Andrews translates it as "Catalan soup with boiled meats and vegetables, in two courses"—it is a dish that arouses feelings about Catalan tradition, family, and the holidays. The soup is served with a large pasta called *galets*, and the meat, vegetables, and *pilota* are served separately. Roasting a turkey is also a popular Catalan tradition. Many of these leftover meats later reappear in one of the most emblematic Catalan dishes, *canelons*. *Escudella* is served as the first course of the Christmas Day meal, followed by stuffed capon or turkey. Dessert on that day consists of *torrons* (almond nougat) and *neules* (rolled thin wafers), accompanied by *cava*, the Catalan sparkling wine. *Canelons* are served the following day, on December 26, Sant Esteve, when family members gather again to eat the traditional dish. An option to make this rich dish even richer is to add truffle to the *canelon*'s béchamel sauce. The recipe we offer here for *escudella* is adapted from Anna's family recipe and from her experience living and shopping for ingredients in the United States. She suggests some personal tricks to save time in the process of making the soup and to achieve a clear broth to serve with the pasta. We also share Anna's family's recipe for *panellets*, a traditional dessert eaten for All Saints Day.

Escudella i carn d'olla

Serves four.

INGREDIENTS

1 veal shank, cross cut
1 beef short ribs
2 pork spare ribs, chopped
2 slices pork belly (about 1 inch thick)
2 pork shanks
¼ of a chicken (a stewing hen if possible)
2 fresh blood sausages (uncured and without rice; omit if you cannot find them)
4 Yukon Gold potatoes

2 carrots
1 parsnip
1 turnip
1 celery stalk (optional)
1 cup of chickpeas, soaked overnight
½ a large cabbage
10 ounces large *lumaconi* pasta (this pasta replaces *galets*; use the largest pasta shape available to you)
Salt to taste
6 liters of water (about 1 ½ gallons)

For the *pilota*

5½ ounces ground beef (or veal)
5½ ounces ground pork
1 garlic clove, chopped
1 egg
1 tablespoon chopped parsley

1–2 tablespoons pine nuts (optional)
Salt and pepper to taste
2 tablespoons bread crumbs
Enough bread crumbs to bread the *pilota*

PREPARATION

Anna recommends using a pasta pot with a strainer insert, so that vegetables can be added to the soup later to keep the broth clear. If not, improvise with a steamer basket. The trick is to steam the vegetables rather than boiling them in order to keep their texture firm and retain more flavor.

First, cut all the vegetables into large pieces. Put all of the meat ingredients except the blood sausage (if using) and the *pilota* in a pot with enough cold water to cover. Bring to a boil then simmer the meat for an hour (reaching the boiling point slowly produces less foam and other impurities). Skim off foam and impurities as needed. After an hour, add the garbanzo beans in the pot in a pasta insert or steamer basket. After another hour, add the vegetables (except the potatoes). Meanwhile, make the *pilota*. Mix all the ingredients and form into a large meatball. If you would like more texture for the meatball, use the pine nuts. After it is formed into a ball, roll it in bread crumbs. The ball should be about the size of a fist. After the soup has simmered for three hours, add the blood sausages (if using) and the *pilota* to the broth and the potatoes to the basket or insert. Salt the broth at this point. Simmer for another 30 minutes, and when everything is cooked, separate the broth from the meats and vegetables. If the broth is cloudy, you can pass it through a fine strainer, cheesecloth, or *chinois*. Boil the pasta in the soup and serve it first as an appetizer. Separate the meat from the bones and serve it along with the vegetables, the *pilota* (cut in enough pieces for everyone), and the blood sausages (if using).

VARIATIONS
Instead of a large *pilota*, you can make small meatballs, one for each guest. The soup can also be made with rice or small pasta rather than large pasta. The *galets*, traditionally used on Christmas, sometimes are stuffed with the meat of the *pilota*. The large pasta may be parboiled separately in a pot of salted water and added to the soup five minutes before serving.

Panellets

Panellets are Catalan sweets made and eaten during the All Saints Day celebration on November 1. They are extremely easy to make and even easier to eat. They are a marzipan sweet made from a mix of almond meal and boiled or baked potatoes or sweet potatoes. Here we offer the traditional version in which the sweets are rolled in pine nuts as well as a coconut variation. Makes about 30.

INGREDIENTS

8 ounces ground almond
8 ounces sugar
Zest of one lemon
6 ounces boiled or baked potato, mashed

1 egg, separated
4 ounces pine nuts
2.5 oz. unsweetened shredded coconut

PREPARATION
Heat the oven to 325° Fahrenheit. In a bowl, mix the sugar with the lemon zest and add the ground almond. Beat the egg yolk, mixing about three-quarters of it into the mashed potato. Reserve the remaining yolk to add to the mixture later in case it is too dry. Although you can mix the ingredients by hand, it is much easier to use a standing mixer fitted with a paddle. Combine the mashed potato and the sugar-and-almond mixture for about a minute until it becomes a workable dough. If too dry, add the rest of the egg yolk; if too wet, mix in a bit more ground almond. The dough needs to be moist but dry enough to work with your hands. For coconut *panellets*, divide the dough at this point, mixing half the dough with two-thirds of the coconut until well blended. Roll the dough in 1- to 2-inch balls and place them on a baking sheet lined with a silicon baking sheet or aluminum foil. Roll balls made with coconut into the remaining shredded coconut and the plain dough in the pine nuts. If the nuts do not adhere to the dough, roll the balls into the egg white first or gently press the nuts into the rolled balls until they are covered completely. Bake about 10–15 minutes until the nuts and the coconut are nicely golden. You can broil them on low for a few minutes to achieve the desired toasted color, but be very careful not to burn them. Cool and serve. *Panellets* are best when served fresh.

VARIATIONS
There are many variations of *panellets*. You can use chopped almonds instead of the coconut, chocolate powder, and so forth. For chocolate *panellets*, add about two tablespoons of cocoa powder to the dough and then roll them in cocoa powder before baking. You can also use pistachios or fruit liquors to flavor the sweets, like raspberry liquor.

OLD NEW SWEETS

The most popular and best-known Catalan dessert is probably *crema catalana*, which many would argue is similar to the French crème brûlée. Colman Andrews explains that some purists claim that *crema catalana* is the cream and not the burnt sugar on top, and there are places where the dessert is served without the burnt sugar, making it indeed a wholly original Catalan dessert. Andrews also notes that some Catalans claim the invention of the crème brûlée, though the English also claim some responsibility in creating this dessert.[34] Rather than wading into this debate, we close our recipe collection with a dish that existed in Catalan culture as well as in many European countries for many, many centuries. Despite its historic existence everywhere on the continent, it still retains its popularity in Catalonia today. We find it interesting because it reflects the evolution of a medieval dish from savory to sweet across the centuries and illustrates the popularity Catalan medieval cooking enjoys today. *Menjar blanc*, which we discussed earlier in the book, is presented here as a dessert in an updated recipe. The text is adapted from the *Corpus del patrimoni culinari català*, which includes two versions of the recipe, one made with rice flour and the other with almonds. We choose the former since it is the most unusual version of the dessert.[35] We also include Ferran Adrià's adaptation of *menjar blanc*, an early dish in which he experimented with savory and sweet ingredients as well as different textures and served in his elBulli restaurant. In this case, he tops the *menjar blanc* with tomato ice. Both recipes serve four.

Menjar blanc

In the medieval text *Llibre d'aparellar de menjar*, recently published in a critical edition, *menjar blanc* is a dish made with chicken or capon breasts, rice, almonds, and sugar and is considered a great "spoon" delicacy.[36] The recipe omitted the meat at some point in its history and now is a dessert, though still eaten with a spoon.

INGREDIENTS

4 cups whole milk (plus a little more)
²/₃ cup rice flour
²/₃ cup of sugar

1 cinnamon stick
1 lemon peel
Ground cinnamon

PREPARATION

Bring the milk to a slow boil in a pot with the cinnamon stick, lemon peel, and sugar. Take the pot off the heat and remove the cinnamon stick and lemon peel. Slowly add the rice flour along with a bit of cold milk. Return to the heat and cook until thick, stirring continuously. Once the desired thickness is achieved, remove the pot from heat. Divide the dessert among four small terrines and cool them in the refrigerator. When ready to serve, dust with ground cinnamon.

Tomato Ice, Fresh Oregano, and *Menjar Blanc*

by Ferran Adrià

INGREDIENTS

300 grams tomatoes
A bit of chopped fresh oregano

1 tablespoon extra-virgin olive oil
Salt

For the *menjar blanc*

50 grams sliced almonds
50 grams salted water (the original recipe calls for seawater; see note below)

75 grams tap water
1 envelope gelatin powder

PREPARATION

To make the tomato ice, quarter the tomatoes and blend them. Season the tomato juice with the oregano, oil, and salt. Put the seasoned juice in the freezer, stirring it every 30 minutes until it is frozen into ice crystals.

Soak the sliced almonds in the salted and tap water for twelve hours in the refrigerator. Dissolve the gelatin in cold water as instructed in the package and set aside. Crush the soaked almonds in a blender and pass it through a *chinois*. Add a spoon of the resulting almond milk to the dissolved gelatin mixture and slowly heat it without boiling. Once the gelatin is fully dissolved, add the rest of the almond milk and put it in the refrigerator until the mixture sets.

To serve, spoon *menjar blanc* in a martini glass, top with tomato ice, and serve.

NOTE

In Barcelona, seawater is sold in markets. You can substitute the seawater with a combination of tap water and salt. The desired salinity is 1 liter of water to 35 grams of table salt.

A Ferran Adrià recipe, inspired by the classic *menjar blanc*: tomato ice, fresh oregano, and *menjar blanc* (1992). *Photograph by Francesc Guillamet; image provided by elBullifoundation.*

The recipes collected and adapted in this chapter capture the way in which Catalan dishes have historically built their flavors from (mostly) local ingredients. These recipes also are recognized as part of the traditional Catalan way of cooking. However, there are other traditional Catalan dishes that are missing from this collection, such as *canelons*, *fricandó*, and *esqueixada*, which visitors to the city will encounter on the menus of Barcelona's restaurants. Although they are indeed traditional and delicious preparations, they do not quite capture the culinary Catalan language that we wanted to outline in this section of the book. The *canelons* and *fricandó* are clear adaptations of Italian cannelloni and French fricandeau. They reflect an important story in the development of Catalan gastronomy: the many foreign influences it received, especially in the nineteenth century, when many cooking professionals from Italy and France crossed the borders to open restaurants. Over the years, these dishes have been fully adapted into Catalan cuisine and have developed a Catalan identity, but because these preparations are more familiar due to their similarities with other popular cuisines, we have decided to set them aside. *Exqueixada*, however, does not quite capture the complexity of the flavors discussed in the chapter. Considering its simplicity, perhaps we should review this indispensable dish for hot summer days: Shred desalted cod with your hands and mix it with chopped tomatoes, onions, olive oil, vinegar, and salt. You may add green or red peppers or garnish with black olives. Bon profit.[37x]

Notes

INTRODUCTION

1. Néstor Luján, *Vint segles de cuina a Barcelona. De les ostres de Barcino als restaurants d'avui* (Barcelona: Folio, 1993), 16.
2. Jaume Fàbrega, *La cuina modernista* (Barcelona: Viena Edicions, 2015), 23.
3. Luján, *Vint segles de cuina a Barcelona*, 16–17.
4. Manuel Vázquez Montalbán, *La cocina de los mediterráneos*, Carvalho gastronómico (Barcelona: Zeta, 2008), 15.
5. Josep Pla, *El que hem menjat*, vol. 22, *Obra completa* (Barcelona: Destino, 1980). This collection of essays was published for the first time in 1972.

CHAPTER 1

1. The deconstructed Spanish omelet and exploding olive were attributed to the chef Ferran Adrià and his culinary team. The powder popcorn was served in the now-closed Comerç 24 by Carles Abellán, a chef who trained with Adrià. Dishes that appeared to be one thing but were another were called *trampantojos*, a combination of the words *trampa* (to trick, trap, or cheat) and *antojo* (craving or snacks).
2. One of the early dishes served at El Celler de Can Roca by Joan Roca called Mussels with Riesling (August 31, 2007).

3. James Graff, "The 2004 TIME 100," *Time*, April 26, 2004, http://content.time.com/time/specials/packages/article/0,28804,1970858_1970890_1971358,00.html, accessed December 19, 2017.

4. Vicente Todolí and Richard Hamilton, *Comida para pensar, pensar sobre el comer* (Barcelona: Actar, 2009).

5. These business arrangements were explained by chef Albert Raurich to Anna Riera during an interview on October 16, 2018.

6. We are not including his ventures outside of Barcelona, such as Heart in Ibiza, a concept developed with his brother and the Cirque du Soleil. More information can be found here: www.heartibiza.com/en/.

7. Brenna Houck, "Willy Wonka Could Have Designed This Barcelona Restaurant," *Eater*, January 23, 2017, www.eater.com/2017/1/23/14342014/enigma -restaurant-barcelona-albert-adria-open.

8. Statement given by the chef during an interview with Anna Riera on November 2, 2018.

9. Laura Price, "How Disfrutar Went from One to Watch to Highest New Entry in the World's 50 Best Restaurants List," *The World's 50 Best Restaurants*, June 7, 2018, www.theworlds50best.com/blog/News/disfrutar-highest-new-entry-worlds -50-best-restaurants.html.

10. Named one of the most important chefs under thirty in Europe in 2017, David Andrés owns the restaurant Somiatruites in Igualada, a town on the outskirts of Barcelona. See www.elperiodico.com/es/extra/20170116/david-andres-lista -forbes-jovenes-lideres-futuro-5747221, accessed September 5, 2018.

11. We should clarify that Chef Ruscalleda had two Sant Pau restaurants, one in Sant Pol that closed in 2018 and the other still in operation in Tokyo. The chef, in a conversation with Anna Riera on October 11, 2018, revealed her plans to relocate her Tokyo Sant Pau restaurant to work with the Kitano Hotel Group.

12. Montse Palacín, *Barcelona Served: Contemporary Catalan Cuisine* (Barcelona: b-guided and Ajuntament de Barcelona, 2005), 109.

13. For Ada Parellada's profile, see Cristina Jolonch's article on www.lavanguardia.com/comer/sitios/20180127/44294763440/semproniana-ada-parellada -cumple-25-anos.html, accessed December 2, 2018.

14. Cristina Jolonch, "Carles Abellán lleva su tapeo a La Diagonal," *La Vanguardia*, December 23, 2017, www.lavanguardia.com/local/barcelona /20171223/433827427561/carles-abellan-lleva-su-tapeo-a-la-diagonal.html, accessed September 11, 2018.

15. See Cristina Jolonch's interview with chef Pérez about his restaurants: www.lavanguardia.com/comer/de-carne-hueso/20181216/453531899335/entrevista-paco -perez-cocinero.html, accessed on December 15, 2018.

16. Pilar Salas, "Juan Manuel Salgado y Adrià Viladomat vuelven a luchar por el Bocuse d'Or," *7caníbales.com*, January 15, 2018, www.7canibales.com/actuali dad/juan-manuel-salgado-adria-viladomat-vuelven-luchar-bocuse-dor/.

17. The restaurant was described as the most beautiful restaurant in the world. See www.lavanguardia.com/comer/sitios/20171116/432905726187/alkimia-res taurante-premio-diseno.html, accessed December 15, 2018.

18. Chris Dwyer, "10 Best New Restaurants of 2016," *CNN Travel*, https://edition.cnn.com/travel/article/best-new-restaurants/index.html, accessed March 15, 2018.

19. Wine lovers or anyone interested in wine should visit Monvinic in Barcelona, where they can taste a great variety of wines from all over the world, especially those from Catalonia, and peruse its impressive library on wines of Spain and the world. Some wine professionals in the city consider Lluís Tolosa's catalog *Barcelona Wine* (Barcelona: Tolosa Wine Books, 2015), published in four languages (Catalan, Spanish, English, and French), the best current compilation of Catalan wine. He also wrote *Guia dels millors 100 vins i caves de Catalunya* (Barcelona: S. L. Espurna Nec & Otium, 2017).

20. According to the 2017 report by the Observatorio Español del Mercado del Vino (OEMV), www.vinetur.com/2017101745135/%EF%BB%BFcataluna-vende -en-el-mercado-internacional-el-75-del-vino-que-produce.html, accessed March 15, 2018. The information about the changes in the Catalan winemaking industry was shared by Lluís Tolossa in an interview with Anna Riera on March 13, 2018.

21. Inés Butrón, *Comer en España: De la subsistencia a la vanguardia* (Barcelona: Península, 2011), 134.

22. Butrón, *Comer en España*, 134.

23. Quoted in Butrón, *Comer en España*, 135.

24. Butrón, *Comer en España*, 135–36.

25. Butrón, *Comer en España*, 136.

26. Butrón, *Comer en España*, 136–37.

27. Butrón, *Comer en España*, 137.

28. Conversations between Anna Riera and Juan Mari Arzak in 2016.

29. Butrón, *Comer en España*, 137. Bocuse's book *La cocina del mercado* was published in English as *Paul Bocuse's French Cooking* (1977).

30. Quoted in Butrón, *Comer en España*, 137.

31. Rafael Nadal, "Homenaje al Motel," *La Vanguardia*, June 3, 2011, www .lavanguardia.com/opinion/articulos/20110603/54165239075/homenaje-al-motel .html, accessed September 15, 2018.

32. Butrón, *Comer en España*, 143.

33. Carmen Casas, "Gran éxito de Ferran Adrià en el VII Congreso de Cocina de Autor," *La Vanguardia*, March 28, 1998.

34. José Ribagorda, "En el 'Zaldiarán' de Vitoria se inició la revolución," *Telecinco.es* (blog), April 23, 2009, www.telecinco.es/blogs/labuenavida/Zaldiaran -Vitoria-inicio-revolucion_6_825915005.html.

35. Butrón, *Comer en España*, 137–38.

36. Francisco de Sert Welsch, *El Goloso. Una historia europea de la buena mesa* (Barcelona: Alianza Editorial, 2007), 398–99.

37. Augstí Fancelli, "El mejor cocinero del mundo," *El País Semanal*, November 27, 2011, https://elpais.com/diario/2011/11/27/eps/1322378823_850215.html. All translations are ours unless otherwise noted.

38. Xacier Moret, *elBulli desde dentro. Biografía de un restaurante*, trans. Josep M. Pinto (Barcelona: RBA Libros, 2007), 111.

39. Moret, *elBulli desde dentro*, 97.

40. The category *cuisine d'auteur* was starting to be used during that time and Adrià's cookbook belongs in that group.

41. Moret, *elBulli desde dentro*, 99.

42. Moret, *elBulli desde dentro*, 99.

43. Moret, *elBulli desde dentro*, 100.

44. Moret, *elBulli desde dentro*, 110–11.

45. Moret, *elBulli desde dentro*, 111.

46. Moret, *elBulli desde dentro*, 111.

47. Moret, *elBulli desde dentro*, 130.

48. Moret, *elBulli desde dentro*, 130–31.

49. According to the website *Foods and Wines from Spain*, elBullitaller "soon became one of the cornerstones of the elBulli structure, catching on and being imitated in Spain and many other countries. With the arrival of Pere Castells and Ingrid Farré, the workshop set up its Scientific Department, where research is carried out on new commercial products that can be used in cuisine" (www.foodswines fromspain.com/spanishfoodwine/tools/foodpedia/who-is-who/4444220.html, accessed March 15, 2018).

50. Robyn Curnow, "Science Creates Gastronomic Storm," *CNN*, June 27, 2005, edition.cnn.com/2005/TECH/06/27/spark.elBulli/index.html, accessed September 14, 2018.

51. Giulia Sgarbi, "Twelve Iconic Dishes of El Bulli," *The World's 50 Best Restaurants*, www.theworlds50best.com/blog/News/12-iconic-dishes-el-bulli-ferran -adria.html, accessed September 15, 2018.

52. Arthur Lubow, "A Laboratory of Taste," *New York Times*, August 10, 2003, www.nytimes.com/2003/08/10/magazine/a-laboratory-of-taste.html.

53. María Paz Moreno, *Madrid: A Culinary History* (Lanham, MD: Rowman & Littlefield, 2018), 72.

54. Curnow, "Science Creates Gastronomic Storm."

55. Pau Arenós, *La cocina de los valientes* (Barcelona: Ediciones B, 2011), 9. The term, however, failed to be embraced by journalists and food critics.

56. Colman Andrews, *Ferran: The Inside Story of El Bulli and the Man Who Reinvented Food* (New York: Gotham, 2010), 177.

57. Interview with the chef on November 2, 2018 (our emphasis).

58. Vicente Todolí and Richard Hamilton, *Comida para pensar, pensar sobre el comer* (Barcelona: Actar, 2009), 51.

59. Information about the foundation and its many initiatives can be found here: www.alicia.cat/en/.

60. Ferran Adrià was invited to speak at Harvard University in 2008. Information about his visit can be found here: www.seas.harvard.edu/news/2008/12/ferran-adri-visits-harvard, accessed September 13, 2018.

61. Mikel Corcuera, *25 Años de la nueva cocina vasca* (Bilbao: Aizkorri, 2003), 80.

62. Rebecca Ingram, "Mapping and Mocking: Spanish Cuisine and Ramón Gómez de La Serna's 'El primer mapa gastronómico de España,'" *Cincinnati Romance Review* 33 (Winter 2012): 78–97.

63. Javier Moreno-Luzón, "The Restoration: 1874–1914," in *The History of Modern Spain: Chronologies, Themes, Individuals*, ed. Adrian Schubert and José Álvarez Junco, trans. Nick Rider (London: Bloomsbury, 2018). Moreno-Luzón notes that unlike Basque nationalism, the Catalan one was successful in forming a political party that "attracted a significant percentage of the electorate to vote for it and so defeated both Conservatives and Liberals. In addition, in contrast with the stance of Basque pro-independence campaigners, the Catalanists of the Lliga also designed plans for the whole of Spain, the aim of which was to ensure that the particularities of Catalonia were recognized within a plurinational and decentralized state" (59).

64. Ferran Agulló, *Llibre de la cuina catalana*, 9th ed. (Barcelona: Editorial Alta Fulla, 1999), 11. This oft-cited quote comes from the prologue of the second expanded edition published in 1933. The cookbook was published for the first time in 1928.

65. Manuel Vázquez Montalbán, *L'art del menjar a Catalunya. El llibre roig de la identitat gastronòmica catalana* (Barcelona: Salsa Books, 2004), 16–17.

66. The year 1982 is significant, as it is usually considered the end of the political transition from dictatorship to democracy in Spain. It was the year that the socialist

party Partido Socialista Obrero Español (PSOE) won the general elections and Felipe González was made president of the Spanish government.

67. *Calçots* differ in the way that they are grown. Planted in trenches, each bulb is buried under additional soil as it grows to enlarge the white part of the onion, resulting in an onion that resembles a leek or scallion. The name refers to the word *calçar*, which in farming refers to adding more soil.

68. Direcció General de Turisme, Generalitat de Catalunya, *Congrés Català de la cuina* (Barcelona: Departament de Comerç i Turisme, 1982).

69. Direcció General de Turisme, Generalitat de Catalunya, *Congrés Català de la cuina*, 3.

70. Butrón, *Comer en España*, 143–44.

71. Vázquez Montalbán, *L'art del menjar a Catalunya*, 13.

72. Vázquez Montalbán, *L'art del menjar a Catalunya*, 12.

73. Butrón, *Comer en España*, 145.

74. Marta Fernández Guadaño, "Y por último, un Melocotón Melba," *Diario Expansión*, July 27, 2011, *Fuera de Serie*, www.fueradeserie.expansion.com/2011/07/29/gastroteca/1311935604.html, accessed December 20, 2018.

75. Philippe Regol, "Escoffier, Adriá y el Melocotón Melba. El último plato para el último vals," *Observación Gastronómica* (blog), https://observaciongastronomica.blogspot.com/2011/08/escoffieradria-y-el-melocoton-melba.html, accessed September 8, 2018.

76. The list of ingredients for Adrià's take on the Melba peach dessert is on Regol's blog, *Observación Gastronómica*.

77. Regol, "Escoffier, Adriá y el Melocotón Melba."

78. Santi Santamaria, *La cocina al desnudo* (Madrid: Ediciones Planeta, 2008).

79. Anton Pujol, "Cosmopolitan Taste: The Morphing of the New Catalan Cuisine," *Food, Culture & Society* 12, no. 4 (2009): 438. Pujol analyzes the feud between the two chefs as the tension between traditional Catalan cooking and a highly sophisticated, cosmopolitan cuisine. He argues that this pull is not limited to culinary culture but reflects a relentless quest by Catalans to achieve cosmopolitanism in all areas.

80. Fiona Govan, "Santi Santamaria's Death Brings End to Feud with Ferran Adrià," *The Telegraph*, February 18, 2011, www.telegraph.co.uk/foodanddrink/8331823/Santi-Santamarias-death-brings-end-to-feud-with-Ferran-Adria.html.

81. Jörg Zipprick, *¡No quiero volver al restaurante!* (Madrid: Foca-Akal, 2009).

82. Miquel Sen, *Luces y sombras del reinado de Ferran Adrià* (Barcelona: La esfera de los libros, 2007); José Berasaluce, *El engaño de la gastronomía española* (Gijón, Spain: Trea, 2018).

83. Quoted in Butrón, *Comer en España*, 227–28; Almudena Villegas, *Manual de cultura gastronómica* (Córdoba: Almuzara, 2008).

84. Regol, "Escoffier, Adriá y el Melocotón Melba."

85. Lauren Collins, "Ranking the World's Best Restaurants," *New Yorker*, October 26, 2015, www.newyorker.com/magazine/2015/11/02/whos-to-judge.

86. Information about the project and the tours can be found here: www.bbva compass.com/our-story/bright-futures/roca-brothers.html, accessed September 14, 2018.

87. Anna Riera, "Sueño, luego existo," *El Periódico de Catalunya*, May 16, 2013.

88. Interview given by Joan Roca to the authors on June 21, 2017, at El Celler de Can Roca, Girona, Spain.

89. Toni Massanés and David Ortiz Ripoll, *From the Earth to the Moon* (Barcelona: Generalitat de Catalunya, 2016).

CHAPTER 2

1. Joan Santanach, ed., *The Book of Sent Soví: Medieval Recipes from Catalonia*, trans. Robin Vogelzang (Boydell & Brewer, 2008), 18.

2. Isabel Moyano Andrés, "La cocina escrita," in *La cocina en su tinta* (Madrid: Biblioteca Nacional de España, 2010), 20.

3. Rudolf Grewe, "Catalan Cuisine, in a Historical Perspective," in *National and Regional Styles of Cookery: Oxford Symposium 1981 Proceedings*, ed. Alan Davidson (London: Prospect Books, 1981), 170.

4. Francesc Xavier Hernàndez Cardona, *Barcelona & Catalunya. Història d'un binomi* (Barcelona: Rafael Dalmau, 2017), 7.

5. Felipe Fernández-Armesto, *Barcelona: A Thousand Years of the City's Past* (Oxford: Oxford University Press, 1992), 5.

6. Hernàndez Cardona, *Barcelona & Catalunya*, 21.

7. Robert Hughes, *Barcelona* (New York: Vintage Books, 1993), 57.

8. Hughes, *Barcelona*, 57–58.

9. Hughes, *Barcelona*, 57.

10. Grewe, "Catalan Cuisine, in a Historical Perspective," 171.

11. Néstor Luján, *Vint segles de cuina a Barcelona* (Barcelona: Ediciones Folio, 1993), 19–20.

12. Rafael Chabrán, "Medieval Spain," in *Regional Cuisines of Medieval Europe: A Book of Essays*, ed. Melitta Weiss Adamson (New York: Routledge, 2002), 129.

13. Melitta Weiss Adamson, *Food in Medieval Times* (Westport, CT: Greenwood Press, 2004), 115–16.

14. Hughes, *Barcelona*, 58.

15. Hughes, *Barcelona*, 64–65.

16. Luján, *Vint segles de cuina catalana*, 21.

17. Chabrán, "Medieval Spain," 130.

18. Luján, *Vint segles de cuina catalana*, 23.

19. Grewe, "Catalan Cuisine, in a Historical Perspective," 171; Adamson, *Food in Medieval Times*, 115–16.

20. Grewe, "Catalan Cuisine, in a Historical Perspective," 171–72.

21. Hughes, *Barcelona*, 70.

22. Hughes, *Barcelona*, 70.

23. Adamson, *Food in Medieval Times*, 116. In recent years, restaurants in Barcelona have rediscovered their connection with *garum* and have included it in dishes on their menu, as is the case of Dos Pebrots, opened in 2017 by chef Albert Raurich, known for his work as head chef at Ferran Adrià's elBulli.

24. Hughes, *Barcelona*, 71.

25. Hughes, *Barcelona*, 74.

26. Grewe, "Catalan Cuisine, in a Historical Perspective," 172.

27. Eliana Thibaut i Comalada, *Cuina medieval catalana. Història, dietética i cuina* (Valls, Spain: Cossetània Edicions, 2006), 62.

28. Grewe, "Catalan Cuisine, in a Historical Perspective," 172.

29. Thibaut i Comalada, *Cuina medieval catalana*, 63.

30. Grewe, "Catalan Cuisine, in a Historical Perspective," 173; Thibaut i Comalada, *Cuina medieval catalana*, 63.

31. Grewe, "Catalan Cuisine, in a Historical Perspective," 173.

32. Chabrán, "Medieval Spain," 131.

33. Adamson, *Food in Medieval Times*, 116. Later in the eighteenth and nineteenth centuries, the French would influence Spain on the order in which dishes were served and the use of printed menus.

34. Thibaut i Comalada, *Cuina medieval catalana*, 102.

35. Chabrán, "Medieval Spain," 132.

36. Bernard Rosenberger, "Arab Cuisine and Its Contribution to European Culture," in *Food: A Culinary History from Antiquity to the Present*, ed. Jean-Louis

Flandrin, Massimo Montanari, and Albert Sonnenfeld (New York: Columbia University Press, 1999), 221.

37. Rosenberger, "Arab Cuisine and Its Contribution to European Culture," 217–18.

38. Chabrán, "Medieval Spain," 132–33; Thibaut i Comalada, *Cuina medieval catalana*, 304.

39. Colman Andrews notes that in Murcia there is a pasta called *aletria*. *Catalan Cuisine: Europe's Last Great Culinary Secret* (Boston: Harvard Common Press, 1999), 196.

40. Andrews, *Catalan Cuisine*, 196–97.

41. Mestre Robert, *Llibre del Coch. Tractat de cuina medieval*, ed. Veronika Leimgruber (Barcelona: Curial, 2012), 59–60.

42. Manuela Marín, "From Al-Andalus to Spain: Arab Traces in Spanish Cooking," *Food & History* 2, no. 2 (2004): 36–37.

43. Marín, "From Al-Andalus to Spain," 37–38. María Rosa Menocal's popular *The Ornament of the World: How Muslims, Jews and Christians Created a Culture of Tolerance in Medieval Spain* (2003) offers this narrative of cultural and religious harmony.

44. Miguel-Ángel Motis Dolader, "Mediterranean Jewish Diet and Traditions in the Middle Ages," in *Food: A Culinary History from Antiquity to the Present*, ed. Jean-Louis Flandrin, Massimo Montanari, and Albert Sonnenfeld (New York: Columbia University Press, 1999), 227.

45. Motis Dolader, "Mediterranean Jewish Diet and Traditions in the Middle Ages," 238.

46. Quoting Jaume Riera, Motís Dolader, "Mediterranean Jewish Diet and Traditions in the Middle Ages," 239.

47. Marín, "From Al-Andalus to Spain," 39–40.

48. Hughes, *Barcelona*, 77–78.

49. Hughes, *Barcelona*, 78–79.

50. Hughes, *Barcelona*, 79.

51. Hughes, *Barcelona*, 80–81.

52. Hughes, *Barcelona*, 80. The genealogy of Guifré el Pelós is entertaining, as his father is reputed to have slayed a dragon. Hughes follows this tangled story in his account of the origins of the city of Barcelona (*Barcelona*, 81–83).

53. Hughes, *Barcelona*, 83.

54. Hughes, *Barcelona*, 84.

55. Hughes, *Barcelona*, 87.

56. Hughes, *Barcelona*, 94.

57. Antoni Riera-Melis, "Society, Food and Feudalism," in *Food: A Culinary History from Antiquity to the Present*, ed. Jean-Louis Flandrin, Massimo Montanari, and Albert Sonnenfeld (New York: Columbia University Press, 1999), 251–52.

58. Riera-Melis, "Society, Food and Feudalism," 255.

59. Riera-Melis, "Society, Food and Feudalism," 256–57.

60. Luján, *Vint segles de cuina catalana*, 30.

61. Riera-Melis, "Society, Food and Feudalism," 253.

62. Riera-Melis, "Society, Food and Feudalism," 257.

63. Riera-Melis, "Society, Food and Feudalism," 258.

64. Riera-Melis, "Society, Food and Feudalism," 258–59.

65. Hughes, *Barcelona*, 95.

66. Hughes, *Barcelona*, 95.

67. Hughes, *Barcelona*, 96.

68. Hughes, *Barcelona*, 97.

69. Riera-Melis, "Society, Food and Feudalism," 253.

70. Hughes, *Barcelona*, 98.

71. Hughes, *Barcelona*, 105.

72. Hughes, *Barcelona*, 105–7.

73. Hughes, *Barcelona*, 105.

74. Hughes, *Barcelona*, 108.

75. Hughes, *Barcelona*, 108.

76. Hughes, *Barcelona*, 109–10.

77. Hughes repeats a common misconception that the use of spices in medieval times was to disguise the smell and taste of rancid meat. It has been sufficiently documented that this was not the case.

78. Hughes, *Barcelona*, 113–15.

79. Hughes, *Barcelona*, 119–20.

80. Hughes, *Barcelona*, 120–21.

81. Hughes, *Barcelona*, 155.

82. The novel was later adapted into a TV series in 2017 and is currently available through Netflix.

83. Chabrán, "Medieval Spain," 133–34.

84. Quoted in Chabrán, "Medieval Spain," 135.

85. Chabrán, "Medieval Spain," 135.

86. David Fernández de Castro, *Barcelona i el vi* (Barcelona: Editorial Mediterrània, 2017), 24–25.

87. Fernández de Castro, *Barcelona i el vi*, 25.

88. Grewe, "Catalan Cuisine, in a Historical Perspective," 174. A picture of the *bresquet* is available in the blog *Medieval Spanish Chef,* available at the following link: www.medievalspanishchef.com/2012/04/bresquet-with-14th-c-recipe -for-eel-in.html.

89. Luján, *Vint segles de cuina catalana*, 53.

90. Grewe, "Catalan Cuisine, in a Historical Perspective," 174.

91. Grewe, "Catalan Cuisine, in a Historical Perspective," 175.

92. Thibaut i Comalada, *Cuina medieval catalana*, 25. The author writes that Platina declared that Catalan cooks were the best in the world. Though he has praised them, Platina did not in fact make such a statement. We thank Ken Albala for the clarification.

93. Thibaut i Comalada, *Cuina medieval catalana*, 102.

94. Luján, *Vint segles de cuina catalana*, 53–54.

95. Santanach, *The Book of Sent Soví: Medieval Recipes from Catalonia*, 11. The first edition of the manuscript was published by Rudolph Grewe in 1979.

96. Santanach, *The Book of Sent Soví*, 11–12.

97. Santanach, *The Book of Sent Soví*, 12. The first two cookbooks, *Llibre d'aparellar de menjar* and *Llibre de totes maneres de potages*, have been published by Editorial Barcino in 2015 and 2017, respectively.

98. Santanach, *The Book of Sent Soví*, 13.

99. Santanach, *The Book of Sent Soví*, 17–20.

100. Santanach, *The Book of Sent Soví*, 20–21.

101. Grewe, "Catalan Cuisine, in a Historical Perspective," 174.

102. Santanach, *The Book of Sent Soví*, 41.

103. Santanach, *The Book of Sent Soví*, 22. The 2015 edition of the *Llibre d'aparellar de menjar* includes a graphic explanation of the recipe with instructions for tying the head and tail to prevent it from burning during cooking, since the feathers must be intact for the final presentation of the dish (82–83).

104. Grewe's comment about the peacock sauce are mentioned in Santanach, *The Book of Sent Soví*, 22.

105. Hughes, *Barcelona*, 135.

106. Santanach, *The Book of Sent Soví*, 23–24.

107. Santanach, *The Book of Sent Soví*, 75.

108. Thibaut i Comalada, *Cuina medieval Catalana*, 48.

109. Santanach, *The Book of Sent Soví*, 24.

110. Santanach, *The Book of Sent Soví*, 24. Santanach notes that the similarity between *genestada* and *menjar blanc* can be argued since the the recipes appear consecutively in the manuscript's index and also in the *Llibre d'aparellar* (segle

XIV, the manuscript found in the *Biblioteca Nacional de Catalunya*), which was published in book form in 2015.

111. Santanach, *The Book of Sent Soví*, 57. In this edition, there is a note about the "ground substance"—*comolt*—which probably refers to a specific ingredient. In a quote from Grewe's edition reprinted in 2003, it is explained as a "thoroughly ground or liquid element that is added to a sauce to improve its flavor."

112. Grewe, "Catalan Cuisine, in a Historical Perspective," 176.

113. Santanach, *The Book of Sent Soví*, 53.

114. Chabrán, "Medieval Spain," 138.

115. Isabel Moyano Andrés, "La cocina escrita," in *La cocina en su tinta* (Madrid: Biblioteca Nacional de España, 2010), 20.

116. Andrews, *Catalan Cuisine*, 19.

117. Terence Scully, *The Neapolitan Recipe Collection: Cuoco Napoletano* (Ann Arbor: University of Michigan Press, 2000), 18–19.

118. Scully, *The Neapolitan Recipe Collection*, 18.

119. Chabrán, "Medieval Spain," 139.

120. Moyano Andrés, "La cocina escrita," 23.

121. Moyano Andrés, "La cocina escrita," 20–21.

122. Pérez does not know *aigua rosada* refers to rose water and therefore incorrectly speculates about the literal translation, "pink water."

123. Luján, *Vint segles de cuina catalana*, 54–60.

124. Chabrán, "Medieval Spain," 140.

125. Andrews, *Catalan Cuisine*, 134. Andrews offers a modern-day take on the *Llibre del coch* recipe *Emperador en cassola*, which combines a sweet and sour sauce (using orange juice and golden raisins or sultanas), herbs (parsley, mint, marjoram), and nuts (almonds and pine nuts) and is served with the fish (134).

126. Chabrán, "Medieval Spain," 140.

127. Andrews, *Catalan Cuisine*, 246. In fact, *blancmanger* is neither French or Catalan. It is a recipe derived from the East, and a version still exists today in Turkey. Thanks to Ken Albala for the explanation.

128. Andrews, *Catalan Cuisine*, 246.

129. Rafael Conde, "Alimentación y sociedad: las cuentas de Guillema de Montcada (A.D. 1189)," *Medievalia. Revista de estudios medievales* 3 (1982): 11–15. In the introduction of the recent edition of the *Llibre d'aparellar de menjar*, a study follows one of these records to illustrate the diet of the noble class. The information contained in the recent study is similar to the diet we illustrate here: Antoni Riera i Melis, "El context historic dels receptaris medieval catalans. 2. La cuina i la taula de la noblesa: l'ostetació de la qualitat," in *Llibre d'aparellar de menjar* (Barcelona: Editorial Barcino, 2015), 21–51.

130. Conde, "Alimentación y sociedad," 16.

131. Teresa Vinyoles Vidal, "La vida quotidiana i l'espai domèstic al segle XIII," in *Jaume I: Commemoració de VIII centenari de naixement de Jaume I*, ed. M. Teresa Ferrer i Mallol, vol. 2 (Barcelona: Institut d'Estudis Catalans, 2013), 141.

132. Vinyoles Vidal, "La vida quotidiana i l'espai domèstic al segle XIII," 141.

133. Vinyoles Vidal, "La vida quotidiana i l'espai domèstic al segle XIII," 142.

134. Vinyoles Vidal, "La vida quotidiana i l'espai domèstic al segle XIII," 142.

135. Vinyoles Vidal, "La vida quotidiana i l'espai domèstic al segle XIII," 144.

136. Riera-Melis, "Society, Food and Feudalism," 258–59.

137. Antoni Riera-Melis, "Alimentació i poder a Catalunya al segle XII: Aproximació al comportament alimentari de la Noblesa," *Revista d'etnologia de Catalunya* 2 (1993): 14–15.

138. Riera-Melis, "Alimentació i poder a Catalunya al segle XII," 15.

139. Riera-Melis, "Alimentació i poder a Catalunya al segle XII," 16.

140. Quoting the translation of the work of Jaume Roig that appears in Hughes, *Barcelona*, 124.

141. Luján, *Vint segles de cuina catalana*, 42–44.

142. Xavier Renedo and David Guixeras, eds., *Frances Eiximinis. An Anthology*, trans. Robert Hughes (Barcelona: Barcino/Tamesis, 2008), 159–60.

143. Riera-Melis, "Society, Food and Feudalism," 266.

144. Hughes, *Barcelona*, 169.

145. Hughes, *Barcelona*, 170–71.

CHAPTER 3

1. Modesto Martí de Sola, *Barcelona y su provincia. Guía-itinerario descriptiva, estadística y pintoresca* (Barcelona: Establecimiento Tipográfico "La Academia," 1888), 36. All translations are ours, unless specified otherwise.

2. Cayetano Cornet i Mas, *Guía completa del viajero en Barcelona* (Barcelona: I. López Editor—Librería Española, 1866), 174. Our translation.

3. *Xocolateries* were establishments where hot chocolate and other nonalcoholic beverages were served.

4. José Coroleu, *Barcelona y sus alrededores. Guía histórica, descriptiva y estadística del forastero* (Barcelona: Jaime Seix, 1887), 272; Luciano García del Real, *Barcelona. Guía Diamante* (Barcelona: Librería de Francisco Puig, 1896), 15–16. The latter guidebook is bilingual, published in Spanish and French. The other guidebooks mentioned in the chapter are in Spanish.

5. Michael A. Vargas, *Constructing Catalan Identity: Memory, Imagination, and the Medieval* (Cham, Switzerland: Palgrave Macmillan, 2018), 23.

6. Vargas includes a useful breakdown of the political events of Catalonia from 897 to 2017 in *Constructing Catalan Identity*, 25–27.

7. Antoni Segura i Mas and Elisenda Barbé i Pou, "Catalonia: From Industrialization to the Present Day," in *A Companion to Catalan Culture*, ed. Dominic Keown (Woodbridge, Suffolk, UK: Tamesis, 2011), 71.

8. Isabel Moyano Andrés, "La cocina escrita," in *La cocina en su tinta* (Madrid: Biblioteca Nacional de España, 2010), 23.

9. Robert Davidson, "Barcelona: The Siege City," in *A Companion to Catalan Culture*, ed. Dominic Keown (Woodbridge, Suffolk, UK: Tamesis, 2011), 97.

10. Davidson, "Barcelona: The Siege City," 97.

11. John Payne, *Catalonia: History and Culture* (Nottingham, UK: Five Leaves Publication, 2004).

12. Payne, *Catalonia*, 71. Ralph E. Giesey explains that this is the oath in which the people of Aragon supposedly addressed their new king, starting with a proud "We who are as much as you" and, after stating their conditions to accepting him, ending with the open threat, "If not, not." Ralph E. Giesey, *If Not, Not: The Oath of the Aragonese and the Legendary Laws of Sobrarbe* (Princeton, NJ: Princeton University Press, 1968), vii.

13. Henry Kamen, "A Forgotten Insurrection of the Seventeenth Century: The Catalan Peasant Rising of 1688," *The Journal of Modern History* 49, no. 2 (1977): 226. For Kamen, this incident explains why the popular Catalan uprisings have failed throughout the region's history: successful uprisings require the support of the ruling (or upper) classes.

14. Payne, *Catalonia*, 72.

15. *Els segadors*, literally "the reapers," was a term also used to describe peasants in general. Here is a fragment of the Catalan anthem translated by Hughes: "Now is the hour, reapers, / the time to be on your guard! / For when June comes round again, / we'll sharpen our tools well! / (chorus) A good sickle-cut! / A good sickle-cut / if they want to take our wheat! / A good sickle-cut!" Robert Hughes, *Barcelona* (New York: Vintage Books, 1993), 180.

16. Kamen, "A Forgotten Insurrection of the Seventeenth Century," 212–13.

17. Kamen, "A Forgotten Insurrection of the Seventeenth Century," 215.

18. Payne, *Catalonia*, 73.

19. Felipe Fernández-Armesto, *Barcelona: A Thousand Years of the City's Past* (Oxford: Oxford University Press, 1992), 118.

20. Fernández-Armesto, *Barcelona*, 124–26.

21. Payne, *Catalonia*, 74.

22. Albert Garcia Espuche, *Barcelona 1700* (Barcelona: Editorial Empúries, 2010).

23. Jaume Fàbrega, *La cuina del 1714. Història i receptes* (Barcelona: Viena Edicions, 2014). The suggested culinary route can be followed through the following website: http://patrimoni.gencat.cat/ruta1714. When renovations for the market El Born started in the late 1970s, they revealed traces of the besieged city. These archaeological remains were preserved and the old market building converted into El Born Centre de Cultura i Memòria. The restaurant in the building, El 300 del Born, owned by the group Moritz, has a menu with dishes related to the battles of the period and the siege of 1714.

24. *Becos* were inns in Barcelona run by immigrants from Switzerland and Italy. They were already in existence in the eighteenth century but became very popular in the nineteenth century. They served simple and nutritious meals. A popular inn was Beco del Racó, run by an Italian from Sardinia. The establishment was famous for its hare stew, meat stew with potatoes, Catalan stew with meatball soup, and *fricandó*. Néstor Luján, *Diccionari Luján de gastronomia catalana* (Barcelona: Edicions La Campana, 1990), 29–30.

25. Fàbrega, *La cuina del 1714*, 13.

26. Fernández-Armesto, *Barcelona*, 127.

27. Fernández-Armesto, *Barcelona*, 130–31. The Palau Moja currently houses in its basement the Catalan Heritage House, where visitors can learn about the region's history and its cuisine with local organic ingredients.

28. Robert Hughes, *Barcelona* (New York: Vintage Books, 1993), 198.

29. Hughes, *Barcelona*, 198. La Rambla is a boulevard that stretches from Plaça Catalunya toward the sea, which also serves to geographically orient the city's residents, who refer to either the mountain or the water when giving directions. La Rambla has different sections: Rambla de Canaletes, Rambla des Estudis, Rambla de Sant Josep (where the famed fresh food market La Boquería is located), Rambla del Caputxins, and Rambla de Santa Mònica. These names also indicate church properties that used to be in the vicinity.

30. Hughes, *Barcelona*, 194.

31. Hughes, *Barcelona*, 195.

32. Fernández-Armesto, *Barcelona*, 132.

33. Hughes, *Barcelona*, 195.

34. The Catalan press Curial has published eleven volumes that cover the years 1769–1816 as of this writing.

35. Moyano Andrés, "La cocina escrita," 27.

36. María Paz Moreno, *Madrid: A Culinary History* (Lanham, MD: Rowman & Littlefield, 2018), 34–37.

37. María de los Ángeles Pérez Samper, *Barcelona, corte. La visita de Carlos IV en 1802* (Barcelona: Cátedra de Historia General de España, 1973), 19.

38. Pérez Samper, *Barcelona*, 95.

39. Pérez Samper, *Barcelona*, 99–102.

40. María de los Ángeles Pérez Samper, *Mesas y cocinas en la España del siglo XVIII* (Gijón, Spain: Ediciones Trea, 2011), 185–86. Pérez Samper quotes from volume 6 of the *Calaix de sastre*, 1802–1803, by the Baró de Maldà (Rafael d'Amat i de Cortada).

41. Pérez Samper, *Mesas y cocinas en la España del siglo XVIII*, 186.

42. Pérez Samper, *Mesas y cocinas en la España del siglo XVIII*, 187–88.

43. Payne, *Catalonia. History and Culture*, 79–80. Towns like Begur have a large number of houses built by *indianos*, and a few of them are open to the public.

44. Payne, *Catalonia*, 79–80.

45. Payne, *Catalonia*, 80.

46. Pérez Samper, *Mesas y cocinas en la España del siglo XVIII*, 131–32.

47. Pérez Samper, *Mesas y cocinas en la España del siglo XVIII*, 374.

48. Luján, *Diccionari Luján de gastronomia catalana*, 174.

49. Pérez Samper, *Mesas y cocinas en la España del siglo XVIII*, 133–34.

50. Pérez Samper, *Mesas y cocinas en la España del siglo XVIII*, 143–44.

51. Pérez Samper, *Mesas y cocinas en la España del siglo XVIII*, 144–45.

52. Jaume Fàbrega, *La cuina modernista* (Barcelona: Viena Edicions, 2015), 58–62.

53. Information about the arrival of *havanera* to Spain and Catalonia can be found here: www.fundacioem.com/en/the-havanera. There are yearly events in Calella de Palafrugell, Escala, and other towns along the Costa Brava. Yearly updated information can be found online.

54. Fàbrega, *La cuina modernista*, 60.

55. Fàbrega, *La cuina modernista*, 58–59.

56. Fàbrega, *La cuina modernista*, 59.

57. Payne, *Catalonia*, 80–81.

58. A novel describing this world at the end of the century is Eduardo Mendoza's *The City of Marvels* (1986). Perhaps a more entertaining version of this struggle set in the early twentieth century is Mendoza's critically acclaimed crime novel, *The Truth about the Savolta Case* (1975).

59. Núria Bàguena i Maranges, *Cuinar i menjar a Barcelona (1850–1900)* (Barcelona: CIM Edicions, 2007), 18.

60. Bàguena i Maranges, *Cuinar i menjar a Barcelona*, 20–21.

61. Glòria Baliu and Ignasi Riera, *La cuina del XVIII* (Barcelona: Sd Edicions, 2003), 17.

62. Jaume Fabre and Josep M. Huertas, *Cent anys de vida quotidiana a Catalunya. Del fogó de carbó a l'antena parabòlica* (Barcelona: Edicions 62, 1993), 186.

63. Fabre and Huertas, *Cent anys de vida quotidiana a Catalunya*, 187–88.

64. Baliu and Riera, *La cuina del XVIII*, 18. The authors quote from Codina's *El temps dels albats* (93).

65. Bàguena i Maranges, *Cuinar i menjar a Barcelona*, 21.

66. David Fernández de Castro, *Barcelona i el vi* (Barcelona: Editorial Mediterrània, 2017), 88.

67. Fernández de Castro, *Barcelona i el vi*, 88–94.

68. Hughes, *Barcelona*, 222.

69. Payne, *Catalonia*, 82.

70. Payne, *Barcelona*, 83.

71. Albert Balcells, *Catalan Nationalism: Past and Present*, ed. Geoffrey J. Walker, trans. Jacqueline Hall (New York: St. Martin's Press, 1996), 22.

72. Balcells, *Catalan Nationalism*, 23–24.

73. Payne, *Catalonia*, 83.

74. Robert S. Lubar, "Art and Anarchism in the City of Bombs," in *Barcelona and Modernity: Picasso, Gaudí, Miró, Dalí*, edited by William H. Robinson, Jordi Falgàs, and Carmen Belen Lord (New Haven, CT: Cleveland Museum of Art and Yale University Press, 2007), 111.

75. Payne, *Catalonia*, 84.

76. Baliu and Riera, *La cuina del XVIII*, 16. The list of food consumed by workers comes from *Higiene industrial* (1856) by the doctor Pedro Felipe Monlau.

77. Baliu and Riera, *La cuina del XVIII*, 17. Joaquim Font i Mosella, the author of *Consideraciones sobre los inconvenientes que irrogan a la salud de los jornaleros y a la pública de Barcelona en las fábricas en especial las de vapor* (Considerations about the factory inconveniences that damage the health of workers and the public health of Barcelona, especially steam factories) (1852), makes these observations about the eating habits of factory workers.

78. Baliu and Riera, *La cuina del XVIII*, 17. Hughes describes Cerdà's work, *A Statistical Monograph on the Working Class of Barcelona in 1856*, as "the first serious attempt to study the living space of the city and its patterns of movement and transport, its services, health, and the general working conditions of its trades" and a "dense catalog of social suffering" (*Barcelona*, 280).

79. William H. Robinson and Carmen Belen Lord, "Introduction," in *Barcelona and Modernity: Picasso, Gaudí, Miró, Dalí*, ed. William H. Robinson, Jordi Falgàs, and Carmen Belen Lord (New Haven, CT: Yale University Press, 2007), 7.

80. Hughes, *Barcelona*, 280–81. Hughes points to the naming of the streets in the new expansion and the work of the poet Victor Balaguer as proof of the desire to invoke the glories of Catalonia's past. The names used include "Catalan conquerors (Roger de Llúria, Bernat de Rocafort); medieval dynasties (Borrell, Comte d'Urgell); the countries of Catalunya's lost Mediterranean empire (Corsega [*sic*], Calabria, Napols [*sic*], Sardenya, Sicilia); its ancient political institutions (Consell de Cent, Diputació, Corts Catalanes); the three kingdoms of the Crown of Aragon (Aragó, Mallorca, and València); political heroes (Pau Claris, Rafael Casanova); emblematic sites of the Catalan resistance to Napoleon (Bruc, Girona, Bailen [*sic*]); and a whole array of poets and writers from the Middle Ages (Ausiàs March) to figureheads of the Renaixença (Balmes and Aribau)" (288).

81. Hughes, *Barcelona*, 282–85.

82. Quoted in Hughes, *Barcelona*, 288–89.

83. Hughes, *Barcelona*, 286.

84. Robinson and Lord, "Introduction," 8.

85. Balcells, *Catalan Nationalism*, 25–26.

86. Balcells, *Catalan Nationalism*, 25. As Balcells explains, basic schooling was in Castilian, the official language. The use of Catalan was difficult because it lacked standard rules for spelling and usage and, when written, was a medieval, archaic language different from its spoken form. It is therefore not surprising that many texts about Catalonia by Catalans in the nineteenth century were written in Castilian.

87. Balcells, *Catalan Nationalism*, 26.

88. Robinson and Lord, "Introduction," 8.

89. Robinson and Lord, "Introduction," 9.

90. Paco Villar, *Barcelona, ciutat de cafès (1880–1936)* (Barcelona: Viena Edicions, 2013), 12.

91. María del Mar Serrano, *Las guías urbanas y los libros de viaje en la España del siglo XIX* (Barcelona: Universitat de Barcelona, 1993), 70–72.

92. Serrano, *Las guías urbanas y los libros de viaje en la España del siglo XIX*, 40–41.

93. From Andersen's *Viaje por España*, quoted in Villar, *Barcelona, ciutat de cafès (1880–1936)*, 12.

94. Villar, *Barcelona*, 13.

95. Villar, *Barcelona*, 13.

96. Villar, *Barcelona*, 13–14.

97. Villar, *Barcelona*, 15.

98. Villar, *Barcelona*, 14.

99. Villar, *Barcelona*, 52–53.

100. Villar, *Barcelona*, 56.

101. Villar, *Barcelona*, 14.

102. Villar, *Barcelona*, 16.

103. Bàguena i Maranges, *Cuinar i menjar a Barcelona*, 84.

104. Bàguena i Maranges, *Cuinar i menjar a Barcelona*, 81.

105. Colman Andrews, *Catalan Cuisine: Europe's Last Great Culinary Secret* (Boston: Harvard Common Press, 1999), 23.

106. Andrews, *Catalan Cuisine*, 23; Bàguena i Maranges, *Cuinar i menjar a Barcelona*, 82.

107. Bàguena i Maranges, *Cuinar i menjar a Barcelona*, 82.

108. Luján, *Vint segles de cuina catalata*, 94–95.

109. Villar, *Barcelona*, 31.

110. Villar, *Barcelona*, 16.

111. Villar, *Barcelona*, 17.

112. Villar, *Barcelona*, 17–18.

113. Lluís Permanyer, *La Barcelona d'ahir. L'esplendor de la burgesia* (Barcelona: Angle Editorial, 2015), 105.

114. Lluís Permanyer, "Una esquina codiciada," *La Vanguardia*, May 23, 2006.

115. Lluís Permanyer, *Barcelona nocturna* (Barcelona: Efadós and Ajuntament de Barcelona, 2016), 86.

116. Villar, *Barcelona*, 29. "Can" in this context in Catalan means "in the home or business place of," much like the French *chez*.

117. Villar, *Barcelona*, 30.

118. Villar, *Barcelona*, 31.

119. Villar, *Barcelona*, 31.

120. Villar, *Barcelona*, 33–34.

121. Villar, *Barcelona*, 34. Notice the two Spanish wines awarded gold medals during the World's Fair.

122. Fàbrega, *La cuina modernista*, 31.

123. *Rostit* means "slow cooked" and usually indicates meat slowly cooked in oil in a terra-cotta or cast-iron casserole. In this case, however, it could also indicate a vegetable dish slow cooked with some type of meat—for example, *cansalada* (a Catalan version of fatty salt pork).

124. Bàguena i Maranges, *Cuinar i menjar a Barcelona*, 136.

125. Fàbrega, *La cuina modernista*, 84.

126. Villar, *Barcelona*, 70.

127. Villar, *Barcelona*, 70.

128. Villar, *Barcelona*, 71.

129. Villar, *Barcelona*, 19.

130. Villar, *Barcelona*, 28–29.

131. Villar, *Barcelona*, 23–24.

132. Villar, *Barcelona*, 204.

133. The original café closed in 1903, but it was reopened and restored to its original condition in 1989.

134. Francesc M. Quílez i Corella, "Graphic Art of the Quatre Gats," in *Barcelona and Modernity: Picasso, Gaudí, Miró, Dalí*, ed. William H. Robinson, Carmen Belen Lord, and Jordi Falgàs (New Haven, CT: Yale University Press, 2007), 95.

135. Villar, *Barcelona*, 242.

136. Villar, *Barcelona*, 242. The anecdotes about the ambiance and the clientele are from Ricard Opisso and Màrius Verdaguer, a writer from Menorca, and both are quoted in the book.

137. Cristina Mendoza, "Quatre Gats and the Origins of Picasso's Career," in *Barcelona and Modernity: Picasso, Gaudí, Miró, Dalí*, ed. William H. Robinson, Carmen Belen Lord, and Jordi Falgàs (New Haven, CT: Yale University Press, 2007), 80–81.

138. Mendoza, "Quatre Gats and the Origins of Picasso's Career," 81.

139. Villar, *Barcelona*, 244.

140. Mendoza, "Quatre Gats and the Origins of Picasso's Career," 81.

141. Mendoza, "Quatre Gats and the Origins of Picasso's Career," 81.

142. Mendoza, "Quatre Gats and the Origins of Picasso's Career," 80–81.

143. Mendoza, "Quatre Gats and the Origins of Picasso's Career," 82.

144. Villar, *Barcelona*, 250.

145. Quílez i Corella, "Graphic Art of the Quatre Gats," 95. Quílez mentions that given the drafts of the menu that Picasso prepared (and that are in the Picasso Museum), he did not take this task lightly.

146. Quoted in Villar, *Barcelona*, 253.

147. Villar, *Barcelona*, 253.

148. Villar, *Barcelona*, 254.

149. Villar, *Barcelona*, 253.

150. Pilar Vélez, "The Decorative Arts of the Modernist Era: European Art Nouveau Plus the Local Tradition," in *Barcelona and Modernity: Picasso, Gaudí, Miró, Dalí*, ed. William H. Robinson, Carmen Belen Lord, and Jordi Falgàs (New Haven, CT: Yale University Press, 2007), 165.

151. Vélez, "The Decorative Arts of the Modernist Era," 166.

152. Francesc M. Quílez i Corella, "The Art of the Poster," in *Barcelona and Modernity: Picasso, Gaudí, Miró, Dalí*, ed. William H. Robinson, Carmen Belen Lord, and Jordi Falgàs (New Haven, CT: Yale University Press, 2007), 69.

153. *Orxata* or *horchata* (in Spanish). Those ones in Spain are made with *chufa* (tiger nuts) and the ones in Mexico, which are popular in the United States, are made with rice.

154. Pérez Samper, *Mesas y cocinas en la España del siglo*, 383.

155. Pérez Samper, *Mesas y cocinas en la España del siglo XVIII*, 384.

156. Pérez Samper, *Mesas y cocinas en la España del siglo XVIII*, 386.

157. Pérez Samper, *Mesas y cocinas en la España del siglo XVIII*, 388.

158. Bàguena i Maranges, *Cuinar i menjar a Barcelona*, 107.

159. Fàbrega, *La cuina modernista*, 22–23. Néstor Luján points out that even though the origin of *fricandó* (a cooking method applied to different dishes since the sixteenth century) is French, it has clearly adapted Catalan traits (like the *canelons*) and has become, thanks to the creativity of the region's cooking, a popular dish. *Diccionari Luján de gastronomía catalana*, 79.

160. Fàbrega, *La cuina modernista*, 23.

161. *Sofregit* allows for variations, but its main ingredient is onions slowly cooked until melted. It is a recipe that already appears in some form in the medieval text *Sent Soví* and is a classic Catalan start to many dishes. We discuss the sauce more extensively in chapter 6.

162. Fàbrega, *La cuina modernista*, 23–24.

163. *La cuynera catalana*, facsimile edition of 1851 (Barcelona: Maxtor, 2010). The title follows the original Catalan, prior to the standardization of its modern spelling.

164. *La cuynera catalana*, 9–10.

165. M. Carme Queralt, ed., *La cuinera catalana. Regles útils, fàcils, segures i economiques per cuinar bé. Receptari anónim del segle XIX* (Valls, Spain: Cossetània Edicions, 2009), 12–13.

166. Moyano Andrés, "La cocina escrita," 29–30.

167. Inés Butrón, *Comer en España: De la subsistencia a la vanguardia* (Barcelona: Península, 2011), 80.

168. *Teca* means "meal" in colloquial Catalan.

169. Lara Anderson, *Cooking Up the Nation: Spanish Culinary Texts and Culinary Nationalization in the Late Nineteenth and Early Twentieth Century* (Suffolk: Boydell and Brewer, 2013).

170. Rebecca Ingram, "Mapping and Mocking: Spanish Cuisine and Ramón Gómez de La Serna's 'El primer mapa gastronómico de España,'" *Cincinnati Romance Review* 33 (Winter 2012): 78–97.

171. Dionisio Pérez, *Guía del buen comer español* (Madrid: Patronato Nacional de Turismo, 1929). Néstor Luján criticizes Pérez for "over-Castilianizing" the gastronomic history of the Iberian Peninsula (*Vint segles de cuina catalana*, 55–56).

CHAPTER 4

1. Information obtained from https://ajuntament.barcelona.cat/comerc/ca/directori-de-comerc/mercats-municipals, accessed August 9, 2018.

2. The Santa Caterina market reopened in 2005 after undergoing an extensive renovation that started in the late 1990s.

3. Nadia Fava, Manel Guàrdia, and José Luis Oyón, "Barcelona Food Retailing and Public Markets, 1876–1936," *Urban History* 43, no. 3 (2016): 455.

4. Manuel Guàrdia i Bassols and José Luis Oyón, "Introduction: European Markets As Makers of Cities," in *Making Cities through Market Halls: Europe, 19th and 20th Centuries* (Barcelona: Ajuntament de Barcelona, Institut de Cultura Museu d'Història de Barcelona, 2015), 11.

5. Manuel Guàrdia i Bassols, José Luis Oyón, and Nadia Fava, "The Barcelona Market System," in *Making Cities through Market Halls Europe, 19th and 20th Centuries* (Barcelona: Ajuntament de Barcelona and Institut de Cultura Museu d'Història de Barcelona, 2015), 262.

6. The rebellion started during the St. James's holiday, which was celebrated with a bullfight. Historians have explained that the uprising took a strong anticlerical sentiment because of a previous military incident during which some Catalan army volunteers were slaughtered in Reus. There had been rumors that members of the clergy had participated in the cruel killing of the soldiers. After the unsatisfactory bullfight, the crowd started booing and throwing wooden benches into the arena, which they then entered to kill the bulls. Their anger not satisfied, a mob was quickly formed and marched down Las Ramblas burning down convents.

7. Montserrat Miller, "Mercats noucentistas de Barcelona: Una interpretació dels seus orígens i significant cultural," *Revista de l'Alguer* 4 (December 1993): 94.

8. Miller, "Mercats noucentistas de Barcelona," 94–95.

9. Miller, "Mercats noucentistas de Barcelona," 95.

10. Miller, "Mercats noucentistas de Barcelona," 95–96.

11. Carme Batlle i Gallart, *Fires i mercats. Factors de dinamisme econòmic i centres de dociabilitat (Segles XI a XV)* (Barcelona: Rafael Dalmau, Editor, 2004), 10.

12. Batlle i Gallart, *Fires i mercats*, 11.

13. Batlle i Gallart, *Fires i mercats*, 26–30.

14. Batlle i Gallart, *Fires i mercats*, 100–102.

15. Batlle i Gallart, *Fires i mercats*, 18.

16. Miller, "Mercats noucentistas de Barcelona," 97.

17. Miller, "Mercats noucentistas de Barcelona," 98–99.

18. Miller, "Mercats noucentistas de Barcelona," 97.

19. Guàrdia i Bassols, Oyón, and Fava, "The Barcelona Market System," 276.

20. Miller, "Mercats noucentistas de Barcelona," 97–98.

21. Guàrdia i Bassols, Oyón, and Fava, "The Barcelona Market System," 262.

22. Guàrdia i Bassols, Oyón, and Fava, "The Barcelona Market System," 262.

23. Genís Arnàs and Matilde Alsina, *Mercats de Barcelona (Segle XIX)* (Barcelona: Alberí Editor; Ajuntament de Barcelona, 2016), 52.

24. Arnàs and Alsina, *Mercats de Barcelona*, 70–77.

25. Guàrdia i Bassols, Oyón, and Fava, "The Barcelona Market System," 263.

26. Miller, "Mercats noucentistas de Barcelona," 99.

27. However, the idea for the avenue was not forgotten; the plan was floated again as late as 1907 without success.

28. Arnàs and Alsina, *Mercats de Barcelona*, 52–56.

29. Arnàs and Alsina, *Mercats de Barcelona*, 49–51.

30. Guàrdia i Bassols, Oyón, and Fava, "The Barcelona Market System," 267–68.

31. Guàrdia i Bassols, Oyón, and Fava, "The Barcelona Market System," 264.

32. Guàrdia i Bassols, Oyón, and Fava, "The Barcelona Market System," 269.

33. Guàrdia i Bassols, Oyón, and Fava, "The Barcelona Market System," 270.

34. Guàrdia i Bassols, Oyón, and Fava, "The Barcelona Market System," 273.

35. Núria Bàguena i Maranges, *Cuinar i menjar a Barcelona (1850–1900)* (Barcelona: CIM Edicions, 2007), 27–28.

36. Bàguena i Maranges, *Cuinar i menjar a Barcelona*, 28.

37. Bàguena i Maranges, *Cuinar i menjar a Barcelona*, 28.

38. Bàguena i Maranges, *Cuinar i menjar a Barcelona*, 30–31.

39. Fava, Guàrdia, and Oyón, "Barcelona Food Retailing and Public Markets," 457.

40. Jaume Fàbrega, *La cuina modernista* (Barcelona: Viena Edicions, 2015), 29.

41. Fàbrega, *La cuina modernista*, 29.

42. Fàbrega, *La cuina modernista*, 29.

43. Bàguena i Maranges, *Cuinar i menjar a Barcelona*, 37–38.

44. Bàguena i Maranges, *Cuinar i menjar a Barcelona*, 38.

45. Bàguena i Maranges, *Cuinar i menjar a Barcelona*, 38–39.

46. The word *queviures* means "edibles" in Catalan. In Spanish, it designates food shops, and according to the Catalan linguist Joan Coromines, its use comes from Andalusia. The meaning could refer to the adjectives "plentiful" or "complete." Inés Butrón follows the history of these shops in her recently published *Colmados de Barcelona: Historia de una revolución comestible* (Barcelona: SD Ediciones, 2019).

47. Bàguena i Maranges, *Cuinar i menjar a Barcelona*, 40. Another name for them were *mantequerias* (*manteca* means "lard").

48. Lluís Permanyer, "El Colmado de Juan Nepomuceno Conde Núñez," *La Vanguardia*, December 16, 2001.

49. Lluís Permanyer, "El Colmado cobró otra dimensión con Martignole." *La Vanguardia*, December 30, 2001.

50. Néstor Luján explains that the *neula*, a wafer that was consumed in the eleventh century, was not rolled until the 1800s. Its name comes from the Latin word *nebula*, "fog," and refers to its light texture. Néstor Luján, *Vint segles de cuina a Barcelona. De les ostres de Barcino als restaurants d'avui* (Barcelona: Folio, 1993), 32.

51. Bàguena i Maranges, *Cuinar i menjar a Barcelona*, 40.

52. Cristina Jolonch, "Los últimos colmados antiguos ya son auténticas reliquias," *La Vanguardia*, February 5, 2017, www.lavanguardia.com/comer/si tios/20170204/413976189543/colmados-antiguos-barcelona-cierres.html, accessed August 23, 2018.

53. Montserrat Miller, *Feeding Barcelona 1714–1975: Public Market Halls, Social Networks, and Consumer Culture* (Baton Rouge: Louisiana University Press, 2015), 80.

54. Miller, *Feeding Barcelona*, 80–81.

55. Miller, *Feeding Barcelona*, 81.

56. Danielle Provansal and Melba Levick, *El mercats de Barcelona* (Barcelona: Ajuntament de Barcelona, 1992), 213–14.

57. Miller, *Feeding Barcelona*, 47.

58. Miller, *Feeding Barcelona*, 47.

59. Miller, *Feeding Barcelona*, 48.

60. Miller, *Feeding Barcelona*, 12.

61. Miller, *Feeding Barcelona*, 12.

62. Fava, Guàrdia, and Oyón, "Barcelona Food Retailing and Public Markets," 461.

63. Miller, *Feeding Barcelona*, 81; Manuel Guàrdia, José Luis Oyón, and Nadia Fava, "De mercado de barrio a mercado central: Trabajo, parentesco y proximidad en torno al Mercado del Born, 1876–1971," *Zainak* 36 (2013): 236.

64. Chris Ealham, *Class, Culture, and Conflict in Barcelona, 1898–1937*, Routledge/Cañada Blanch Studies on Contemporary Spain (London: Routledge, 2005), 105. Also, Bàguena, *Cuinar i menjar a Barcelona*, 37.

65. Fava, Guàrdia, and Oyón, "Barcelona Food Retailing and Public Markets," 461. Miller narrates one of these events: the 1930 festivities that included a cavalcade around the city and a grand market ball. Her detailed account about how the beauty queens representing different markets were elected and the various interests at play in the organization of these events offers a captivating view of the functioning of markets and their social and political significance in Barcelona (*Feeding Barcelona*, 1–26).

66. Fava, Guàrdia, and Oyón, "Barcelona Food Retailing and Public Markets," 461–62; Guàrdia, Oyón, and Fava, "De mercado de barrio a mercado central," 237–38.

67. Guàrdia i Bassols, Oyón, and Fava, "The Barcelona Market System," 279.

68. Temma Kaplan, "Female Consciousness and Collective Action: The Case of Barcelona, 1910–1918," *Signs* 7, no. 3 (1982): 560–64.

69. Guàrdia i Bassols, Oyón, and Fava, "The Barcelona Market System," 279–80.

70. Guàrdia, Oyón, and Fava, "De mercado de barrio a mercado central," 238. The Spanish Civil War marked a painful time in the history of Barcelona's markets. In addition to the problems in the supply and distribution of food during the struggle, the purge by Francoists to eliminate civil servants and merchants who belonged to the Spanish Republic decimated the markets (Guàrdia i Bassols, Oyón and Fava, "The Barcelona Market System," 287).

71. The website for Mercabarna (www.mercabarna.es/en/) offers useful information about its services, including downloadable reports that identify food purchasing trends in the city and its markets.

72. The gastronomy campaign on the commemoration of the 1714 siege is examined in a forthcoming article, "*Catalanidad* in the Kitchen: Tourism, Gastronomy and Identity in Modern Contemporary Barcelona" by Leigh K. Mercer and H. Rosi Song for the *Bulletin of Spanish Studies* (Glasgow, UK) in 2019. Two of the cookbooks that were published are Jaume Fàgrega's *La cuina del 1714. Història i receptes* (Barcelona: Viena, 2014) and *La cuina del 1714* (Barcelona: Comanegra, 2014). The second book is the collective work of Catalan chefs who offer a modernized version of the traditional dishes.

73. https://elpais.com/ccaa/2017/03/25/catalunya/1490467101_590414.html, accessed August 28, 2018.

74. The Palau Robert had an exhibit on the history of the Roca brothers and their restaurant between 2016 and 2017 called "El Celler de Can Roca from the Earth to the Moon" and one about Ferran Adrià and his elBulli foundation in 2014. Informa-

tion about both exhibits can be found at http://palaurobert.gencat.cat/en/exposicions/ historic/historicSala3/2016/elceller/ and http://palaurobert.gencat.cat/en/exposicions/ historic/historicSala3/2014/2014s3_1_elbullifoundation/, accessed August 28, 2018.

75. The set menu could be linked to the cheap meals served in the nineteenth century, but the current form of the *menú del día* derives from an ordinance during the Franco dictatorship in the 1960s to attract tourists to Spain. It required food establishments to offer a daily fixed menu at an affordable price. The popularity of the daily menu is strong (after its identification with the menu for poor people was shed), and its price and quality varies greatly across the country.

76. Montserrat Crespi-Vallbona and Darko Dimitrovski, "Food Markets from a Local Dimension: La Boqueria (Barcelona, Spain)," *Cities* 70 (2017): 32.

77. From http://ajuntament.barcelona.cat/mercats/ca/noticia/el-mercat-de-santa -caterina-regularza-lacczss-de-grups-de-visitants, accessed August 9, 2018.

78. The group runs some of the most popular restaurants in Barcelona and in other cities, including Madrid: in the Eixample area—Tragaluz, El Japonés, Mordisco, Tomate, Fan Ho; in Diagonal—Rojo, Negro; in the Gothic Quarter—Bar Lobo, Cuines Santa Caterina, Luzia; and on the beach—Agua, Bestial, and Pez Vela.

79. Guàrdia i Bassols and Oyón, "Introduction: European Markets as Makers of Cities," 70.

80. Guàrdia i Bassols and Oyón, "Introduction: European Markets as Makers of Cities," 71.

81. Guàrdia i Bassols and Oyón, "Introduction: European Markets as Makers of Cities," 70.

82. The history behind these renovations are documented in the second volume on Barcelona markets published by Genís Arnàs and Matilde Alsina, *Mercats de Barcelona (Segle XX i XXI)*, (Barcelona: Alberí Editor; Ajuntament de Barcelona, 2018).

83. Ajuntament de Barcelona, *Markets: The Barcelona Experience* (Barcelona: Ajuntament de Barcelona, 2015), 7. The publication was prepared as part of the ninth International Public Markets Conference held in Barcelona on March 26–28, 2015. Information about the conference can be found here: https://publicmarkets. pps.org/9th-international-public-markets-conference, accessed December 19, 2018.

84. Arnàs and Alsina, *Mercats de Barcelona*, 61–62.

CHAPTER 5

1. The popular Italian Inspector Montalbano, created by Andrea Camilleri, is directly linked to Vázquez Montalbán, who gives his name to the detective. An-

other popular police detective, Mario Conde, created by the Cuban writer Leonardo Padura, is also greatly influenced by the Pepe Carvalho series. In the case of the Cuban detective, he continually dreams of food rather than eating it because of the island's food scarcity.

2. Carvalho travels to Catalonia and other parts of Spain, eating his way around the country. He also solves crimes abroad like in Buenos Aires and Bangkok. His (mis)adventures eventually lead him to travel around the world while running away from justice.

3. A sample of an itinerary can be found here: www.amigosbarcelona.com/articulo/excursiones-y-rutas-para-conocer-barcelona#la-ruta-de-pepe-carvalho, accessed August 28, 2018.

4. Néstor Luján, *Vint segles de cuina a Barcelona. De les ostres de Barcino als restaurants d'avui* (Barcelona: Folio, 1993), 151–52.

5. Inés Butrón documents the culinary landscape in Spain during these years of hunger in *Comer en España. De la subsistencia a la vanguardia* (Barcelona: Ediciones Península, 2011).

6. Carmen Casas, *Barcelona a la carta. Guia de restaurantes, historia y recetario* (Barcelona: Laia, 1981), 15–16.

7. Casas, *Barcelona a la carta*, 4.

8. Marisol García, "Barcelona: Ciudadanos y visitantes," in *La metaciudad: Barcelona. Transformación de una metrópolis*, ed. Mónica Degen and Marisol García (Barcelona: Anthropos, 2008), 100.

9. Manuel Vázquez Montalbán, *Barcelonas*, trans. Andy Robinson (London: Verso, 1992), 194.

10. Vázquez Montalbán, *Barcelonas*, 197.

11. Casas, *Barcelona a la carta*, 18–19.

12. Manuel Vázquez Montalbán, *Saber or no saber. Manual imprescindible de la cultura gastronómica*, Carvalho Gastronómico 1 (Barcelona: Zeta, n.d.), 181.

13. Néstor Luján, *Diccionari Luján de gastronomia catalana* (Barcelona: Edicions La campana, 1990), 142.

14. Cristina Jolonch, "Vuelve Casa Leopoldo," *La Vanguardia*, March 9, 2017, www.lavanguardia.com/comer/sitios/20170311/42748026893/reapertura-restaurante-casa-leopoldo-barcelona.html, accessed August 20, 2018.

15. Néstor Luján, *Vint segles de cuina a Barcelona*, 165–67.

16. The restaurant website offers a dossier of its history, available at this link: www.culleretes.com/wp-content/uploads/2016/12/CANCULLERETES_PRESSKIT_ENG.pdf, accessed August 27, 2018.

17. Luján, *Vint segles de cuina a Barcelona*, 171. Luján was married to Paquita's daughter and therefore related to the owners of two of the most emblematic restaurants of the city, Agut and Can Culleretes.

18. Enric González, "Una declaración de amor," *El País*, April 26, 2009, https://elpais.com/diario/2009/04/26/domingo/1240716637_850215.html.

19. Segi Doria, "El restaurante de las estrellas cumple 180 años," *ABC*, December 17, 2015, www.abc.es/espana/catalunya/gente-estilo/abci-caracoles-restaurante-estrellas-cumple-180-anos-201512171653_noticia.html.

20. Luján, *Vint segles de cuina a Barcelona*, 171–72.

21. www.restaurantgaig.com/en/history/, accessed September 1, 2018.

CHAPTER 6

1. Colman Andrews, *Catalan Cuisine: Europe's Last Great Culinary Secret* (Boston: Harvard Common Press, 1999), 187–88.

2. Néstor Luján, *Diccionari Luján de gastronomia catalana* (Barcelona: Edicions La campana, 1990), 9–11.

3. Joan Roca, *Roots: Essential Catalan Cuisine According to El Celler de Can Roca*, translated by Adriana Acevedo Alemán (Librooks, 2012), loc. 149 of 2022, Kindle.

4. Luján, *Diccionari Luján de gastronomia catalana*, 161.

5. Ferran Agulló, *Llibre de la cuina catalana*, 9th ed. (Barcelona: Editorial Alta Fulla, 1999), 25.

6. Jaume Fàbrega, *L'essencia de la cuina catalana* (Barcelona: Comanegra, 2013), 23.

7. Luján, Diccionari *Luján de gastronomia catalana*, 124.

8. Luján, Diccionari *Luján de gastronomia catalana*, 124.

9. Manuel Vázquez Montalbán, *L'art del menjar a Catalunya. El libre roig de la identitat gastronómica catalana* (Barcelona: Salsa Books, 2004), 237.

10. Andrews, *Catalan Cuisine*, 129.

11. Fàbrega, *L'essencia de la cuina catalana*, 29.

12. Agulló, *Llibre de La cuina catalana*, 30–31.

13. Fàbrega, *L'essencia de la cuina catalana*, 29–30.

14. A detailed explanation of the dish (in Spanish) can be found at the following website: www.afuegolento.com/articulos/474/jornadas-gastronomicas-alrededor-de-un-plato-el-niu-el-nido. Curiously, the recipe on the site uses tomatoes in the *sofregit*. Accessed August 1, 2018.

15. Manuel Vázquez Montalbán, *Carvalho Gourmet. Las recetas de Carvalho*, vol. 3 (Barcelona: Planeta, 2012), 119.

16. Fàbrega, *L'essencia de la cuina catalana*, 133.

17. Luján, *Diccionari Luján de gastronomia catalana*, 33.

18. Andrews, *Catalan Cuisine*, 88.

19. Andrews, *Catalan Cuisine*, 88–89.

20. Agulló, *Llibre de la cuina catalana*, 31.

21. Luján, *Diccionari Luján de gastronomia catalana*, 150–51.

22. Luján, *Diccionari Luján de gastronomia catalana*, 22.

23. Andrews, *Catalan Cuisine*, 226.

24. Fàbrega, *L'essencia de la cuina catalana*, 236.

25. Luján, *Diccionari Luján de gastronomia catalana*, 129–30.

26. Cruaña's obituary provides information about his career as a restauranteur: www.thedailymeal.com/eat/influential-catalan-restaurateur-llu-s-crua-dies-79, accessed August 22, 2018. Information about the opening of his New York City restaurant can be found here: www.nytimes.com/1991/09/06/arts/restaurants-611891.html, accessed August 22, 2018.

27. The origins of both the dish and the sauce are debated, but the sauce is supposedly based on the *sauce américaine* that accompanied a lobster dish created in the late nineteenth century by a French cook who had spent time in the United States (https://es.wikipedia.org/wiki/Salsa_americana, accessed August 22, 2018). The *salsa americana* recipe is in Rondissoni's cookbook, which describes it as a classic sauce used in the preparation of shellfish dishes. Manel Guirado, *El llegat de Rondissoni* (Barcelona: Ara Llibres, 2017), 274–75.

28. Vázquez Montalbán, *L'art del menjar a Catalunya*, 233–34.

29. Luján, *Diccionari Luján de gastronomia catalana*, 61.

30. Luján, *Diccionari Luján de gastronomia catalana*, 40–41.

31. Josep Lladonosa i Giró, *Plats amb història: Vivències i opinions* (Barcelona: Editorial Empúries, 2003), 23–24.

32. Suzanne Goin, *The A.O.C. Cookbook* (New York: Alfred A. Knopf, 2013), 57.

33. Luján, *Diccionari Luján de gastronomia catalana*, 63–64.

34. Andrews, *Catalan Cuisine*, 247.

35. Institut Català de la Cuina, *Corpus del patrimoni culinari català* (Barcelona: RBA La Magrana, 2016), 263.

36. Joan Santanach, *Llibre d'aparellar de menjar* (Barcelona: Editorial Barcino, n.d.), 159.

37. The Catalan version of the French *bon appétit* or the Spanish *buen provecho*.

Bibliography

Adamson, Melitta Weiss. *Food in Medieval Times*. Westport, CT: Greenwood Press, 2004.

Adrià, Ferran. *elBulli: El sabor del mediterráneo*. Barcelona: Ed. Empúries, 1993.

Agulló, Ferran. *Llibre de la cuina catalana*. 9th ed. Barcelona: Editorial Alta Fulla, 1999.

Ajuntament de Barcelona. *Markets: The Barcelona Experience*. Barcelona: Ajuntament de Barcelona, 2015.

Albala, Ken, ed. *The Food History Reader: Primary Sources*. London: Bloomsbury Academic, 2014.

Anderson, Lara. *Cooking Up the Nation: Spanish Culinary Texts and Culinary Nationalization in the Late Nineteenth and Early Twentieth Century*. Suffolk: Boydell and Brewer, 2013.

Andrews, Colman. "Influential Catalan Restaurateur Lluís Cruañas Dies at 79." *The Daily Meal*, November 18, 2016. Accessed August 22, 2018. www.thedaily meal.com/eat/influential-catalan-restaurateur-llu-s-crua-dies-79.

———. *Ferran: The Inside Story of El Bulli and the Man Who Reinvented Food*. New York: Gotham, 2010.

———. *Catalan Cuisine: Europe's Last Great Culinary Secret*. Boston, MA: Harvard Common Press, 1999.

Arenós, Pau. *La cocina de los valientes*. Barcelona: Ediciones B, 2011.

Arnàs, Genís, and Matilde Alsina. *Mercats de Barcelona (segles XX i XXI)*. Barcelona: Alberí Editor; Ajuntament de Barcelona, 2018.

———. *Mercats de Barcelona (segle XIX)*. Barcelona: Alberí Editor; Ajuntament de Barcelona, 2016.

Bàguena i Maranges, Núria. *Cuinar i menjar a Barcelona (1850–1900)*. Barcelona: CIM Edicions, 2007.

Balcells, Albert. *Catalan Nationalism: Past and Present*. Edited by Geoffrey J. Walker. Translated by Jacqueline Hall. New York: St. Martin's Press, 1996.

Baliu, Glòria, and Ignasi Riera. *La cuina del XVIII*. Barcelona: Sd Edicions, 2003.

Batlle i Gallart, Carme. *Fires i mercats. Factors de dinamisme econòmic i centres de sociabilitat (segles XI a XV)*. Barcelona: Rafael Dalmau, Editor, 2004.

Berasaluce, José. *El engaño de la gastronomía española*. Gijón, Spain: Trea, 2018.

"Biografía del restaurador Ramón Cabau Guasch, un suicida en el mercado de la Boquería de Barcelona." *Historia de la cocina y la gastronomía*. Accessed September 6, 2018. www.historiacocina.com/es/ramon-cabau.

Butrón, Inés. *Colmados de Barcelona: Historia de una revolución comestible*. Barcelona: SD Edicions, 2019.

———. *Comer en España: De la subsistencia a la vanguardia*. Barcelona: Península, 2011.

Can Culleretes press kit. Accessed September 1, 2018. www.culleretes.com/wp-content/uploads/2016/12/CANCULLERETES_PREfSSKIT_ENG.pdf.

Casas, Carmen. "Gran éxito de Ferran Adrià en el VII Congreso de Cocina de Autor." *Vanguardia*, March 28, 1998.

———. *Barcelona a la carta. Guía de restaurantes, historia y recetario*. Barcelona: Laia, 1981.

Castells, Irene Castells. "Els rebomboris del pa de 1789 a Barcelona." *Recerques: història, economia, cultura*, no. 1 (1970): 51–81.

Chabrán, Rafael. "Medieval Spain." In *Regional Cuisines of Medieval Europe: A Book of Essays*, edited by Melitta Weiss Adamson, 125–52. New York: Routledge, 2002.

Cia, Blanca. "Toda una vida en el Born." *El País*. March 25, 2017. Accessed August 28, 2018. https://elpais.com/ccaa/2017/03/25/catalunya/1490467101_590414.html.

Collins, Lauren. "Ranking the World's Best Restaurants." *New Yorker*, October 26, 2015. Accessed September 8, 2018. www.newyorker.com/magazine/2015/11/02/whos-to-judge.

Conde, Rafael. "Alimentación y sociedad: Las cuentas de Guillema de Montcada (A.D. 1189)." *Medievalia. Revista de estudios medievales* 3 (1982): 7–21.

Corcuera, Mikel. *25 años de la nueva cocina vasca*. Bilbao: Aizkorri, 2003.

Cornet y Mas, Cayetano. *Guía completa del viajero en Barcelona*. Barcelona: I. López Editor—Librería Española, 1866.

Coroleu, José. *Barcelona y sus alrededores. Guía histórica, descriptiva y estadística del forastero*. Barcelona: Jaime Seix, 1887.

Crespi-Vallbona, Montserrat, and Darko Dimitrovski. "Food Markets from a Local Dimension: La Boqueria (Barcelona, Spain)." *Cities* 70 (2017): 32–39.

Curnow, Robyn. "Science Creates Gastronomic Storm." *CNN*, June 27, 2005. Accessed September 7, 2018. edition.cnn.com/2005/TECH/06/27/spark.elbulli/index.html.

Davidson, Alan. *National & Regional Styles of Cookery: Proceedings: Oxford Symposium 1981*. Oxford Symposium, 1981.

Davidson, Robert. "Barcelona: The Siege City." In *A Companion to Catalan Culture*, edited by Dominic Keown, 97–116. Woodbridge, Suffolk: Tamesis, 2011.

Direcció General de Turisme. Generalitat de Catalunya. *Congrés català de la cuina*. Barcelona: Departament de Comerç i Turisme, 1982.

"Disfrutar." *The World's 50 Best Restaurants*. Accessed September 11, 2018. www.theworlds50best.com/The-List-2018/11-20/Disfrutar.html#.

Doria, Sergi. "El restaurante de las estrellas cumple 180 años." *ABC*, December 17, 2015. Accessed September 1, 2018. www.abc.es/espana/catalunya/gente-estilo/abci-caracoles-restaurante-estrellas-cumple-180-anos-201512171653_noticia.html.

Dwyer, Chris. "10 Best New Restaurants of 2016." *CNN Travel*. Accessed March 15, 2018. https://edition.cnn.com/travel/article/best-new-restaurants/index.html.

Ealham, Chris. *Class, Culture, and Conflict in Barcelona, 1898–1937*. Routledge/Cañada Blanch Studies on Contemporary Spain. London: Routledge, 2005.

Fabre, Jaume, and Josep M. Huertas. *Cent anys de vida quotidiana a Catalunya. Del fogó de carbó a l'antena parabòlica*. Barcelona: Edicions 62, 1993.

Fàbrega, Jaume. *La cuina modernista*. Barcelona: Viena Edicions, 2015.

———. *La cuina del 1714. Història i Receptes*. Barcelona: Viena Edicions, 2014.

———. *L'essencia de la cuina catalana*. Barcelona: Comanegra, 2013.

Falcones, Ildefonso. *Cathedral of the Sea: A Novel*. New York: New American Library, 2014.

Fancelli, Agustí. "El mejor cocinero del mundo." *El País Semanal*, November 27, 2011. Accessed August 3, 2018. https://elpais.com/diario/2011/11/27/eps/1322378823_850215.html.

Fantozzi, Joanna. "Surprises in Ranking for Daniel, Jean-Georges, and David Chang as Second Half of World's 100 Best Restaurants Announced." *The Daily Meal*, May 26, 2015. Accessed September 8, 2018. www.thedailymeal.com/

news/eat/daniel-drops-out-pellegrino-s-world-s-50-best-restaurants-second-half
-top-100-announced/052615.

Fava, Nadia, Manel Guàrdia, and José Luis Oyón. "Barcelona Food Retailing and
Public Markets, 1876–1936." *Urban History* 43, no. 3 (2016): 454–75.

Fernández de Castro, David. *Barcelona i el vi*. Barcelona: Editorial Mediterrània, 2017.

Fernández Guadaño, Marta. "Y por último, un Melocotón Melba." *Diario Expansión*, July 27, 2011. Accessed September 8, 2018. www.fueradeserie.expansion
.com/2011/07/29/gastroteca/1311935604.html.

Fernández-Armesto, Felipe. *Barcelona: A Thousand Years of the City's Past*. Oxford: Oxford University Press, 1992.

García, Marisol. "Barcelona: Ciudadanos y visitantes." In *La metaciudad: Barcelona. Transformación de una metrópolis*, edited by Mónica Degen and Marisol
García, 97–113. Barcelona: Anthropos, 2008.

García del Real, Luciano. *Barcelona. Guía Diamante*. Barcelona: Librería de Francisco Puig, 1896.

Garcia Espuche, Albert. *Barcelona 1700*. Barcelona: Editorial Empúries, 2010.

Giesey, Ralph E. *If Not, Not: The Oath of the Aragonese and the Legendary Laws
of Sobrarbe*. Princeton, NJ: Princeton University Press, 1968.

Goin, Suzanne. *The A.O.C. Cookbook*. New York: Alfred A. Knopf, 2013.

González, Enric. "Una declaración de amor." *El País*, April 26, 2009. Accessed September 4, 2018. https://elpais.com/diario/2009/04/26/domingo/
1240716637_850215.html.

Govan, Fiona. "Santi Santamaria's Death Brings End to Feud with Ferran Adria."
The Telegraph, February 18, 2011. Accessed September 14, 2018. www.telegraph
.co.uk/foodanddrink/8331823/Santi-Santamarias-death-brings-end-to-feud-with
-Ferran-Adria.html.

Graff, James. "The 2004 Time 100." *Time*, April 26, 2004. Accessed September 9, 2018. http://content.time.com/time/specials/packages/article/0,28804,197
0858_1970890_1971358,00.html.

Grewe, Rudolf. "Catalan Cuisine, in a Historical Perspective." In *National and Regional Styles of Cookery. Oxford Symposium 1981 Proceedings*, edited by Alan
Davidson, 170–78. London: Prospect Books, 1981.

Grewe, Rudolf, ed. *Llibre de Sent Soví: Receptari de cuina*. Barcelona: Editorial
Barcino, 1979.

Guàrdia i Bassols, Manuel, and José Luis Oyón. "Introduction: European Markets
As Makers of Cities." In *Making Cities through Market Halls Europe, 19th and
20th Centuries*, 11–71. Barcelona: Ajuntament de Barcelona, Institut de Cultura
Museu d'Història de Barcelona, 2015.

————. *Making Cities through Market Halls Europe, 19th and 20th Centuries*. Barcelona: Ajuntament de Barcelona, Institut de Cultura Museu d'Història de Barcelona, 2015.

Guàrdia i Bassols, Manuel, José Luis Oyón, and Nadia Fava. "The Barcelona Market System." In *Making Cities through Market Halls Europe, 19th and 20th Centuries*, 261–96. Barcelona: Ajuntament de Barcelona, Institut de Cultura Museu d'Història de Barcelona, 2015.

————. "De mercado de barrio a mercado central: Trabajo, parentesco y proximidad en torno al Mercado del Born, 1876–1971." *Zainak* 36 (2013): 231–46.

Guirado, Manel. *El llegat de Rondissoni*. Barcelona: SOM Ara Llibres, 2017.

Gutiérrez, Sonia. "David Andrés: 'Forbes ha valorado el esfuerzo y la valentía de emprender.'" *El Periódico*, January 16, 2017. Accessed September 5, 2018. www .elperiodico.com/es/extra/20170116/david-andres-lista-forbes-jovenes-lideres -futuro-5747221.

Hernàndez Cardona, Francesc Xavier. *Barcelona & Catalunya. Història d'un binomi*. Barcelona: Rafael Dalmau, 2017.

"History." *Restaurant Gaig* (blog). Accessed September 1, 2018. www.restaurant gaig.com/en/history/.

Houck, Brenna. "Willy Wonka Could Have Designed This Barcelona Restaurant." *Eater*, January 23, 2017. Accessed September 11, 2018. www.eater .com/2017/1/23/14342014/enigma-restaurant-barcelona-albert-adria-open.

Hughes, Robert. *Barcelona*. New York: Vintage Books, 1993.

Ingram, Rebecca. "Mapping and Mocking: Spanish Cuisine and Ramón Gómez de la Serna's 'El primer mapa gastronómico de España.'" *Cincinnati Romance Review* 33 (Winter 2012): 78–97.

Institut Català de la Cuina. *Corpus del patrimoni culinari català*. Barcelona: RBA La Magrana, 2016.

Jolonch, Cristina. "Paco Pérez: 'Haber avanzado por el camino que abrió *El Bulli* no es copiar.'" *La Vanguardia*, December 16, 2018. Accessed December 15, 2018. www.lavanguardia.com/comer/de-carne-hueso/20181216/453531899335/ entrevista-paco-perez-cocinero.html.

————. "Los Hermanos Torres abren el restaurante de sus sueños." *La Vanguardia*, June 30, 2018. Accessed September 11, 2018. www.lavanguardia.com/comer/sitios /20180630/45485068710/cocina-hermanos-torres-les-corts-restaurante.html.

————. "El Restaurante Semproniana cumple 25 años." *La Vanguardia*, January 26, 2018. Accessed December 2, 2018. www.lavanguardia.com/comer/sitios /20180127/44294763440/semproniana-ada-parellada-cumple-25-anos.html.

———. "Carles Abellán lleva su tapeo a La Diagonal." *La Vanguardia*, December 23, 2017. Accessed September 11, 2018. www.lavanguardia.com/local/barcelona/20171223/433827427561/carles-abellan-lleva-su-tapeo-a-la-diagonal.html.

———. "Vuelve Casa Leopoldo." *La Vanguardia*, March 9, 2017. Accessed September 1, 2018. www.lavanguardia.com/comer/sitios/20170311/42748026893/reapertura-restaurante-casa-leopoldo-barcelona.html.

———. "Los últimos colmados antiguos ya son auténticas reliquias." *La Vanguardia*, February 5, 2017. Accessed August 13, 2018. www.lavanguardia.com/comer/sitios/20170204/413976189543/colmados-antiguos-barcelona-cierres.html.

Kamen, Henry. "A Forgotten Insurrection of the Seventeenth Century: The Catalan Peasant Rising of 1688." *The Journal of Modern History* 49, no. 2 (1977): 210–30.

Kaplan, Temma. "Female Consciousness and Collective Action: The Case of Barcelona, 1910–1918." *Signs* 7, no. 3 (1982): 545–66.

La cuina del 1714. Receptas actualitzades. Una ruta gastronòmica a través de la nostra història. Barcelona: Comanegra, 2014.

La cuynera catalana. Facsimile edition of 1851. Barcelona: Maxtor, 2010.

Lladonosa i Giró, Josep. *Plats amb història: Vivències i opinions.* Barcelona: Editorial Empúries, 2003.

Lo, Karen. "Petition Calls World's 50 Best Restaurants Awards Sexist, Self-Pleasing, and Lacking Sanitary Criteria." *The Daily Meal*, May 21, 2015. Accessed September 8, 2018. www.thedailymeal.com/news/eat/petition-calls-world-s-50-best-restaurants-awards-sexist-self-pleasing-and-lacking-sanitary/52115.

Lubow, Arthur. "A Laboratory of Taste." *New York Times*, August 10, 2003. Accessed September 7, 2018. www.nytimes.com/2003/08/10/magazine/a-laboratory-of-taste.html.

Luján, Néstor. *Vint segles de cuina a Barcelona. De les ostres de Barcino als restaurants d'avui.* Barcelona: Folio, 1993.

———. *Diccionari Luján de gastronomia catalana.* Barcelona: Edicions La campana, 1990.

Marín, Manuela. "From Al-Andalus to Spain: Arab Traces in Spanish Cooking." *Food & History* 2, no. 2 (2004): 35–52.

Martí de Sola, Modesto. *Barcelona y su provincia. Guía-itinerario descriptiva, estadística y pintoresca.* Barcelona: Establecimiento tipográfico "La Academia," 1888.

Massanés, Toni, and David Ortiz Ripoll. *From the Earth to the Moon.* Barcelona: Generalitat de Catalunya, 2016.

Mendoza, Cristina. "Quatre Gats and the Origins of Picasso's Career." In *Barcelona and Modernity: Picasso, Gaudí, Miró, Dalí*, edited by William H. Robinson, Carmen Belen Lord, and Jordi Falgàs, 80–91. New Haven, CT: Yale University Press, 2007.

Mendoza, Eduardo. *The Truth about the Salvota Case*. London: Harville Press, 1993.

———. *City of Marvels*. Translated by Bernard Molloy. London: Harvill Press, 1990.

Menocal, Maria Rosa. *The Ornament of the World: How Muslims, Jews, and Christians Created a Culture of Tolerance in Medieval Spain*. Boston: Little, Brown, 2002.

Miller, Bryan. "Restaurants." *New York Times*, September 6, 1991. Accessed August 22, 2018. www.nytimes.com/1991/09/06/arts/restaurants-611891.html.

Miller, Montserrat. "Monográficos." *Historia de la cocina y la gastronomía*. Accessed July 27, 2018. www.historiacocina.com/es/monograficos-2.

———. *Feeding Barcelona 1714–1975: Public Market Halls, Social Networks, and Consumer Culture*. Baton Rouge: Louisiana University Press, 2015.

———. "Mercats noucentistas de Barcelona: Una interpretació dels seus orígens i significant cultural." *Revista de l'Alguer* 4 (December 1993): 93–106.

Montanari, Massimo. *Medieval Tastes: Food, Cooking, and the Table*. Translated by Beth Archer Brombert. New York: Columbia University Press, 2015.

Moreno, María Paz. *Madrid: A Culinary History*. Lanham, MD: Rowman & Littlefield, 2018.

Moreno-Luzón, Javier. "The Restoration: 1874–1914." In *The History of Modern Spain: Chronologies, Themes, Individuals*, edited by Adrian Schubert and José Álvarez Junco, translated by Nick Rider, 45–63. London: Bloomsbury, 2018.

Moret, Xavier. *elBulli desde dentro. Biografía de un restaurante*. Translated by Josep M. Pinto. Barcelona: RBA Libros, 2007.

Motis Dolader, Miguel-Ángel. "Mediterranean Jewish Diet and Traditions in the Middle Ages." In *Food: A Culinary History from Antiquity to the Present*, edited by Jean-Louis Flandrin, Massimo Montanari, and Albert Sonnenfeld, 224–44. New York: Columbia University Press, 1999.

Moyano Andrés, Isabel. "La cocina escrita." In *La cocina en su tinta*, 17–59. Madrid: Biblioteca Nacional de España, 2010.

Nadal, Rafael. "Homenaje al Motel." *La Vanguardia*, June 3, 2011. Accessed September 15, 2018. www.lavanguardia.com/opinion/articulos/20110603/54165239075/homenaje-al-motel.html.

Olivella, Daniel, and Caroline Wright. *Catalan Food: Culture and Flavors from the Mediterranean*. New York: Clarkson Potter, 2018.

Palacín, Montse. *Barcelona Served: Contemporary Catalan Cuisine*. Barcelona: b-guided and Ajuntament de Barcelona, 2005.

Payne, John. *Catalonia: History and Culture*. Nottingham, UK: Five Leaves Publication, 2004.

Pérez, Dionisio. *Guía del buen comer español*. Madrid: Patronato Nacional de Turismo, 1929.

Pérez Samper, María de los Ángeles. *Mesas y cocinas en la España del siglo XVIII*. Gijón, Spain: Ediciones Trea, 2011.

———. *Barcelona, Corte. La visita de Carlos IV en 1802*. Barcelona: Cátedra de Historia General de España, 1973.

Permanyer, Lluís. *Barcelona nocturna*. Barcelona: Efadós and Ajuntament de Barcelona, 2016.

———. *La Barcelona d'ahir. L'esplendor de la burgesia*. Barcelona: Angle Editorial, 2015.

———. "Una esquina codiciada." *La Vanguardia*, May 23, 2006. Accessed July 29, 2018. http://hemeroteca.lavanguardia.com/preview/2001/12/16/pagina-7/34218814/pdf.html?search=El%20Colmado.

———. "El Colmado de Juan Nepomuceno Conde Núñez." *La Vanguardia*, December 16, 2001. Accessed August 13, 2018. http://hemeroteca.lavanguardia.com/preview/2001/12/16/pagina-7/34226109/pdf.html?search=El%20Colmado.

———. "El Colmado cobró otra dimensión con Martignole." *La Vanguardia*, December 30, 2001. Accessed August 13, 2018. http://hemeroteca.lavanguardia.com/preview/2001/12/16/pagina-7/34218814/pdf.html?search=El%20Colmado.

Pizarro, José. *Catalonia: Recipes from Barcelona and Beyond*. Melbourne, Australia: Hardie Grant Books, 2017.

Pla, Josep. *El que hem menjat*. Vol. 22. *Obra completa*. Barcelona: Destino, 1980.

Pomés Leiz, Juliet. *Catalan Cuisine*. Translated by Pere Bramon and Neil Charlton. Barcelona: Zahorí de Ideas. Fundació Institut Català de Cuina i de la Cultura Gatronómica, 2014.

Price, Laura. "How Disfrutar Went from One to Watch to Highest New Entry in The World's 50 Best Restaurants List." *The World's 50 Best Restaurants*, June 7, 2018. Accessed September 11, 2018. www.theworlds50best.com/blog/News/disfrutar-highest-new-entry-worlds-50-best-restaurants.html.

Provansal, Danielle, and Melba Levick. *Els mercats de Barcelona*. Barcelona: Ajuntament de Barcelona, 1992.

Pujol, Anton. "Cosmopolitan Taste. The Morphing of the New Catalan Cuisine." *Food, Culture & Society* 12, no. 4 (2009): 437–55.

Queralt, M. Carme, ed. *La cuinera catalana. Regles útils, fàcils, segures i economiques per cuinar bé. Receptari anónim del segle XIX.* Valls, Spain: Cossetània Edicions, 2009.

Quílez i Corella, Francesc M. "Graphic Art of the Quatre Gats." In *Barcelona and Modernity: Picasso, Gaudí, Miró, Dalí,* edited by William H. Robinson, Carmen Belen Lord, and Jordi Falgàs, 93–95. New Haven, CT: Yale University Press, 2007.

———. "The Art of the Poster." In *Barcelona and Modernity: Picasso, Gaudí, Miró, Dalí,* edited by William H. Robinson, Carmen Belen Lord, and Jordi Falgàs, 69–71. New Haven, CT: Yale University Press, 2007.

Regol, Philippe. "Escoffier, Adriá y el Melocotón Melba. El último plato para el último vals." *Observación Gastronómica* (blog). Accessed September 8, 2018. https://observaciongastronomica.blogspot.com/2011/08/escoffieradria-y-el-melocoton-melba.html.

Renedo, Xavier, and David Guixeras, eds. *Frances Eiximinis. An Anthology.* Translated by Robert Hughes. Barcelona: Barcino/Tamesis, 2008.

Ribagorda, José. "En el 'Zaldiarán' de Vitoria se inició la revolución." *Telecinco.es* (blog), April 23, 2009. Accessed September 13, 2018. www.telecinco.es/blogs/labuenavida/Zaldiaran-Vitoria-inicio-revolucion_6_825915005.html.

Richardson, Paul. *Barcelona: Authentic Recipes Celebrating the Foods of the World.* Williams-Sonoma Foods of the World. Birmingham, AL: Oxmoor House, 2004.

Riera, Anna. "Sueño, luego existo." *El Periódico de Catalunya,* May 16, 2013.

Riera i Melis, Antoni. "El context històric dels receptaris medievals catalans. 2. La cuina i la taula de la noblesa: L'ostentació de la qualitat." In *Llibre d'aparellar de menjar,* edited by Joan Santanach, 21–51. Barcelona: Editorial Barcino, 2015.

Riera-Melis, Antoni. "Society, Food and Feudalism." In *Food: A Culinary History from Antiquity to the Present,* edited by Jean-Louis Flandrin, Massimo Montanari, and Albert Sonnenfeld, 251–67. New York: Columbia University Press, 1999.

———. "Alimentació i poder a Catalunya al segle XII: Aproximació al comportament alimentari de la noblesa." *Revista d'etnologia de Catalunya* 2 (1993): 8–21.

Robert, Mestre. *Llibre del coch. Tractat de cuina medieval.* Edited by Veronika Leimgruber. Barcelona: Curial, 2012.

Robinson, William H., Jordi Falgàs, and Carmen Belen Lord. *Barcelona and Modernity: Picasso, Gaudí, Miró, Dalí.* New Haven, CT: Cleveland Museum of Art and Yale University Press, 2007.

Robinson, William H., and Carmen Belen Lord. "Introduction." In *Barcelona and Modernity: Picasso, Gaudí, Miró, Dalí,* edited by William H. Robinson, Jordi Falgàs, and Carmen Belen Lord, 2–19. New Haven, CT: Yale University Press, 2007.

Roca, Joan. *Roots: Essential Catalan Cuisine According to El Celler de Can Roca.* Translated by Adriana Acevedo Alemán. Barcelona: Librooks, 2012. Kindle.

Rochefort, Yann de, Zack Bezunartea, and Marc Vidal. *Boqueria: A Cookbook, from Barcelona to New York.* New York: Absolute Press, 2018.

Rosenberger, Bernard. "Arab Cuisine and Its Contribution to European Culture." In *Food: A Culinary History from Antiquity to the Present,* edited by Jean-Louis Flandrin, Massimo Montanari, and Albert Sonnenfeld, 207–23. New York: Columbia University Press, 1999.

Saiz, Yaiza. "El restaurante más hermoso del mundo está en Barcelona." *La Vanguardia,* November 15, 2017. Accessed December 15, 2018. www.lavanguardia .com/comer/sitios/20171116/432905726187/alkimia-restaurante-premio-diseno .html.

Salas, Pilar. "Juan Manuel Salgado y Adrià Viladomat vuelven a luchar por el Bocuse d'Or." *7caníbales.com,* January 15, 2018. Accessed September 11, 2018. www.7canibales.com/actualidad/juan-manuel-salgado-adria-viladomat-vuelven -luchar-bocuse-dor/.

Santamaria, Santi. *La cocina al desnudo.* Madrid: Ediciones Planeta, 2008.

Santanach, Joan, ed. *Llibre d'aparellar de menjar.* Barcelona: Editorial Barcino, 2015.

———. *The Book of Sent Soví: Medieval Recipes from Catalonia.* Translated by Robin Vogelzang. Boydell & Brewer, 2008.

Scully, Terence. *The Neapolitan Recipe Collection: Cuoco Napoletano.* Ann Arbor: University of Michigan Press, 2000.

Segura i Mas, Antoni, and Elisenda Barbé i Pou. "Catalonia: From Industrialization to the Present Day." In *A Companion to Catalan Culture,* edited by Dominic Keown, 71–96. Woodbridge, Suffolk: Tamesis, 2011.

Sen, Miquel. *Luces y sombras del reinado de Ferran Adrià.* Barcelona: La esfera de los libros, 2007.

Serrano, María del Mar. *Las guías urbanas y los libros de viaje en la España del siglo XIX.* Barcelona: Universitat de Barcelona, 1993.

Sert Welsch, Francisco de. *El goloso. Una historia europea de la buena mesa.* Barcelona: Alianza Editorial, 2007.

Sgarbi, Giulia. "Twelve Iconic Dishes of El Bulli." *The World's 50 Best Restaurants*. Accessed September 15, 2018. www.theworlds50best.com/blog/News/12 -iconic-dishes-el-bulli-ferran-adria.html.

Thibaut i Comalada, Eliana. *Cuina medieval catalana. Història, dietética i cuina*. Valls, Spain: Cossetània Edicions, 2006.

Todolí, Vicente, and Richard Hamilton. *Comida para pensar, pensar sobre el comer*. Barcelona: Actar, 2009.

Tolosa, Lluís. *Guia dels millors 100 vins i caves de Catalunya*. Barcelona: S. L. Espurna Nec & Otium, 2017.

———. *Barcelona Wine. Enjoy Wine Tourism in the City*. Barcelona: Tolosa Wine Books, 2015.

Vargas, Michael A. *Constructing Catalan Identity: Memory, Imagination, and the Medieval*. Cham, Switzerland: Palgrave Macmillan, 2018.

Vázquez Montalbán, Manuel. *Carvalho gourmet. Las recetas de Carvalho*. Vol. 3. Carvalho. Barcelona: Planeta, 2012.

———. *La cocina de los mediterráneos*. Carvalho Gastronómico. Barcelona: Zeta, 2008.

———. *Saber o no saber. Manual imprescindible de la cultura gastronómica*. Carvalho Gastronómico 1. Barcelona: Zeta, 2008.

———. *L'art del menjar a Catalunya. El llibre roig de la identitat gastronòmica catalana*. Barcelona: Salsa Books, 2004.

———. *Barcelonas*. Translated by Andy Robinson. London: Verso, 1992.

Vélez, Pilar. "The Decorative Arts of the Modernist Era: European Art Nouveau Plus the Local Tradition." In *Barcelona and Modernity: Picasso, Gaudí, Miró, Dalí*, edited by William H. Robinson, Carmen Belen Lord, and Jordi Falgàs, 165–70. New Haven, CT: Yale University Press, 2007.

Vilar, Pierre. *Breve historia de Cataluña*. Bellaterra, Spain: Edicions UAB, 2011.

Villar, Paco. *Barcelona, ciutat de cafès (1880–1936)*. Barcelona: Viena Edicions, 2013.

Villegas, Almudena. *Manual de cultura gastronómica*. Córdoba: Almuzara, 2008.

Vinyoles Vidal, Teresa. "La vida quotidiana i l'espai domèstic al segle XIII." In *Jaume I: Commemoració de VIII centenari de naixement de Jaume I*, edited by M. Teresa Ferrer i Mallol, 2:133–70. Barcelona: Institut d'Estudis Catalans, 2013.

Warren, Emma. *The Catalan Kitchen. From Mountain to City and Sea: Recipes from Spain's Culinary Heart*. Melbourne, Australia: Smith Street Books, 2018.

Zipprick, Jörg. *¡No quiero volver al restaurante!* Madrid: Foca-Akal, 2009.

Index